THE CATHOLIC WOMAN

The Catholic Woman
Difficult Choices in a Modern World

Jeanne Pieper

Lowell House
Los Angeles

Contemporary Books
Chicago

Library of Congress Cataloging-in-Publication Data

Pieper, Jeanne.
  The Catholic woman : difficult choices in a modern world / Jeanne Pieper.
    p.   cm.
  Includes bibliographical references and index.
  ISBN 1-56565-081-6
  1. Women in the Catholic Church—United States. 2. Catholic Church—United
States—Membership. I. Title.
BX1407.W65P54 1993
282'.082—dc20   93-11781
                                                        CIP

Requests for such permissions should be addressed to:
Lowell House
2029 Century Park East, Suite 3290
Los Angeles, CA 90067
Publisher: Jack Artenstein
Vice-President/Editor-in-Chief: Janice Gallagher
Director of Publishing Services: Mary D. Aarons
Text design: Mary Ballachino/Merrimac Design

Manufactured in the United States of America
10 9 8 7 6 5 4 3 2 1

Dedicated, with love and appreciation,
to Catholic women everywhere

CONTENTS

INTRODUCTION

It was spring of 1956 and I had been badgering my twin sister for months to fill out the college application forms that were stacked on the dresser we both shared.

She kept procrastinating. "I'll do it tomorrow," she said. "After all, our grades are almost the same. If they accept you, they'll accept me later." But I sensed something unusual about her casual attitude.

Finally one night, as we lay side by side in our twin beds in the dark, she confessed. "I think I ought to tell you something," she began.

Before she could continue, I suddenly knew exactly what she was going to tell me. "You're not!" was my immediate shocked reply. "When are you going to tell Mother?"

And that's how I learned that my twin sister was planning on entering the convent. Like a condemned man about to enter death row (1956 was at least 20 years before we writers would change the word "man" to "person"), she filled her "last" summer with almost every teenage experience imaginable. She probably realized that entering the convent would be like entering a time machine that would take her back to the Middle Ages.

She had no idea of what lay ahead. Scores of books, both fiction and non-fiction, have revealed the gory details. Wearing the hot, heavy, long black habit and veil that we all remember and a man's white T-shirt instead of a bra are probably among the better known adjustments she had to make. She had to ask permission to participate in even the most innocuous activity. She was not allowed to ride in a car alone with a man (even her father), nor come home for a visit or call us on the phone, nor come to my wedding or even the baptisms of my four children.

Life inside the convent walls was strict and very undemocratic. Many of the rules and customs were archaic and unreasonable—somewhat similar, perhaps, to the time spent during a fraternity Hell Week or a marine boot camp, but lasting years longer. Nuns her age or older (which is most of them, since the number of girls entering each year fell drastically after the mid-sixties) laughingly tell "horror" stories when they get together to reminisce, and marvel at the fact that they survived.

The Catholic Woman

My sister entered the convent because she was idealistic, because she was inspired by several of the nuns who had taught us in grammar school and in high school, because we had been brought up by our parents to strive to "make a difference" in the world. Beneath her vivacious, daring teenage exterior was a contemplative soul hungry for spiritual wisdom and connection with God.

I, on the other hand, longed for exactly the same connection, but with a man. In fact, I spent the summer before she entered so obsessed by my own first romantic infatuation that I was barely aware of what she must have been going through.

Nevertheless, I was as entrenched in the rigid rules of Catholicism as she was. I never once considered having sex before marriage (which happened six years after that summer), even though I dated my husband for five years and "petted" enthusiastically with him much of that time, and we spent a (secret) two-week vacation alone together in Mexico before we were engaged. I used Thomas Aquinas' five proofs of the existence of God continually in intellectual arguments, never missed Mass on Sunday or ate meat on Friday, and was convinced that if I ever practiced artificial birth control I would, in conscience, have to leave the Church.

Today, my sister is still a nun. In fact, she is one of the leaders of her order. And I still consider myself a practicing Catholic. In fact, I am probably much more involved with religion and the Church than I was before. But the similarity with our 18-year-old selves ends there.

"I ask myself, What's the magic number?" my sister says plaintively during our discussion about the writing of this book. "How many teachings of the Church can you disagree with and still be a Catholic?" She goes on to explain how she has agonized over the actual meanings of certain doctrines and has concluded, intellectually, that they are really metaphors and are not meant to be taken literally. We don't even begin to talk about her anger at the institutionalized sexism in the Church. We've had that conversation many times in the past and I know (and echo) her sentiments and frustration.

As for me, not only did I use artificial birth control after my last child was born some 24 years ago, but I also came to believe that the Church's teachings on the subject are not only ridiculous and hypocritical but immoral, as are the Pope's teachings about the impossibility of ordaining women to the priesthood. I go to Mass on Sunday often, but consider that any other day

Introduction

that's more convenient is equally as good. The point is to give yourself the opportunity to connect with God, rather than be obsessive about rules and a calendar.

Obviously, if both my sister and I still feel we are practicing Catholics, the Church has changed a lot in the last 40 years, and, if we are representative at all, so have its members changed, particularly those who are female.

What are these changes? How did they come about? What other changes are on the horizon? The purpose of this book is to explore these and other questions, not only by finding out what other women (and men) have written on this subject, but by talking directly with a wide variety of women. The interviews in this book, while not ignoring feminist leaders actively working for change or those women who are employed by the Church, will focus on the average woman in the pew.

What are some of the issues that haunt or inspire these Catholic women? Do they share many opinions on the Church? If not, how wide is the spectrum of views among them? How do women today reconcile feminist ideas prevalent in our 1990s society with the patriarchal policies of the Catholic hierarchy? What makes them angry, and if they are angry, how do they cope?

Why do converted Catholic women join, and why do born Catholic women stay? How do young Catholic women, in their teens and twenties, view their membership in the Church? What can Catholic women teach one another and the world at large? What are some of their expectations regarding the future for women in the Church? These are just a few of the questions this book will consider.

Many of the women I interviewed are exemplary Catholics by any definition. A surprisingly high percentage assist at Mass more often than once a week, some even daily. Others, even a few of the women religious (nuns) quoted, might not be considered practicing Catholics by the Pope or the bishops. But for this book, our definition of *Catholic* is any woman who cares deeply about being Catholic and the issues that we are discussing, regardless of the actions (or lack of participation) this concern has led her to.

My grandmother used to warn me not to talk about religion or politics. These subjects were always bound to stir up a controversy, she explained, something every good hostess or guest wanted to avoid. Fortunately, the women interviewed for this book either never knew my grandmother or refused to take her words seriously. For them, religion is a vital part of their lives, something personal, intense, and very important. Even those who have left the institutional Catholic church still care deeply about the issues raised here. I thank them all for their honesty and their sharing.

I think now is the place to explain that I am neither a theologian nor a biblical scholar. The last formal (in a classroom, taught by a priest) religion class I attended was in 1957 as a freshman in college. The theology in this book is what I remember from my childhood classes and what I have picked up by reading and by listening to others who do have master's and doctorates in philosophy, theology, and religious studies. Furthermore, this book represents ideas formed by both being, and talking with, the average woman in the pew. For my entire life, I have been an active and interested lay Catholic. Religion in general, and the Catholic church in particular, plays (and always has played) an important part in my life and I have been researching most of the topics found in this book for over 30 years.

There are many times, as I write these pages, that I wish I had more formal religious education on a particular subject. However, if I did, perhaps I would be writing heavy theological treatises, rather than a book like this, which I hope to be honest, accurate, fun to read, and very accessible and easy to understand by both Catholics and non-Catholics alike.

A few words about how the research for this book was done are also in order. Although I tried to be objective and talk to women who held a variety of opinions, my research was more open-ended than scientific. I chose to interview primarily women who I knew, or had been told, were "excited" about being Catholic. While I believe that these women really do represent the views of the majority of Catholic women who actively take part in the Church today, they were not chosen by any demographic or numeric formula. Although I often asked leading questions during an interview, each woman chose what she wanted to talk about. Furthermore, no attempt was made to quantify any opinions about any subject by actually adding them up.

The majority of the women interviewed must be considered middle-class or upper-middle-class Americans, even those belonging to a Community of Religious Women. And although a few women quoted here can call themselves minority, most of them are white Americans of European heritage.

Additional research also came from other current books written on the subject of the Catholic church. I particularly thank Jane Redmont, author of

Introduction

Generous Lives; Margaret Murphy, author of *How Catholic Women Have Changed;* and Kathleen Fitzgerald and Claire Breault, editors of *Whatever Happened to the Good Sisters?* for sharing with me the stories of nearly 500 additional Catholic women.

Other thank-you's are in order. I owe a debt of gratitude to my parents, Marian and Glenn Bramble, and my uncle, Monsignor Keith Bramble, for introducing me to the Catholic faith as a child and for fostering my love for my religion. I particularly thank my brother, Father Don Bramble, OP, and my twin sister, Sister Joanna Marie Bramble, CSJ, for their help and encouragement in this project, and especially for sharing their lives, opinions, beliefs, and experiences as well as their specialized knowledge about the Catholic church. Hardly a week went by while I was researching and writing this book that one or the other did not call me with some new insight, or send me a must-read article (underlined, with notes penciled in the margin), or tell me about a certain book to read or a woman to interview. We are all indebted to my editor, Bud Sperry of Lowell House, for thinking up and campaigning for this project and for his assistance in its completion.

Even more important, I sincerely thank my husband, Jim, for his patience, love, support, and understanding during the many evenings and weekends that I deserted him for a date with the telephone or my word processor!

DATES THAT HELP
TELL THE STORY

1953:   Sisters Formation Conference starts program of college education for nuns *before* they enter the classroom as teachers.

1958–1963:   Pope John XXIII

1960s and before   No women as students or teachers at seminaries.

1960s: Use of birth control pill by women becomes widespread.

1961:   Nuns begin to heed call for missionaries in Latin America.

1962–1965:   Second Vatican Council

1963:   Pope John XXIII's encyclical on World Peace and Social Policy of the Church.

1963–1968:   Pope Paul VI

1963:   Betty Friedan publishes *The Feminine Mystique.*

1964:   U.S. Civil Rights Act of 1964 prohibits job discrimination on basis of sex, race, religion, or national origin.

1964:   Nuns begin to modify dress, examine old rules.

1966:   Vatican II tells Religious Orders to update their constitutions.

1966:   National Organization for Women founded by Betty Friedan.

1968: Pope Paul VI's encyclical *Humanae Vitae* reaffirms Church condemnation of artificial birth control.

1968: Los Angeles Cardinal McIntyre and Immaculate Heart Sisters clash over changes in rules.

1968: Mary Daly publishes *The Church and the Second Sex*.

1970s: Many Church authorities begin to try to stop the feminization of American nuns.

1972: Equal Rights Amendment (ERA) prohibiting sex discrimination passes U.S. Congress.

1973: U.S. Supreme Court legalizes abortion.

1973: Mary Daly publishes *Beyond God the Father*.

1973: U.S. participation in the Vietnam War ends.

1975: Women's Ordination Conference formed.

1977: Vatican declaration says no ordained ministry can be open to women.

1978: John Paul II elected Pope.

1979: Pope John Paul II visits the United States and Sister Theresa Kane publicly asks him to consider dialogue about the question of women's ordination.

1980s: More than one-quarter of students enrolled in Roman Catholic theological schools in the United States are women. Feminist theology gains momentum.

1980s: Many orders of religious women begin to invite associate membership.

1982: Due to Vatican pressure, women religious (nuns) are publicly prevented from distributing Communion at a joint meeting of women and men vowed religious leaders in San Francisco.

1982: ERA fails to win ratification.

1983: Vatican tells U.S. bishops to investigate American nuns.

1984: Geraldine Ferraro runs for vice president.

1984: 24 nuns sign *New York Times* ad asking for dialogue about abortion.

1985: U.N. conference in Nairobi, Africa, ends Decade of the Woman.

1987: Vatican takes stand against such current medical practices relating to conception as in vitro fertilization, artificial insemination, and surrogate motherhood.

1992: After four rewrites, bishops' Pastoral Letter on women receives less than the required two-thirds majority vote and is tabled.

CHAPTER ONE

---◦•◦•◦---

A Glance at Our Past

Once upon a time—a time not more than 30 years ago—it was easy to be a woman. We knew exactly what we could and could not do, and most of us followed these rules.

There were exceptions, of course. Some of us were forced to be "different," either because we had a brave personality or because of difficult circumstances. But the rest of us knew that there were certain truths we did not question. As hard as it is to believe today, before the 1960s most women, including myself, thought the following:

1. Men automatically should be paid more than women.
2. In any election (from grammar school class officers to the U.S. government) only men could run for president and only "girls" for secretary.
3. "Girls" of any age must always wear skirts to school, work, or church, regardless of the weather.
4. Women could not be announcers on television or radio, not even for commercials, because their voices were too high.

The list is long and varied. It goes on and on. From our vantage point today, some of these "rules" seem trivial, others intrinsically evil and incomprehensible. But at the time, few, if any, of them made us angry. We simply took these rules for granted.

We Catholic women were even luckier. We had another list of rules to follow: Church rules so explicit that we were never in doubt about what we should do in almost any situation. Some of these rules were mainly operational, such as not eating meat on Friday and fasting from midnight (not even taking water) before receiving Holy Communion. Others were tied to morality, such as staying pure in thought and body (for some reason it was always the girl's fault if anything sexual happened on a date), not missing Mass on Sunday, not practicing birth control, not getting divorced. Most of us took both the operational and the moral rules equally seriously.

"I was 14 and our whole eighth-grade class was at Mass the morning of our confirmation," my sister Joanna relates. "When it was time to go to Communion, I suddenly remembered I had licked an envelope before coming to Church. I started worrying that I had broken my fast by doing so, but I was too embarrassed not to go up to Communion when the time came. After all, we had all gone to Confession the day before, and I was sure everyone would think I had committed some horrible sin in the last 24 hours if I stayed in my seat and didn't walk up to the Communion rail with the rest of the class."

By refusing to risk such embarrassment, Joanna then spent the rest of the day worrying that she had committed a mortal sin by receiving Communion that morning without fasting since midnight. Even worse, she worried that she would soon be compounding that sin into a sacrilege by getting confirmed with her class that evening without first confessing her morning sin.

She now laughs as she tells me this tale, which I had never heard before. "Of course, I went through the confirmation ceremony anyway," she continues. "However, this incident must have bothered me for years, at least subconsciously, because I remember bringing it up to a priest in confession five or six years later when I was in the convent's novitiate. The problem wasn't that my actions that day were sins—by then I knew they weren't—but that I had thought they were a sin and had done them anyway."

My sister and I were hardly brought up scrupulously, despite what you may think after reading her story. It was just that our family, as well as our friends, believed you had to follow each and every rule of the Church carefully in order to be a practicing Catholic. Even our father, an avid golfer and fisherman, never missed Mass on Sunday, regardless of where he was, what he was doing, or how inconvenient getting to Mass might be. If we arrived even five minutes late, we had to go home and return—on time—to a later Mass.

We believed that if you deliberately broke a law of the Church or of God, you would commit a sin. If the offense was particularly serious, the sin would be considered mortal, which meant you would end up in hell if you died without receiving absolution from a priest in confession, or, if that was impossible, making a perfect act of contrition on your deathbed. A "perfect act of contrition" meant being sorry for your sin because the deed had offended God, not because your sin would send you to hell if you didn't repent.

For decades, if not centuries, missing Mass on Sunday headed many Catholics' lists of "likely and easy to commit" mortal sins. Jane H., who grew up in the twenties and thirties, recalls, "I always went to church when I was supposed to. It was the thing to do. You'd go out partying, and even though you could hardly make it up in the morning, you just always got up and went to Mass. I remember when I went to friends' houses and they had meat on Friday, or it was a Holy Day of Obligation and you had to go to Mass, even though it wasn't Sunday. It was sometimes embarrassing, but it was just something that you did."

GROWING UP CATHOLIC: RELIGIOUS AND INTELLECTUAL IMMATURITY

The large Catholic school system was built primarily to teach the many rules about being a Catholic. There were catechism classes after school and on weekends for those who could not attend these schools during the day.

What's more, we were not only isolated by neighborhood and school, we were actively discouraged from having too much contact with non-Catholics. We were particularly forbidden to read the King James version of the Bible or attend non-Catholic religious services and activities. I remember a major discussion at our Catholic grammar school in the late 1940s between our mother, who was a scout leader, and the school principal when our Girl

Scout troop wanted to take swimming lessons. This meant we would all have to become members of the YWCA, a Protestant organization. Fortunately, reason won out (but not without a fight), and we were finally allowed to pay our dues at the Y and learn to swim.

While perhaps we were not formally taught that outside the Church there is no salvation, that was what many of us believed. Somehow that thought seemed easier to grasp than the idea that millions of non-Catholics throughout the world would miraculously receive "Baptism of Desire" on their deathbeds so they, too, could get to heaven. Those few of us, however, who had any contact with non-Catholics were harder to convince. "I remember reciting the catechism about who is saved," France tells me. "But I did not believe that anyone who believed that the Catholic Church was the one true Church and did not belong to it was damned."

"My mother belonged to the Latter-day Saints and my father was Catholic, and we went to Mormon services as well as to Catholic Mass," Cynthia explains. "I would wear my Catholic school uniform to the LDS Sunday school, which really upset the Mormons. Both of these religions were very dogmatic, and the one wouldn't recognize the other. I just thought what each one taught about the other was stupid. I knew that my Mom wasn't going to go to hell, and that my Dad wasn't going to go to hell. And I grew up in a Jewish neighborhood, so I had lots of different examples of how people are saved."

Rose Catherine agrees. "I come from a mixed marriage. My father died when I was very young. My mother was Protestant, so even when I was little, and I was told that no one but Catholics could get to heaven, I thought, *This is crazy, I don't believe it.* Even in the late 1930s, I was excluding things the Church told me to believe, because I was exposed to people other than Catholics."

The rest of us, however, just took it on faith that you had to be a practicing Catholic to get to heaven. Margaret Murphy, in her book *How Catholic Women Have Changed,* uses these words to describe the way we used to be: *accepting, intimidated, unquestioning, unaware, complacent, doctrinaire, judgmental.* According to her, until the 1960s Catholic women accepted as truth what their parents, their husbands, and the Church told them.

Rose Marciano Lucey agrees. "In the 1940s and the 1950s, in my experience, there was no attempt by the Church to get laypeople to think for themselves, or to analyze the gospels. They were just to go to church and do what they were told," Rose tells me. "I was brought up to believe that the

Church had all the answers and that my role was to be obedient. I was to do what I was told by the pastor and the parish priests. When I went to Saturday catechism classes, we never asked any questions."

When Rose and her husband married in the early 1940s, the priest told them that the primary reason for marriage was to have children. That was all the premarital instruction he offered them.

"I had 10 pregnancies," Rose continues, "because we believed everything the Church was telling us about birth control. I remember learning that two doctors had come up with the rhythm theory and had written a book about it. It was a small book, and we hid it under the counter in our bookstore [the family business]. It was not on display.

"Rhythm wasn't against the Church. It was just that you had to fulfill three requirements to use it. You had to be in dire poverty, or the woman had to be in danger of dying if she had more children. I forget what the third one was. Rhythm was just for emergencies. But you just didn't talk about it much."

There were a lot of things we did not question or talk about in those days. Although many of us could recite pages and pages of the Baltimore catechism word for word, we did not spend much time debating these pages. We didn't spend much time debating what we would be when we grew up either. For most of us, that would be married, and we knew that having any other job would be "just marking time" until that happened.

For Cassandra, marriage came earlier than it did for many of us. She graduated from high school when she was 16, got married at 17, and thought she knew exactly what to expect. "I would walk out of church after the wedding ceremony and then God would bless me with seven children," she recalls.

A week after her first wedding anniversary, however, Cassandra's right ovary ruptured, and she was in and out of the hospital for the next seven years. "It was awful," she sighs. "For the first time in my life I felt guilt, because I knew that the reason I couldn't get pregnant was because I was being punished for something, and I would fill in the blank with some past sin: because I didn't go to Church for the first 16 years of my life, or because I really am no good and should not have married such a good husband. All sorts of craziness. It took a very good person—my husband—to keep me together and keep the family together."

Unlike Cassandra, many of us who went to college during the 1950s and 1960s were not as focused on getting married and having babies. We competed equally with men in the classroom and often won. But we too believed we'd be a "failure" if we weren't at least engaged by the time we graduated.

Since I was one of the top seniors in the School of International Relations at the University of Southern California in 1960, the president of our school asked me to help him recruit junior college transfer students. I remember driving back to school with him after one such lecture. He complimented me on the talk I had given, then added sadly, "It is such a shame. You'd be so good in this field. But you are a warm and loving girl and you will be much better off married."

Neither at school nor at home was there even a hint of how to combine the two paths of marriage and career. When I married a year and a half later, I swore to both myself and my husband that I was not planning on becoming "just a housewife" upon marriage.

Nevertheless, about 10 months later I was a mother. I had asked the doctor who gave us our premarital blood tests how many days you had to abstain from having sex in the middle of the month to make sure you wouldn't get pregnant. He had laughingly refused to reply, telling me to come back after the honeymoon!

THE MAGIC AND MYSTICISM OF THE CHURCH

In the 1950s women made up only 31% of the work force. Our job options were not all that exciting either. We could be nurses, teachers, or secretaries. But Catholic girls had one additional option, something dramatic, mysterious, and guaranteed to get them to heaven: They could enter the convent! And in the 1940s and 1950s, scores of them did.

Fifty-six nuns and ex-nuns tell their stories in Kathleen Fitzgerald and Claire Breault's collection of essays, *Whatever Happened to the Good Sisters?* In it, one writer, who does not give her name, reports, "I had this enormous, exaggerated desire to give myself to a cause, but at that time there was no Peace Corps or Vista Volunteers."

For Rita Bresnahan, writing in the same book, the convent offered a safe harbor and a lifetime direction: "It felt almost that I didn't have a choice, that it was my destiny."

Theresa, now in her sixties and still a nun, entered the convent in 1946 at age 14. She tells me, "I was making this great big sacrifice of my life. I was following St. Theresa's example, giving my whole life to God like she did, never dreaming what it was going to include. My mother was happy and willing for me to enter, but I didn't realize that she would cry herself to sleep at night because she missed me."

Those entering in the 1960s were just as idealistic. Mary Ann Butkiewicz, who entered in 1966, writes: "I wanted to live with people who were special . . . people like myself who had left behind self, family, friends, and possessions to exhilarate their spirits with a sense of joy, peace and love that one can only find when living and working with people in love with the same bridegroom, Christ."[1]

Vivian was 27 when she entered the Sisters of Immaculate Heart of Mary. She still writes "IHM" after her name today, but I can clearly hear the embarrassment in her voice when she speaks to me.

"Because of my own narrowness of vision and because of how we had been taught, I thought that the way you served the Church was to become a sister or a priest," she explains. "I believed lay folks were definitely second-class citizens, and that they were out there to pay, pray, and obey. I wanted something more than that. I wanted to be of service to the world, and I never questioned the men who made up the hierarchy of the Catholic church. I thought they were specially gifted, called by God, and that they had the only way to know the will of God."

Obviously something more than rules was working in the Church to create such idealistic young women. Rosalind Camardella writes, "The Church of my youth was full of ritual. The heady fragrance of incense, gently spiraling from ornate, gleaming vessels; the comforting flicker of red votive candles; even the unintelligible Latin prayers, all served to wrap my belief in reverence and stir my young soul to awe. There was no need to understand doctrines and dogmas. My sense of God was immediate, direct and real."[2]

My good friend Sharon feels the same way. "I loved the candles, the incense, the pageantry, the sense of mystery," she tells me. "I never felt it anywhere else. And it gave me an identity. We moved a lot when I was a child, and I wasn't sure what I was or how I fit in, but I always knew I was a Catholic, and that identity meant a lot."

Today, this sense of belonging continues to excite Sharon. "I can go into any Catholic church, anywhere in the world, and I always have a sense of belonging. I always feel welcome. It is like having friends all over the world. When I was in high school, I went to daily Mass. I think it was to belong and also for approval, and maybe a little because of fear, but mostly because I loved the liturgy, the ritual of Mass. There was something in it that calmed me down, made me feel good."

Now the mother of five children, Sharon's sense of the Church as community was strengthened during her college years in the late 1950s. "A Dominican priest would gather us all up around the altar for Mass, and it was very loving and family like. I felt a bonding with the people, and this was and is very important for me. I went to Immaculate Heart College, which was celebrating Mass in a festive way. It was pre–Vatican II, but with balloons and music, banners, artwork . . . and it was very touching to me."

A Wealth of Fond Memories

Despite the many (often insulting) jokes about attending Catholic schools, the women interviewed for this book had nothing but praise for most of the sisters and priests they knew in their childhood.

"I had the good fortune of liking every priest I met as a child. I always felt something very good and kind in them," Sharon insists. "One priest in the small town where I grew up really helped my mother. He was a very loving man. My parents had been married out of the Church and my mother had all this guilt, and he got her back on track to resolve this issue, even though they didn't get married in the Church until I was 18," Sharon explains.

Carolyn, an attorney who, like Sharon, still goes to daily Mass, had a similar experience. "My mother had a breakdown after a miscarriage, and the nuns and priests were very kind to her. My mom always relied on the Church for help and always got help there."

"I think we had a feeling about the nuns as being disciplinarians in grammar school, but that was good. If I hadn't followed their example and instilled fear in my own children when they were growing up, I would have been overwhelmed," explains Colleen, now the mother of 14 and grandmother of 26. "But I felt very close to the nuns in high school and college. They taught me how to approach living in the world and as a family. The education that I received from these sisters has greatly influenced my life and my feelings toward the Church and my faith."

Girls who entered the convent also had close emotional ties to the nuns who taught them. "My eighth-grade teacher was my first mentor, model, guide and confidant. I loved her and felt her love for me," Sister Mary Joseph remembers decades later. [3]

Sister Pat, at 13, saw the nuns who taught her as "spirited, joyful, and intelligent; warm, prayerful, and self-reliant. They were always right there for us, decorating the gym for the prom or building sets or pinning costumes. They moderated club activities and coordinated service projects. They affirmed my fledgling discoveries and encouraged a lifelong commitment to spiritual growth." [4]

Despite their closeness to the nuns who were their teachers, each new class of young girls entering the convent did not have a clue about what lay ahead. Vivian explains, "The nun who I talked to said, 'It is wonderful if you want to come, but believe me, it is not easy.' I had no idea what that meant, but I soon found out!"

CONVENT LIFE BEFORE THE LATE 1960S

Although many women today, those still in the convent and those who have left, insist that a lot of good things happened to them during these years, it is the horror stories that stand out.

"In the early sixties, during my second year in the convent, I was sent on a trip back to my hometown to recruit new people, and I talked to my ex-fiance," Betty relates. "Of course, when I got back to my convent, I told Mother Superior that I had done this, since I was supposed to tell her everything."

Because she talked to her old boyfriend, Betty was not allowed to make her vows as a nun that year and had to go through another year of postulancy. That wasn't the incident that bothered her the most, however. Even though she was going to the same college as her sister, she was not allowed to speak to her. One afternoon she saw her sister—whom she hadn't spoken to for a year—on campus. Betty said, "Hi, how are Mom and Dad?" and then obediently reported this conversation to Mother Superior when she got back to the convent that night. Her punishment for that was to make the Stations of the Cross twice a day on her knees for a month. She couldn't even get up between stations.

Betty says, "We never talked in religious life at all except for one hour on Sunday evening each week. Although we could talk in class at the college we were all going to, we were *not* allowed to talk to any laypeople between classes."

Such enforced silence was an old tradition for many orders of nuns. Sister Pat entered the convent in 1942. "We asked permission to speak to someone. We even asked permission to go up a flight of stairs to another floor. I formed close friendships but was always warned against 'particular' friendships [a convent euphemism for both cliquish behavior and homosexual liaisons]. The professed sisters were also off limits. We were not to talk to them except on special days when they could come over and visit. My brother was a Marine. We had no idea what was going on overseas during the war and we were not to ask. We were removed and apart from the world."[5]

Rose Catherine tells me she was not particularly bothered by difficult convent rules, but she had no illusions that they would make her a better person. "It was the mid-forties," she explains, "and I just thought the rules were necessary for order in a large group. But Superiors told us that they would deliberately make things difficult for us on purpose, to test us, and I could not see any reason for this. Life was difficult enough."

Although she loved teaching, what Rose Catherine mostly remembers is always being tired. "Those were the days of big classes, and we taught without any credential or experience. I had a first-grade classroom with 89 children in it. I taught five different classes about five different subjects in high school in the mornings, and then taught the first grade in the afternoon. I made 4,000 altar breads [Communion hosts] every week, and went to college on Saturdays," Rose continues. In addition to all these chores, Rose and the other sisters spent eight to nine hours praying in chapel each day.

Even after the "boot camp" of the early years was finished, life in the convent was still extremely regimented and hierarchical. Assignments were changed at will by the Superior each year and were accepted obediently with little, if any, discussion, regardless of the emotional or practical hardship such arbitrary uprootings brought with them.

Even those women who were respected professional teachers, nurses, and administrators by day turned into "little girl nuns" when they returned to their convents in the evening. Once there, almost every aspect of their lives was governed by the regulations of canon law, community custom, or the dictates of the Mother Superior. Although many sisters might occasionally grumble to themselves or a trusted friend, few dared to suggest out loud that the definitions of the nature of religious life, regulations governing individual behavior, or the conduct of convent affairs might be suitable matters for disagreement, much less for noncompliance.

LEADING THE WAY IN A CHANGING CHURCH

Yet, along with blind obedience to often ancient convent traditions, American Catholic nuns were rapidly becoming the largest group of highly educated women in the world. Starting in the mid-fifties, the Sisters Formation Movement advocated that all nuns receive a college degree before beginning to teach. Slowly but surely, each order began to comply with the growing mandate to educate its members, even sending those women who already had degrees back to school to work on master's and doctorates. Some even went to secular universities.

In retrospect, it is not surprising that many of these seemingly docile and religious women, living in community with one another, still idealistic but now newly educated, with neither husbands nor children to distract them, would be among the first to embrace the massive social and philosophical changes of the 1960s, particularly the ideas of very vocal feminists. It is also not surprising that some of their sisters in religion would fight equally hard to retain century-old traditions of convent lifestyle and government.

To say that these women went from living in the Middle Ages to the 21st century in a decade or so without bloodshed may be only technically true, for there were many emotional casualties along the way. But few groups have been able to change the status quo from within so quickly or so completely as did Catholic nuns. Compared to them, many laywomen often felt that their own lives and beliefs were all but standing still. The fact is, however, that by the 1990s, Catholic women today—whether lay or religious—increasingly have more in common with one another than ever before. Paradoxically, it is their willingness to acknowledge, accept, and even honor diversity that is bringing about this new unity.

The history of the transformation of Catholic women over the last three decades is an interesting one, as we will see in the next two chapters. However, the story of where we are now, in the 1990s, which the rest of this book will attempt to analyze, is even more fascinating.

THE 1960S AND 1970S

Most people think of the 1960s as a mixture of tremendous turmoil and excitement. To be fair, we need to include much of the 1970s in this decade as well. The U.S. State and Defense Departments, race relations, recreational drugs, the sexual revolution, age-old family and moral values—almost no segment of society was exempt from the tidal wave of change and innovation. The common thread running through many movements of the day was that reform was needed everywhere. For fifteen or more years, the status quo was challenged on every side, even in the Catholic church.

"I grew up in a hurricane," Margaret explains. "When I was a child, the

Catholic church was a safe and secure place for everyone as well as for myself. In the early 1960s, it was what you hung on to when everything else was changing. But that idea soon blew away as well."

One of the first things to change in the Church was the language used to say Mass. "In 1961, when I graduated from grammar school," Margaret remembers, "Mass was in Latin. When I graduated from high school in 1965, we had the New Latin Mass. By the time I graduated from college, everything was in English."

More than just words was changing. Pope John XXIII called the bishops of the world, along with other advisers, to a series of meetings held in Rome between 1962 and 1964. He died before these conferences ended, but his successor, Pope Paul VI, completed his work. Called Vatican II, each session was much like a corporate retreat in which almost every aspect of Church policy and practice was open for discussion and study. 2,540 bishops and a few heads of religious orders of men had voting rights. [6] The repercussions from this massive undertaking are still being felt today.

Although the documents coming out of Vatican II at first were read only by the very involved, by the early 1970s even the casual Catholic realized that something monumental had taken place, primarily because of the many changes to the way Mass was being said each Sunday. The altar was turned around so that the priest could face the people. A time was set aside for people to greet one another during the service. A whole new list of songs in English had to be written or found, and were borrowed at first from the Protestants.

Religious orders of both men and women were asked to review their constitutions and bring them up to date. All members were to be consulted, and any changes were to be decided democratically, rather than imposed from the top down as before. Even within the institutional Church itself, there was a new openness to other religions. Dialogue, both among the leaders and among the grassroots, was initiated between groups of Catholics and almost every other major religion as the Ecumenical Movement got under way. The laity were not only encouraged to participate in the Church but told they were valued members with worthwhile ideas and jobs to do. They discovered that they, too, had positive roles to play in each other's salvation.

The Excitement of Experimentation— The Pain of Rebirth

Many people, even non-Catholics, rejoiced that the long-locked windows of the Catholic church had been opened. Yet not every aspect of this Church renewal was seen as positive, nor were these years happy ones for many Church members caught up in a whirlpool of questioning and evaluation about how new ideas should be defined or implemented. These years were particularly volatile for men and women whose whole identities were tied into the fortunes and beliefs of the Catholic church, which was both their employer and, for many, their significant other. By the mid-seventies, thousands of priests had sought dispensation from their vows of celibacy or had left the Church entirely, and the exodus of women religious (nuns) was under way as well. Some left because change was too fast, others out of frustration that it was too slow. "There was a massive identity crisis," says one priest.

"Change of such magnitude, accomplished at such a fast pace, is fraught with conflict," Sisters Lora Ann Quinonez and Mary Daniel Turner explain. Vatican-mandated meetings within each order of nuns, called renewal chapters, gave members of religious communities the opportunity to discuss important matters openly, often for the first time. Much to their initial surprise, the membership of each group began to realize that there was disagreement among some members even over fairly substantive issues such as religious beliefs. Inventing a process to handle such differences was often painful and time-consuming.

"Sisters were neophytes in handling overt conflict, reaching consensus, and distinguishing idea from proponent," Quinonez and Turner recall. "They sometimes 'fought to the death.' When conflict arose, it often strengthened the resolve of both the disapproving and the disapproved to persist in their ways."[7]

Those of us who were "just" housewives and mothers were suffering an identity crisis as well. The closest I ever got to the action of the 1960s was as a witness to an anti–U.S. protest through the streets of downtown Mexico City put on by my fellow students at the University of Mexico after the United States' (aborted) invasion of the Bay of Pigs in Cuba in 1961. Although the demonstration seemed to me to be more in fun than in anger, something like the University of California at Berkeley panty raids of the

time (which I had only read about), I was concerned enough to help organize a briefing session at the U.S. Embassy to answer the questions of all of
us Americans who were studying in Mexico that year.

Back in the States the next spring, however, I got married and immediately
pregnant, which effectively ended my brief stint as a "liberated woman." Ten
years and four children later, I woke up to find my twin sister had traded her
long, billowing black-and-white habit for a polyester pantsuit, and was now
driving a car, picketing for the United Farm Workers, and using lyrics from
Simon and Garfunkel as a teaching tool in her high school English class. I
had never heard of Simon and Garfunkel and had only barely heard of Cesar
Chavez and the California farm workers. I knew my parents and brother
were participating in the civil rights movement and my husband once invited
a man home for dinner who spent the evening talking about how great marijuana was.

Besides cleaning house, gardening, and taking care of my children, I
longed for some intellectual stimulation or feeling of community. We would
go to Mass on Sunday and see other families with young children, but I
never got to know any of them beyond just saying hello. Even when our first
child started Catholic school, the only activity for young mothers was to sell
hot dogs at lunch once a week. Eventually, I heard about a group that met
one morning a month and had free baby-sitting. It could have been the
Communist party for all I cared, but fortunately it turned out to be the
League of Woman Voters.

These few sentences are my total personal recollection of the 1960s.
Many other Catholic women interviewed for this book, however, who have
longer and more interesting stories to relate about these years, talk about the
ways they actively played a part in a rapidly changing church and society.

Silvia fled Castro's Cuba for New England only to find that no American
priest would let her get married in the Church because her husband's bap-
tismal certificate was back in Cuba. "It took over a year for it to arrive," she
explains. "By that time it was so anticlimatic, I didn't care."

But once their second child was born, they decided to raise their children
Catholic, and they went back to the Church. "They were opening up a parish,
and I really liked it and I got involved. They had adult education and they
told me that the Church had changed a lot while we had been gone," Silvia
recalls. "Everyone was really into Vatican II changes and it all made sense to

me. I ended up getting a master's degree in the Pastoral Ministry Program at a nearby Catholic seminary that had opened its doors to women students."

Nancy was just beginning her studies to become a doctor. She left her Catholic college after one year because she discovered that graduates from that college were not getting into medical school. It was the first time she realized that the entire world wasn't Catholic and that not everyone thought the way Catholics think. "I didn't believe that the other kids were really sleeping with their boyfriends. I had never heard of marijuana. It was a big shock! But I still stayed thinking of myself as Catholic, and doing what I thought I should be doing as far as I could." She eventually became a psychiatrist.

Uneven Changes

The speed of Church changes—some major, some minor—depended primarily on the mood of the pastor or the local bishop, which meant that there were usually two groups of dissatisfied people in every parish or diocese: those who thought the changes were too abrupt and those who were upset at their slowness. Angry fights were not uncommon.

Carolyn, a law student at the time, reminisces. "One Easter, the guitar player sang 'Bridge over Troubled Water' and 'Let the Sun Shine In' as we left Mass and many people were furious that a Simon and Garfunkel song and a song from a musical that had nude people in it [Hair] were being sung at church."

Theological and procedural disagreements, and sometimes actual fights, occurred between different priests as well as between the laity. When Liz left the convent and returned home, she went to her parish looking for a way to continue the rich prayer life she had enjoyed during her year and a half as a nun. Instead, she discovered that her parish was ultraconservative, as was her city's archbishop.

One Sunday, a liberal priest happened to be visiting in her parish, and said Mass. He read some of the documents coming out of Rome to the congregation during his sermon, which inspired some parishioners and angered others. The pastor in charge of her parish found this very threatening and reported the priest to the chancery office (the bureaucratic offices of the Church in each area). "The visiting priest was only attempting to instill the spirit of Vatican II, and he met such resistance in the parish and instilled so much hope in other members of the parish that a year or so later, in order to restore peace, the archbishop pulled the diocesan priests out of the parish and started over with some conservative priests from Spain," Liz recalls.

Liz started college and met her husband, an ex-seminarian, and they both became involved in religious education for the grammar-school children of the parish. They attempted to start a discussion group with the other teachers, mostly college students like themselves. According to Liz, "the pastor fought it tooth and nail. Unless he could control the discussions, there would be no such group, and his approach was definitely not Vatican II."

Fortunately for Liz and her husband, a group of nuns and priests invited them to join their discussion group about the changes coming out of Vatican II. "There was a lot of anger, and of course some people were picketing for civil rights. And there was a lot of pressure put on people against this, even from the chancery office," Liz remembers. "It was very difficult. But at the same time I experienced community as well as innovative liturgies,[8] even liturgical dance, during these years. It was a very meaningful experience!"

Rosemary reports that after graduating from a Catholic college, she worked diligently at having children, making a home, and volunteering in the church. "And I enjoyed it," she insists. "Through teaching children, I relearned my faith in light of Vatican II. That led to much work in liturgy at the parish level. For a while I had some influence, as long as the pastor was supportive and thought liturgy vital to community spirituality. However, whenever a pastor or associate changed, our ideas and philosophy were expected to bend to meet the new priest's personal preferences on whatever topic."

Cynthia and her husband joined Vista (the U.S. domestic version of the Peace Corps) after college and worked with the poor in Arizona. "As a young girl I had wanted to be a missionary in Africa," she tells me. "Vista came out of my Catholic idea that you were supposed to help others."

Her attempts to find a vital Catholic community, however, were disappointing. "I was really out of the Church much of that time," she admits. "I'd move to a new parish and check it out, and then realize I didn't belong there either. The only place I found people I could identify with was in Denver, and they were women religious. And then I knew that I was not insane, that I really was a Catholic. I mean, they thought like I did, and they were nuns!"

A New Leadership Role for American Nuns

Of all the people in the Catholic church, American nuns make up the group that entered into the new spirit of change with the most enthusiasm. Many of them insist, however, that change in the convent started back in the late 1950s and would have continued even if Vatican II had never taken place.

According to Doris, "The convent in the 1960s was an exciting place to be. Everybody seemed to have some new insight, some passionate cause which was always contagious. We talked about everything and anything. Also, the many hours we had for study and reflection gave us the chance to examine our souls in a way few people can do."[9]

Now highly educated and still highly idealistic, together often 24 hours a day, the American nuns met the challenges of the sixties head-on, often painfully. Sister Mary Glennon talks about the experience of her order of nuns during these years. "We moved slowly, like a lot of communities. Many people were in denial that all of this was happening. Then, like everyone else, we had to face reality. It wasn't just Vatican II. It was the whole world that was changing. And we came through it kicking and screaming. We had all these meetings, and meetings, and more meetings. We rewrote our constitution over and over again. Vatican II brought new life. We were impregnated with new life from the Holy Spirit at work in the Church, and there were no better women to take hold of that new life and bring it to birth."

But these were very difficult years for Mary and her fellow sisters. "We took it very, very seriously," she continues. "And at great cost, both personally and communally, we came through these changes. I have talked to women going through divorce who said that when they were through with the divorce, they didn't know who they were. They had to start over, because they had given even their name away.

"So when all this was over, after the pain and the agony and the crucifixion of divorce, I felt a lot in common with these women. It was probably 20 years . . . . These years were incredibly painful, totally agonizing, when you saw the exodus of the sisters. And these were our friends, our companions on the journey! They left for various reasons. The rigidity and the self-discipline had been kind of the glue that held everything together. And suddenly we were being told that everything was to change. The idea had been that we would enter religious life to leave the world behind and worldly things behind. Then Vatican II came along and said that the world is created by God, and the world is good, and so leaving it behind is no longer appropriate. It was like turning the ship around in mid-ocean, and not getting very clear directions on where to go next.

"We voluntarily did all these things. We didn't see it coming, it just happened. But we were ready for it. The whole world was ready for it. Women have the power to bring about the new. Pain and joy go together in giving birth. With Vatican II, the women religious accepted the challenge and ran with it."

A New Spiritual World

"Experimentation" was the cry of the 1970s, and the Catholics were no exception. Groups banded together, incorporating many of the new psychological outlooks of the time. Utopia, or something like it, was surely around the corner if we just could get our act together.

By now the Christian Family Movement (CFM), following Belgium's Cardinal Joseph Cardijin's early 1900s challenge to laypeople to "observe, judge, and act," had expanded to almost every part of the United States. A worldwide network of more than 100,000 action-oriented and educated laity were eager and able to integrate the call of the Council documents into their lives.

A quote from the 1970 CFM study guide, *The Family in Revolution*, gives us a hint about some of the topics each small group worked on that year. "Things like protest, militancy, racism, busing, housing and restless students are all around us. There are quieter and personal revolutions too: what is happening to the old people, to the family and its money, how men and women express their feelings in and out of marriage." [10]

The Marriage Encounter Movement, introduced to the United States by Spain's Father Gabriel Calvo through the CFM in 1967, soon swept like wildfire through the parishes of America. Over the next 20 years, hundreds of thousands of Catholic couples (as well as celibate priests and nuns) signed up for this very well structured and intense weekend experience. Protestant and Jewish couples either attended the Catholic Marriage Encounter or sponsored similar weekends of their own. Marriage Encounter is still in existence today, with Engaged Encounter probably its most dynamic component.

There was nothing psychologically revolutionary about these weekends. Much of what was taught was, or is, being written in popular self-help books on couple communication. But actually experiencing these techniques, in a sheltered, highly emotionally charged, and spiritual atmosphere with 30 or 40 equally "turned-on" couples is something that must be lived through to be believed. Marriage Encounter's secret weapon is the "ten and ten daily dialogue" where couples first write privately about a topic for 10 minutes, exchange what they have written, and then practice feeling what the other person has written for 10 more minutes. "Feelings are not good or bad" and "Love is a Daily Decision" are its mottoes.

Jerry and Joan were present at the first U.S. Marriage Encounter. They had been in the CFM for five years, had made a very intense spiritual retreat (a Cursillo), and thought their marriage was great and they knew everything about each other. After listening to one couple tell some of their marriage experiences, they were given a series of topics to write about concerning their marriage and then share with each other. Jerry and Joan remember: "We were painfully honest, playing the game to the hilt, expressing our real feelings about marriage, our spouse, and then risking sharing our answers with each other. We confided to each other things we mistakenly thought we could never discuss, in a spirit of love and acceptance. By the end of the day, we felt we had discovered each other for the first time. Our minds and hearts stood naked before each other. The Marriage Encounter team merely set the climate for us and the ground rules." [11]

It was an earth-shaking experience for Jerry and Joan, just as it was for many of the couples who have participated in these weekends. I can honestly say that for me personally, it was the most intense and educational weekend of my life and for many, many years (maybe even today, more than 20 years later) I classified all psychological and marital events in my life as "before M.E." or "after M.E."

Another equally exciting phenomenon that swept through the Church in the 1970s was the Charismatic Movement. Cassandra had never heard about it until she accidentally showed up at their meeting in her parish church one night. "I didn't understand what they were talking about at the Charismatic meeting and I disagreed with most of it. Some of the people were talking in tongues and there were all sorts of singing and praying. It was like a zoo! I was very confused. I came home all upset that the meeting I thought I was going to had not happened. Anyway, that night, when I went to bed, I had what I can only call a pure religious experience.

"In a dream, or whatever, I was lifted up off my bed and I could see my husband asleep next to me, and I was all aglow—on fire—and there was just this hand on me. It didn't frighten me. I felt called forward. I felt it was a sign or an invitation to come ahead. And that was what I did."

Soon after, Cassandra enrolled in junior college to become a teacher and eventually got her master's in religious education from her local Catholic university.

"I went to school full-time," she says, smiling. "I worked part-time and raised my two children full-time. My husband was very supportive. In the 1970s anything was possible. CFM was first, then Marriage Encounter, and then the Charismatic renewal. I was right in the middle of it all. It was a source of strength for me. It never leaves you."

Sharon's experiences were similar. She was living in St. Louis, and an older woman in her neighborhood who was interested in post–Vatican II changes organized an informal faith group for the younger mothers. A friend Sharon met in this neighborhood group invited her to a Life in the Spirit seminar.

"I had no idea what it was, I just wanted to get out of the house," Sharon says. "So I went, and it was very positive, and all they talked about was the love of God. It had beautiful singing and I liked it. I missed a lot of meetings, and the next time I went I had not done any of the preparation, so I had no idea what to expect. But we broke into small groups praying for each other, and I had a very intense transforming experience. I felt the power of God within me. I had never experienced anything like that. It was the first time I felt connected to God, not the Church, but to God, and it was very transforming."

Sharon continued going to other seminars, classes, workshops, and prayer services. Now, 20 years later, her children grown, she is studying for a master's degree in theology. "All these years," she explains, "I was gradually getting permission to take charge of my own religious life. And the Church became the community that fed me and nurtured me, rather than something that told me what to do. But that took a lot of years!"

Barbara entered her order of nuns in the 1950s. Today she is one of the leaders of her large religious community. The 1970s still remain a special time for her. It started when she began a master's program in theology at the University of San Francisco.

"It was like a total opening up to me about what religion was all about, what spirituality was all about," she relates. "It became a real, living experience for me. And I began to share what I was learning with the other sisters. But I soon found out that it wasn't theology that they wanted from me, so I began to develop some rituals around which we could share, and we all found this very valuable."

After receiving her degree, Barbara moved to Tucson, Arizona, where she took a class offered by the Tucson Ecumenical Council. Only three Catholics were in the group; the rest were Protestants. And the first thing they did was read Mary Daly's hot-off-the-press book, *Beyond God the Father.* Barbara could relate to the anger in it. "Many of the things she talked about had happened to me at USF, but at the time I hadn't realized how male-dominated it was. For one thing, the sisters had to have more classes as prerequisites to get their advanced degrees than the priests did, because it was just assumed that the seminary training was more valuable than that of the convent."

The real gift of the group was that it became a women's consciousness-raising group for Barbara over the following years. Its influence spread beyond Arizona. Rachel (then a nun, today married) was a member of this group, and she put on a weekend retreat for my sister Joanna and a group of her convent friends. It was held at the United Farm Workers meeting hall in Delano, California. There were about 60 women there, all nuns, wearing everything from habits to blue jeans. I, their token laywoman, was also invited.

We slept (what little sleep we got!) in sleeping bags on the floor. It was my and many of the nuns' first introduction, both intellectually and emotionally, to the women's movement; the first time most of us ever saw or participated in a feminist liturgy; the first time we had even a hint of the emerging philosophy of feminist spirituality; our first premonition about where Catholic women might be more than 20 years later when the 20th century was rushing to a close. Looking back, I know now that the seeds for this book began to germinate that weekend.

Adjusting to Change

Not everyone's memories of the 1960s and 1970s are so positive. Sherry Tyree, a founding member of and spokeswoman for Women for Faith and the Family, considers these years the birthplace of the heresies that are being propagated today by people, primarily nuns and liberal laywomen who, she claims, if they were honest, would no longer pretend to be Catholics. After working in the civil rights movement in the mid-sixties, Sherry taught religion and English at a Catholic grammar school between 1970 and 1974.

"Thank goodness I didn't keep up with classes in religion during that time," she tells me. "I don't know how I would have reacted to some of them. There were lots of pretty silly theology being taught. I was only aware that something funny was going on. Here I was teaching religion and I was having to call all over the place to find rosaries, because the religion books didn't include anything about the rosary. That was a period when the nuns were leaving and forsaking teaching. I think they left because the Church was going through a very unstable time and they were throwing the baby out with the bathwater."

In 1962, there were 173,351 American nuns. In 1988, there were 106,102, almost all middle-aged or older.[12] Not only were fewer and fewer young women joining the convent each year, more and more older women were leaving religious life, many after years of being a nun. Many of their departures, particularly in the 1960s, were particularly difficult.

Rita remembers: "I felt no sense of joy or freedom. Only a heaviness, a terrible heaviness. When I left the order I was instantaneously whisked back in time . . . a 36-year-old woman just turned 17. Never had I felt so painfully self-conscious, never so ugly, so scared, so confused and dependent . . . so totally inadequate to meet the world."[13]

Kathy's story is similar, but it has a happy ending. She tells me, "It took tremendous courage for me to leave the convent. I really thought I was leaving to nothing, that no one would ever want me, choose me. But the first five years I was out of the convent, I dated all the time, and I was so surprised. I really wanted to get married, but none of them was right. It is so sad when people leave the convent to get married, like I did, and they don't end up with either a loving husband or a loving community of other nuns. But I found this wonderful husband . . ."

Deciding to leave the convent was also traumatic for Betty. It was definitely not the thing to do in 1967. "I had the closest thing to what I would call an existential crisis where you see yourself, and yet you put yourself outside of yourself, and you can't really cope. We could go walking during meditation time, and I would go as far away as I could go, and just scream bloody murder and cry out as loud as I could to try and get the horrendous turmoil out of my body."

When she arrived home, her surprised parents were so upset that she had left the convent that they cried. They said they disowned her. They let her stay the night, but they wouldn't let her go to church with them the next morning (a Sunday), or eat at the same table with them, or be seen with them. For a long time afterward, she could not even go to church at her parents' parish, and she slept on the floor of her sister's apartment. She bought material with the $25 she had been given by the nuns when she left and made clothes so she would have something to wear to school the next week. She got the college to agree they would let her continue on in the classes she had been in as a nun. Finding a job was more difficult, because no one wanted to hire her when they found out she was an ex-nun.

"For the rest of the year, I slept about two to three hours a night, worked as a nurse full-time, went to school full-time and lived on the candy and apples and stuff the patients in the hospital would give me." Eventually her parents forgave her and came to her graduation.

Nuns were not the only women having problems adjusting to the changes or relating to the Church during these years. Carolyn started law school in 1971. After she graduated, she got very active in politics. It was not always a happy fit.

"There is a real anti-Catholicism in liberal politics, because you get with people who have knee-jerk reactions," she explains. "In liberal politics you have groups with special agendas. You have the feminists, and the pro-choice, and the Zionists . . . . The list is long. They are as bad as people on the right. They can be terrible. I got caught up in a lot of that agenda. It was creating a lot of conflict, not with my beliefs, but with the institutional Church. I was particularly angry when the Pope went to Ireland and he talked about women's roles being virgin or mother. And I thought, *where does that put me? I'm a lawyer.*"

Terry ended up at a Catholic women's college in the Midwest. She had to pay the tuition herself because her father refused to waste that kind of money on a girl. She particularly remembers her fourth-year religion class. "The class was taught by a Jesuit priest who had a definite drinking problem and hated women. And I remember thinking, *why is this man teaching at a women's college if he hates women so much?* Everyone was afraid of him, because he held it over our heads that if we didn't pass his class we couldn't graduate."

According to Terry, "the only women on campus who were involved with the Church were the nerds . . . . You knew they were going to become nuns. There wasn't anything about them that was attractive. The nuns who taught us were very old-fashioned; they were still wearing their full habits then [1974–1979] and today they are still wearing long black dresses and veils."

Cassandra began to understand the women's movement the hard way. Her husband was in school, and she was supporting the family as a book-keeper. Then the company was bought out, and only one person—a man—in her department kept his job. Worse still, she had to train him to take over her job as well. Angry, she asked her now former bosses why they didn't just keep her instead of having her train him. And they answered that he was a man, so he needed the job more. Suddenly Cassandra became aware of how little society valued women or their work.

"It didn't take me very long to figure out that the same kind of thing was also going on in my parish," Cassandra explains. "I began to wonder, why does the pastor ask me if I have my husband's permission to work before he will consider me for a job as Director of Religious Education? Why does any-one insist that my dress be a certain length [these were the miniskirt years] in order not to offend the Lord, who created my body in the first place?"

Such "subversive" ideas began to ferment slowly in Cassandra and were fed by other experiences and conversations with other women, many of them nuns with newly raised feminist consciences, whom she met at the Catholic university where she was studying. Then an ex-nun who was Direc-tor of Religious Education at another parish became her mentor.

The feminist movement in the Catholic church began to take shape slowly for Cassandra and women like her all around the country. One by one, these women started to reach out to one another, some timidly at first, others more aggressively, in order to share new ideas and rituals.

Cassandra's first organized feminist experience with other Catholic women came in the early 1980s at a weekend Women's Ordination Confer-ence put on by a group of laywomen and nuns. She and other women shared their stories, revealed their spiritual joys and problems, and searched for healing and solutions.

As the 1970s came to a close, Cassandra's story was repeating itself throughout the country. Sometimes sponsored by national organizations, more often local and completely grassroot, other women started coming together to pray and to share. For the first time, however, these gatherings were being organized by women for themselves and by themselves, not under the direction of a male priest as had been done in the past.

Almost before anyone really knew what was happening, the feminist movement in the Catholic church began to grow.

THE 1980S

The year 1980 began on a high note for feminist women in the Catholic church. Only a few months earlier, Sister Theresa Kane, as president of both the Sisters of Mercy and the Leadership Conference of Women Religious, publicly asked Pope John Paul II, during his first visit to the United States, to consider the possibility that women be included in all ministries of the Church (meaning ordination). Although some Catholics were upset that she was "washing our dirty laundry in public" (on national television), others were impressed by her courage and her vision. To this day, more than a few Catholic women can remember where they were and what they were doing when they heard Theresa Kane's speech.

At the time, it did not seem like such an impossible request. After all, more and more jobs were opening up for women everywhere, both in society and in the Church. In many parishes women were being allowed to be Eucharistic ministers (those who distribute Communion) and lectors (those who read) during Mass, jobs their husbands and brothers had been given by Vatican II around the end of the 1960s.

Toward a New Solidarity

Considered at the time one of the more positive events of the 1980s was the decision of the U.S. bishops to write a pastoral letter on women in the Catholic church. In accord with their practice to consult experts in the field before writing a pastoral letter, they decided to ask women to tell them about their experiences.

That any men in the Church—particularly bishops—would take women so seriously, let alone solicit their opinions, was such a revolutionary idea that many women found it difficult to believe. Even more unbelievable was the question that was being asked: "How have you been affirmed by society and the Church and how have you been oppressed by society and the Church?"

Feminists were excited and surprised. This had to be the work of the Holy Spirit herself. They were sure that if they had gone into the parishes and talked to women that way on their own, they would have been accused of heresy and inciting riot. Instead, it was the U.S. bishops themselves asking these threatening and radical questions!

One listening session that I led was of a group of women who were all at least 60 years old. Many were decades older. These were women who had been and still were the most faithful participants and workers of their parishes. Yet rarely, if ever, had they been asked their opinion on any substantive issue regarding their personal lives. I found them excited and enthusiastic about sharing their life stories, but extremely skeptical that any men in the Church would really hear what they had to say.

However, the bishops did listen, and the first draft of their Pastoral on Women proved that they did. The problem was how to fit what they heard into an overall policy statement that would be supported by the Vatican. Ten years later, in the fall of 1992, after four tries and extreme pressure from women on both sides of the political spectrum, they gave up.

But all the women involved in the listening sessions were changed by the process. For our parish, it was the first time that any of us had ever talked about real-life issues as a group, the first time that many of us really connected with one another regardless of our personal positions on particular issues.

When I interviewed her, Jane H. reminded me that she had been present at a listening session that I led. "We wrote down all sorts of things, and I thought it was a great evening," she recalls, "but I think that the hierarchy was very upset with what they got out of it—the bishops I mean—and they got the same thing from everyone. Was there any follow-up? I have never heard anything about it since we had that meeting."

Hers was not the only such comment that I heard when conducting interviews. Cynthia headed the group responsible for organizing the listening sessions in her diocese. "That process changed all 21 of us on the committee," she says. "We felt a solidarity with women, felt an affirmation of ourselves and one another. The Church needs to understand how we live and that we are smart, that we know things. They need to know that sometimes women have to make decisions that are difficult. The gentleness of the language of what I heard was what was profound for me. It didn't have the jargon of pro-choice and pro-life. It just said things from the heart."

Polarization Between the Right-Wing and Left-Wing

Not every encounter was as gentle. Inspired by the many women I was meeting, mostly nuns, and intrigued by where they were leading us, I started participating in some of their activities. I saw my role as that of a bridge between the average woman in the pew and the feminist nuns. In fact, I volunteered to lead a workshop entitled "The Average Women in the Pew" at the National Association of Religious Women (NARW) convention when it came to Los Angeles. Almost every laywoman at the convention, and many nuns, signed up for my workshop.

Feeling smug at my new sensitivity and understanding about women in the Church, I confidently started the first workshop with the prayers and procedures that had worked so well during the listening sessions a few months earlier. However, as we broke up into small groups for discussion, I noticed two women (both nuns) leaving the workshop, one in tears. I soon discovered that they were upset because I had started the session with the "Our Father," and even worse, ended with "Glory Be to the Father and to the Son and the Holy Spirit." They were sure I had used these sexist prayers on purpose to humiliate them. Flabbergasted, the only thing I was sure of was that there was a huge chasm between the average woman in the pew and these feminist women, and that the chasm was growing ever larger.

If the feminist nuns were moving too quickly for me, they were centuries ahead of Helen Hitchcock in St. Louis. Fearful that the bishops would hear only angry feminist voices, she gathered together five friends to form a group that would defend the Pope's teachings on all subjects. Called Women for Faith and Family, this group is against almost every aspect of the women's movement and is still active today, trying to push the hierarchy even further right than it naturally is.

The polarization between liberal and conservative viewpoints increased in the 1980s as the liberals got braver and louder and the conservatives started to catch on that the struggle was less about single issues than about a desire to change the entire system, both in the Church and in society.

Instead of teaching middle-class children in the suburbs practically for free, as they had done in the past, many nuns began to work as community organizers with the poor in the inner city. Other people—not only nuns— became involved with social justice struggles in Latin America as well as in the United States. Surprisingly, abortion almost unwittingly became the symbol of the Catholic feminist movement.

When Geraldine Ferraro was running for vice president of the United States, her pro-choice position was attacked by conservative bishops, led by Archbishop O'Conner of New York. Ferraro had been very clear about her position on abortion ever since she was a Congresswoman. She said she personally accepted the Church's doctrine on abortion but felt she could not impose her religious views on others. Furthermore, she had dealt with brutal cases of rape, incest, and child abuse when she had been head of the Special Victim's Bureau for the District Attorney's office, which had affected her greatly.[14]

Soon after Ferraro was condemned for her stand on abortion, 26 nuns joined four priests and 69 Catholic laypeople in signing an advertisement in support of her. To innocent Americans brought up believing in democracy and freedom of speech, the wording of the *New York Times* announcement seemed factual and almost innocuous. "A diversity of opinions regarding abortion exists among committed Catholics," was its main statement.

"It said almost nothing," Sister Maureen Fiedler, one of the signers, tells me when we talk. "A columnist wrote that it was equivalent to the colonists asking King George if they could have a dialogue about this matter of tea. I signed it primarily because I was furious about what the hierarchy was doing to Geraldine Ferraro. It never occurred to me that the Vatican would do anything about it. That was such a medieval notion, that people couldn't even talk about a subject."

Several months later, the head of Fiedler's community of nuns got a letter from the Vatican saying that the nuns who signed the letter either had to retract their signatures or leave the convent. These letters were sent to the heads of the orders involved, not to the individual women.

But this was 1984, not 1954, and women religious in the United States were no longer isolated from one another. Despite instructions to the contrary, the leadership of all of the orders involved consulted with one another concerning what their response to the Vatican should be. The next two years were extremely difficult for all involved as the leaders of each order tried to come up with some solution that their signers could, in conscience, agree to that would placate the Vatican.

Barbara Ferraro (no relation to Geraldine) and Patricia Hussey, two of the women involved, refused any compromise and in the process of their long fight with the Church decided that they were definitely pro-choice. Their book, *No Turning Back*, tells of their ordeal. They eventually left the convent.

Jo'Ann, one of the hundreds of friends of one signer, Sister Marge Tuite, who died soon after, tells me, "Margie was near tears when she talked to me about the possibility that she would be removed from her religious order for doing this. Then she really cried, and she said, 'You know, I am a cultural Catholic. Every fiber of my being has grown up with that Catholic identification and they can't take that away from me.'"

Although Tuite was eventually "cleared" by the Vatican, she did not sign a letter of retraction and never saw the letter that the heads of her order sent to Rome on her behalf to resolve the issue. Many of her friends believe that Tuite's death from cancer was directly attributable to her stress over this incident.

Barbara was not one of the signers, nor was she in the leadership of her order then, as she is now, but she thinks that the Major Superiors involved handled the problem very well. "They all got together and refused to allow themselves to be isolated. There was a lot of strategizing and moderation and working together to compromise."

However, Maureen Fiedler is not as sure that she did the right thing by compromising. "I went through all sorts of problems about whether I was giving up my principles. It was a terrible trauma. Signing the ad felt fine, but compromising with the Vatican on this is what really caused me stress. I would never compromise like that again."

Although she praised the way her order handled the problem, she and many of the signers were upset that the leaders would frequently meet to discuss how they were going to confront the Vatican without including the signers in the meeting.

In the end, most of the women in this confrontation did what women have been doing with men all along: They played a semantic game and offered them a face-saving solution. "A tremendous amount of time went into crafting statements," Patricia Hussey maintains. She, however, refused to go along with playing word games that did not mean retraction to the signers but looked like they meant adherence to the Church's teaching against abortion to the Vatican.[15]

Whether this was a good or bad solution depends on where you stand on the feminist scale and what your tolerance is for ambiguity and compromise. But an even larger Churchwide showdown with feminist American nuns was avoided ("Perhaps only postponed," one nun suggests) which might have happened if many nuns had actually been expelled from their orders. Many women also believe that, because of this incident, the Vatican will think twice before pushing American Catholic women, particularly nuns, into a corner in the future, since so much bad publicity was generated. It is now obvious, even to the Vatican, that women will no longer automatically capitulate to every demand.

Setbacks for Feminists

In retrospect, the decade of the 1980s turned out to be one of anger, frustration, and even burnout for many women who had been at least partially awakened in the 1970s. The Equal Rights Amendment, thought so close to passage, lost its battle for ratification by a three-state margin. Women, recently trained for ministry in the Catholic church, experienced less-than-adequate salaries and unfair hiring practices. On the job, many women discovered that they were expected to accept supervision (often arbitrary) by a male (usually a priest) even though they were doing all the work and were better qualified for their jobs than their bosses.[16]

At a joint meeting of the heads of male and female religious orders in San Francisco in 1982, everyone understood that only men would be present around the altar during the consecration of the bread and wine at Mass. But an effort was made to include the women in the liturgy by asking some of them to help distribute Communion. At the last minute it was decided, supposedly by the dictates of a Vatican representative in attendance, that Church law required that women were only allowed to distribute Communion if there were not enough priests available. Obviously, with the church half full of priests, there were plenty of male alternatives to women. Since this was an on-the-spot dictate, there had been no time to warn the chosen women in advance that their services were no longer needed (allowed). When the women approached the altar to get the hosts that they were to distribute, they were sent back to their seats empty-handed. Rather than humiliate the women, this highly visible and emotionally charged dismissal turned out to be a blessing in disguise for the cause of women because it graphically awakened even the most conservative members of the audience to the issue of sexism in the Church.

The 1980s turned out to be a decade of two steps forward, one and three-quarter steps backward for many women. As the decade came to a close, few women, including the feminist nuns, had enough energy left to worry about the battle of the sexes, even in the Church. With both the national and the world economy in a deep recession, violence and despair threatening to overwhelm our cities, our schools, and even our families, and the Third World struggling to be included as an equal in the 21st century, there was and is simply too much else to be done.

And Catholic women are busy doing it!

"It didn't matter if the hierarchy of the Church couldn't hear what we said in the listening sessions," Cynthia says softly. "And it still does not matter. Because my life goes on without them. And I would love to have the hierarchy join us. I would love to have them be with me. But they can't right now.

"I think marriages have gone through the same changes that the Church has, in the same time frame—I mean, if you go from Vatican II on. Marriage took a radical change in the 1960s, and we see it in the divorce rate. But those of us who survive in marriage are giving an example of how you can survive in the Church."

Many women are refusing to walk away from the Catholic church, but at the same time they will not relinquish their newfound ability to describe their own reality. Even those reluctant to confront are equally unwilling to abandon their vision for the Church and for society. Often involved in social justice causes, perhaps less judgmental and more inclusive than they have been in decades, Catholic women who stay in the Church have internalized, almost without realizing that they are doing so, one of the main messages of Vatican II. Feminists, traditionalists, those exploring new kinds of spirituality, the young, the old, and the in-between—those who stay are all truly convinced that *they* are the Catholic church. And they refuse to hear anyone, even the Pope, who tells them that they are not.

CHAPTER TWO

Parts of a Whole:
The Makeup of Women
in the Catholic Church

It is not only politically incorrect but intellectually dangerous to lump people into categories or stereotypes. People often, however, have enough beliefs or traits in common that they *can* be considered as part of more or less homogeneous groups. Labeling, while neither scientifically nor morally accurate, is a kind of a shorthand writers use to make their books more compact, their points more easily understood.

Years ago, Catholic women could be placed in only two categories: practicing and nonpracticing. But as the 20th century comes to a close, there are many more options. Life, as well as religious choices, is much more complicated than it once was.

Keeping in mind that many women will place themselves in more than one category, let's take a look at where women in the Catholic church might be today if we divided them into groups according to their political and religious points of view.

INTENSE, ANGRY, RADICAL FEMINISTS

These women get the most press because they make the most interesting (maybe *sensational* is a better word) reading and give the public the most vicarious excitement. Although people often write them off as shrill and humorless, many of these women can be extremely funny.

Ruth Fitzpatrick, leader of the Women's Ordination Conference (WOC), works in Fairfax, Virginia, about a half-hour ride from Washington, D.C. She is one of the more visible Catholic feminists in the United States today, and a university scholar as well as a continual thorn in the side of the American bishops.

Barely paid and always overworked, Ruth is famous for the light touches she brings to a serious and, for many, painful list of subjects. Her newsletters to WOC members are a delight to read, despite their often upsetting content. At Halloween, the office pumpkin usually wears a bishop's miter.

At WOC fund-raising/award dinners, musician/songwriter/intense feminist Marsie Silvestro usually *is* the stand-up comic. I suspect that she may be the writer behind such slogans as "Don't throw stones at sinners, throw WOCs at popes." As the dinner plates are cleared away, the excited crowd of women hums "May Procession" songs from their grammar school days when the Blessed Mother is crowned with flowers. Behold, the *Regina Coeli* (a Latin title for Mary, meaning "Queen of Heaven") miraculously appears. A red checkered apron serves as her veil. A silver halo, complete with dangling star, encircles her head. Extra large, dark glasses with bright blue frames cover her eyes as she proceeds to send the giddy women into peals of laughter with Catholic jokes about her son, Jesus, and his Church.

At the last WOC dinner, which was held in Albuquerque in spring of 1993, the *Regina Coeli* was followed by a medley of songs written and sung by Dorothy "Dody" Davies with verses like the following found in "Spiritual Indigestion."

The church of my youth
Says it feeds me the truth
But, with half of the human loaf only,
It's my half that's missing
And so I'm insisting
I'm choking on "holy baloney."

The Holy Book tells us
of males reproducing
Again and again and again
With all that begetting
Say, aren't we forgetting
That babies are not born to men?

The two verses quoted from the original song, "Spiritual Indigestion," with lyrics and music by Dorothy "Dody" Davies, 612 11th St. S.W. Willmar, MN 56201, are contained in two forms:
1. A book of lyrics as poetry titled WOMANVOICE, published by Willmar, MN, © 1990.
2. A cassette tape of original music titled "Expanding The Circle," © 1991.
The song itself has a copyright date of 1989. Inspiration for the title is from Mary Collins' book, Women at Prayer.

But intense feminists certainly don't spend all their time laughing at parties. Some, like Maureen Fiedler and Dolly Pomerleau, work overtime trying to change the Catholic church by lobbying bishops as well as other priests and laypeople through Catholics Speak Out (a project of the Quixote Center in Maryland), which is trying to find a place for democracy within parishes and the rest of the institutional Church. Throughout the United States, there is a long list of other liberal grassroots organizations with similar agendas.

Many radical feminist women, however, who were equally passionate about their new religious and societal insights in the 1970s and 1980s, have left the Church (as much as one ever "stops" being Catholic any more than anyone ever "stops" being Jewish). Others are now so involved in social justice issues that have to do with the poor and the oppressed of the world that they do not have much interest or energy left to focus on the institutional

Church. For them, the issue of sexism in society and the Church is just another in a long list of problems in a worldwide, unjust system where all the power and money reside in the hands of white, middle- and upper-class European and Euro-American males.

According to Sandra Schneiders, who is both a nun and a theologian as well as a prolific writer and lecturer, in her book *Beyond Patching*, these women, when they identify themselves as Catholic "do not belong to the Catholic church, they ARE Catholics. But once they have had their consciousness raised, they can never forget. This often causes a deep, emotionally draining anger that can run from rage to depression."

Schneiders claims that, although these women have been brought up in the Catholic tradition, they increasingly understand that every aspect of it is not just tainted but perverted by the evil of patriarchy. "It is not that the tradition has some problems, but that the tradition IS the problem. And her anger puts her in a double bind."[1]

Cassandra is a perfect example of the kind of anger Schneiders is talking about. A laywoman who has a master's in religious education and is a master catechist of her diocese, Cassandra is often upset with the hierarchy of the Catholic church. Yet she claims that she does not see the institutional Church as irrelevant, despite her angry feelings.

"I think it is a necessary structure to keep chaos from reigning," Cassandra maintains. "But I ignore the hierarchy because *they* consider the institutional Church irrelevant. They only see the hierarchy as relevant. They don't see the Church—the ecclesia—as relevant. They maintain the hierarchy for the sake of the hierarchy. It is the same stuff that was happening in the Old Testament in the time of Christ.

"Today's male church leaders have never heard of new management techniques about collaboration and inclusive patterns for making things happen for the betterment of all people. Instead, they want to keep the hierarchy for the betterment of the hierarchy and infantilize the laity. It is easier to manage, easier to control us that way. That's their bottom line."

One large complication is that many radical feminists depend upon the Catholic church for their livelihood. If they are not actual employees, they are probably members of a Catholic religious organization or some social outreach program that gets at least some of its funding from the institutional Catholic church. If the feminist expresses her anger, she is censored for being angry, strident, and heretical and risks being fired. If she represses it, she destroys her own integrity and psychological well-being.

The well-known lay theologian Rosemary Radford Ruether asserts that "as a feminist, I can come up with only one reason to stay in the Catholic church. You're never going to change it if you leave. So that's why I stay around."[2]

Sister Hortense (not her real name because she works at a company that needs official, institutional Catholic church approval for the educational products they produce) explains: "When I reflect on what it is that we as Roman Catholics believe that is rooted in the Gospel, I have no problem with it. The problems have been caused by patriarchal interpretations. I have no problem with anything in the Gospel. But what is based on patriarchy, ways in which the male church was able to dominate people, mostly poor and uneducated women, because traditionally they have been the most involved . . . that's another thing altogether."

She goes on, her voice perfectly matter-of-fact and unemotional, telling a story of how the sacrament of confession has often been used as a tool of patriarchy. "The woman in a small Irish village would say something in confession about her problems at home—how her husband gets drunk and beats her—and the priest would ask if she had been giving him his husbandly reward, and she would say she found it difficult when he was drunk or has beaten her or the kids. And the priest would be sympathetic and say, 'But it would be better. Why don't you have another baby?' It was the priest who was making life more difficult for her, and the priest who was perpetuating the patriarchy of the village."

My friend Jo'Ann (who worked hard, but with little success, to get me to stop saying "you guys" during my interview with her and two other nuns) insists that one of the most divisive issues among her fellow (that probably is a no-no sexist term also) sisters is the issue of Mass and the Eucharist (Communion).

"I can go to Church with my brother and sister-in-law and the kids as a social activity," she tells me, "but I don't go to Mass generally. What is really difficult for me is when we gather as a group of religious women, we don't just chit-chat. We do faith sharing. We talk about important issues in our lives and the lives of the people with whom we work.

"Then, at the end of the day, we bring in 'stud service' to say Mass. And I have to tell you, this is very difficult for me. Sometimes, the priests who come in are friends of mine, which makes it even more difficult, because I become very hostile, personally, to them. And then I hear that some people think that my reaction proves that Eucharist is not important to me. If it weren't important to me, it wouldn't cause me such pain."

Her friend France agrees. "I have no community at Sunday Mass. It is not a home, and I don't know why I go. It is like being an abused wife." She goes on Sunday, but for her there are many times when she believes it would be more prayerful to not attend.

"For example, yesterday I went to Mass with my sister and her family," she continues. "I was very aware of the words used to introduce the Creed. The celebrant had a good sermon, so that was not a painful experience. But then he said something as simple as 'Let's recite what we all believe,' and there I was. I could say pieces of it, but not 'I believe in God, the Father Almighty,' I couldn't say that. It's not that I couldn't call God Father. It is that 'Father' and 'God' are not the relationship I have. If God is Father, God is also Mother. And then all through the Creed was 'he,' 'he,' 'he.'"

For both Jo'Ann and France, women's ordination is a justice issue, not only because the current policy of male priests discriminates against women, but because there is such a lack of priests to serve the religious needs of the poor in Third World countries.

"As long as there are the haves and the have nots, in terms of Eucharist, then I know that the method of making it available is, in itself, unjust," Jo'Ann assures me. "In Boston, where I grew up, there are plenty of priests. The sisters can even have Mass in their own convent chapel. But my sister in community, who works in Haiti, is the pastor of 19 little mission parishes, and when she visits each parish, like an itinerant preacher, she cannot say Mass or offer the other Sacraments. They may get a 'real' priest once every six months."

It is women like Jo'Ann, France, and Cassandra whom Richard McBriend, chairman of the University of Notre Dame's theology department, refers to in his 1990 *New York Times* article. In it, he claims that, because of the post–1978 Vatican strategy aimed at restoring the Church to the institutional state it was before Vatican II, many of the priests, nuns, and laity are edging to the conclusion that the Church's present leadership is irrelevant, if not inimical, to their deepest religious and human concerns.[3]

The other sister present during my interview with Jo'Ann and France, Mary Anne, answers my question "What kind of a Catholic are you?" with "barely." "But," she says, more philosophically, "if I want to belong to a body of believers, what else is there? It is a big Church. History takes a long time, and it is not always going to be like this. And so I get along with life. One part of me gets very angry, but there is another part that says, 'Hey, I do what I need to do. If they don't like it, that's their problem, not mine.'"

With these closing words, Mary Ann shows she is on the verge of changing groups and becoming a moderate feminist.

MODERATE FEMINISTS

Moderate feminists are a very large group within the Catholic church today, and more and more women are joining their ranks. Their viewpoint is either "What the Pope doesn't know won't hurt him" or they more or less consider the hierarchy of the Catholic church irrelevant to their own spiritual journey. Philosophically, they are pragmatists. They use what they need and don't spend too much time and energy on the rest.

Many of them believe that, for all practical purposes, there are two churches: The Vatican and the real Church. Yet some of them still consider the institutional Church necessary for organizational structure and moral direction, as long as the word coming out of the Vatican is not too reactionary or does not contradict too drastically their own experience. All of them are not convinced that the entire system is hopeless.

Like Mary Anne, many members of this group were once intense, angry, radical feminists. Now, while they may still feel angry now and then, it is rarely their dominant emotion. They are very aware of the many compromises they make every day, in every aspect of their lives, and they have outgrown feeling guilty or inadequate because they are willing to compromise. They refuse to take each individual conflict or difference of opinion too seriously and believe the world, as well as the Church, is large enough for many viewpoints.

Some are taking a "vacation" from working for the institutional Church because this work demanded more compromises than they were willing to make. Cynthia was a campus minister for many years. She recently left that position and is currently bringing a program that helps improve human relationships to public grammar schools. She often thinks about her previous job. "I am missing liturgy," she explains sadly. "I want to teach Church. I want to tell people how wonderful it is, and I can't, especially young people. I can't teach them the lies anymore. I can't teach them that gay people are bad, whether with or without practicing sex. It just isn't true. I can't preach to young girls that they are inferior and that you are not allowed on the altar because you menstruate. That your hands are dirty because you are a woman.

"But I don't leave the Church because I'm not mistreated by Jesus. And I'm not mistreated by all men in the Church. I know many of them value our talents and our insights and would be happy if we could share leadership in the Church with them. But other men in the Church think that they can do it alone. They get a little input, but most of the time they are fine all by themselves. We women can't be that way. We know both men and women need to be included, that we all need to work together. God must be talking to them like God is talking to us. But some men just can't hear it."

She sighs. "The radical feminists stay out there and name the problem. They do it so well. But I can't keep harping about all this and stay married or raise my two sons. It makes my life too difficult. My relationships with men are too important to me."

Bridget, a schoolteacher in her early forties who has a master's degree in theology and has recently entered the convent, thinks the Catholic church has a lot to offer. But she immediately clarifies her point: "Not the hierarchy, but the people who really are the Church. It is the people in the pews that count."

Sister Hortense, from our previous category, said much the same thing. "My education in theology is what has kept me in the Church. And many theologians manage to survive in the Catholic church by becoming very astute at doing what is politically correct. They make certain statements in public that they would never make in private and vice versa. As a catechist in the Roman tradition, I suppose I do a bit of that myself. But for my personal faith life, I don't think of Roman Catholicism as the Vatican hierarchy. I equate it with average people who just happen to be Roman Catholic. And that is a big difference!"

Sharon agrees. "I go to these seminars where we pray for inner healing. People get noisy and relate to each other. And I think, *They aren't threatened about letting us talk. They aren't trying to direct us.* These people are allowing me to relate in the way I need to relate, to experience what God wants me to experience. The Church has a difficult time in trusting in God enough not to let things be so orderly. Order, rather than spirit, has become the priority. We are on a timetable. But the spirit is messy, like nature. Birth is messy, death is messy, nature is messy."

"I think *ignore* is not the right word," another interviewee tells me. "I think *question* is better. Obviously I don't think that it is irrelevant, because I wouldn't go to Church on Sunday if I did. But I retain the right to think for myself on social and political issues that differ from the standard line of the Catholic church."

Sheila's main emphasis is on social action. She currently teaches English as a second language. "I work with the Catholic Worker Movement," she tells me, "which is almost outside the Church, and certainly not related to the hierarchy. I'm able to do what I want to do in the Catholic Worker Movement. It might be different if I were in my twenties and thirties, but there are few rules today that have much to do with me." (This is technically not true, since she also told me that she is married to an ex-priest who was never laicized. They were married by a Baptist minister, and then she converted to Catholicism. They both go to Mass and Communion every week.)

Although Jennifer is in her twenties, she doesn't feel restricted by rules anymore either. "I try to ask myself how would God view it...how would Jesus view it? I think that God is a lot more open-minded than our Church and people in general. When I came back to the Church after being away for a year, I did not feel like I had to answer to anyone in the Church. I did not feel like I needed to go to confession to a priest. I felt that I was answering to God. That was the relationship I felt most broken about."

Jennifer continues, "The Pope is very old, very traditional, and very conservative. And anyone being very conservative right now bothers me. It bugs me, because I feel like who are we, who is anyone, to judge another person.

"I feel the Church is important to establish values and morals and a sense of community and to encourage a sense of spirituality, but I don't really pay much attention to the hierarchy of it. I am willing to let the Church guide me. I feel the Church needs to present a very consistent morality. It needs to be black and white. But we live in a gray world, and we make the choices, based on their black-and-white ideals, which might work if we were all in an ideal situation, but we aren't.

"I am more for individual conscience rather than rules," she concludes. "But a lot of the things that the Church teaches, over time, I am coming to find, do make sense. Most of it is not unreasonable."

On the other end of the age spectrum, Sister Mary Luke Tobin, now in her mid-eighties and the only American Catholic nun to be an actual participant in Vatican II conferences, sums up this category of Catholic women perfectly. "I think people are saying, 'Yes, there are rights and wrongs. And I understand them. But sometimes I am caught in the middle of them and I have to make up my own mind and do the best I can.'

"This is a ship that is listing," she continues, "and I don't know how many years it will take, but I expect the Church will pull itself into a better position. I don't know what it is going to take to do that, but otherwise people will be ignoring the institutional Church, and I think there is too much good, too many riches for that to happen. But, for a while anyway, we are going to see the Vatican hierarchy being ignored."

CODEPENDENT CATHOLICS

If the moderate feminists rid themselves of anger by ignoring the hierarchy of the church, codependent Catholics rid themselves of anger by refusing to acknowledge these feelings.

I hesitate to use the word *codependent*, which is part of the psychological jargon of the day and often just means someone who you think should be angry but who doesn't seem aware enough to say that she is, or brave enough do anything about it. Many times the label is applied to almost any caring, thoughtful person, usually a woman, who is willing to compromise on almost any issue.

In psychology, "codependent" was first used to refer to a person who is "addicted" to maintaining his or her relationship with another person who in turn is addicted to alcohol, drugs, sex, or any other neurotic compulsion. The first time I saw this word used in reference to members of the Catholic church was in Matthew Fox's much-publicized August 1988 letter to Cardinal Joseph Ratzinger (who is head of the Vatican Congregation for the Doctrine of the Faith, formerly known as the Inquisition) in protest to his attempts to silence Fox for his work with creation spirituality.

Since then, Franciscan Michael Crosby has written a book entitled *The Dysfunctional Church: Addiction and Codependency in the Family of Catholicism*. He says that the core issue of his book is "when, for the sake of tradition, Peter's power to bind and loose is absolutized in a way that subordinates the power of the other members of the Church, the word of God itself can be nullified in order to preserve abusive power patterns in the institutional Church."[4]

Crosby claims that this power addiction gets expressed in the addictive process geared to the preservation of the male, celibate, clerical-controlled model of the Church. He insists that clericalism would not exist in the Church and the hierarchical principle would not have effective control if priests and laity did not allow it to happen. But priests and bishops permit and encourage clericalism because their identity is only in their roles.

According to Crosby, to ask priests and bishops to critique patriarchal clericalism in the Church is the same as asking them to self-destruct. He maintains that the laity also helps maintain this clericalism because they, as well as the priests, are addicted to the promise of the organization, which is everything from life everlasting to a sense of belonging to a community, and are therefore willing to endure any amount of bad experiences to hold on to that promise.

Cassandra agrees with Crosby. When she was the director of religious education for her parish, she is sure she often acted in a codependent manner. "I was saving the Church from itself at the expense of my own life. I had grown up in an alcoholic household, so I was an expert at being a codependent. I remember one reconciliation service we had planned during Lent one year, and the priest never showed up, so I made a choice to go along and make it look OK. I said I did it for the people. But my doing so 'saved' the priest, and made him feel it was OK to go on being irresponsible and uncaring, because I would rescue him.

"We had a problem in our family, with a teenage son, and we did an intervention and all four of us (including my husband and daughter) went for 30 days to a 12-step family counseling program. I began to make those connections that what we were doing in this house was very similar to what I was doing in the Church: making excuses, protecting, setting things up so that the patterns of inappropriate behavior could continue."

With this realization, Cassandra soon left her job in the parish. She maintains that many people have similar codependent relationships with the Church that cause them to do different things. "Some people leave one dysfunctional situation for another, like a woman divorcing one alcoholic for another alcoholic. They leave this parish to go to that parish to go to another parish. Or they leave this denomination to go to that denomination. Others stay and pretend that it is normal. They say 'thank you' every time a Eucharistic celebration is spoiled. They give any excuse at all, and that's another way of coping. Or they go home and never come out again. Finally, others are flat out not conscious of it. They've never been *in* enough to be critical. They run in, stay a few minutes, run out. They are not really part of the Church at all.

"For instance, our parish closed its convent this year. It has 16 bedrooms. Yet there were only three nuns living in the house: one teaching at the school, one retired, and one working at a nearby hospital. The last time there were 16 women in that convent was around 1956. Yet the comment from the general congregation was, 'Where are we going to put all the nuns if we close the convent?'"

Toni is a family therapist, and most of her clients are Catholic women. According to her, people, including herself, tend to deal with the Church the same way they deal with other issues in life. "A woman who tends to stuff down her feelings in general will do the same thing about the Church, and often will just kind of deny that there is a problem. She stays involved with the institutional Church because she is supposed to or for some other reason, or she simply gets out of the situation, never acknowledging that the source of the problem could have been dealt with in another way."

Toni believes that there is a tendency in our society to walk away from problems, especially relationship problems. If there is a problem with a particular priest, parish, or rule (such as birth control or divorce and remarriage), a woman may simply walk away from it and not acknowledge that there is a larger issue or that there are other ways to solve these problems.

Probably 70% of the women Toni has worked with are Catholic. Only a few of them are no longer practicing.

"I think that for the people who have evolved beyond a rigid adherence to doctrinal questions—in other words, beyond a kind of fundamentalist approach—the Church's teachings have been helpful rather than harmful. My personal belief is that if by the time a woman is 40 or 50, she still considers herself a practicing Catholic, she probably falls into one of two categories. Either she is just going along with it because she considers it the right thing to do and she doesn't think she has a choice, or she is a woman who has made some kind of peace with it. That means she has come to value what the Church has to offer her and has come to peace with those rules she can't deal with, can't accept. She uses what is useful to her and doesn't worry too much about the rest.

"But there are people who have thought of the Church as a furnished home or sanctuary. And then they find out that it isn't. And what they are left with is a building which was framed, and then windblown—at least that is how they view it. They still hold on to some kind of primitive, childlike view that the Church will provide this warm, comfy, furnished house. And even people, who have grown beyond that kind of preoperational thinking in other areas of their lives, sometimes have held on to it with the Church instead of saying, 'What I have here is the framework, but it is not finished for me. I have to finish it myself.'"

Coming to an adult understanding about one's relationship to the Catholic church is difficult for some women. Seeing problems in its structure, regardless of how apparent they may be, can be even more threatening. But putting one's head in the sand is not an option that will help the Church. A May 1992 editorial in the *National Catholic Reporter* warns us about what can happen if we close our eyes and continue to live in the paralysis of denial. The editorial puts it this way:

> Look around: Many Catholic young disown their religion even as they pursue the spiritual and live meaningful Christian lives. Many intelligent Catholic women see rampant sexism in the church and walk away. Many Catholic parents are increasingly less willing to pay for parish upkeep. Meanwhile, Catholic parishes, schools and hospitals consolidate or close.
>
> Many Catholic priests, overwhelmed, are ridden with depression. Many question their celibacy vows. Priests and the women religious are aging, retiring, their ranks not being replenished.
>
> That aspects—even key aspects of our church institutions—are dying should not be denied. To live in such denial virtually assures we cannot adequately recognize their fruits, mourn their passing, or prepare the passageways to new life.

Refusing to look at what the editorial is talking about is a good example of what is meant when the word *codependency* is linked to the words *Catholic church*.

THE NOTHING-HAS-CHANGED FUNDAMENTALISTS

These women are often very similar in psychology and behavior to the radical feminists. It is only their message that is opposite. In the 1990s their rhetoric sounds even more radical and angry than that of many of the feminists.

The most organized, articulate, and passionate group of Catholic religious fundamentalists are those women who founded and run Women for Faith and the Family (WFF). Begun in September 1984 in St. Louis by six women, WFF has a well-thought-out and specific agenda: to show support for every teaching of the most conservative member of the hierarchy of the Catholic church and to contradict every idea of the feminists (except for one: WFF does acknowledge the need, both economic and psychological, for some women to work outside the home).

In 1984, these women drew up an eight-point statement of fidelity to Church teachings called "The Affirmation for Catholic Women" and began to recruit signatures. They were worried that the U.S. bishops were only hearing the voices of extreme feminists during their listening sessions. They were afraid that the Pastoral, rather than being catechetical in nature, would turn out to be only a response to a limited set of feminists' erroneous concerns. They were particularly incensed with any reference to sexism in the Church.

According to WFF literature, this Affirmation has been translated into at least seven languages and has been circulated worldwide. In March of 1985, 4,000 signatures were sent to the U.S. bishops Women's Pastoral committee. In June, 10,000 signatures were sent to Pope John Paul II. In August 1985, a list of about 17,000 signatures was presented to U.S. bishops. In October 1987, testimony based on 10,000 letters from women was prepared for bishop delegates to the Synod on the Laity, and a list of 30,000 U.S. names of women who had signed the Affirmation was sent to Rome.

WFF claims about 10% of the signers of their Affirmation are nuns, most of whom are from "troubled" (i.e., feminist-dominated) orders. After talking to them and reading their literature, I am sure that WFF believes that they represent the majority of Catholic women, something that all but a very few of the women interviewed for this book would deny.

WFF is actively engaged in lobbying the hierarchy of the Catholic church, and they urge all Catholic women who agree with them to write to their bishops as well. There is no need to list the official beliefs and philosophy of the WFF because they are passionately against virtually every viewpoint expressed by feminists, even moderate ones, in this book. However, I will list just a few of their more interesting ideas in order to give you a flavor of what they are sending to the bishops:

All that Jesus took up from His culture by His teaching or action is normative for every culture of every time and place.

We oppose the systematic elimination from Scripture translations, liturgical texts, hymns, homilies and general usage of "man" as a generic.

Feminist language in the Church is not merely an inconsequential annoyance. Because these new translations frequently alter the substance of the Catholic faith, they jeopardize authentic belief in order to appease feminist reformers.

We recognize that the specific role of ordained priesthood is intrinsically connected with and representative of the begetting creativity of God in which only human males can participate. Human females, who by nature share in the creativity of God by their capacity to bring forth new life, and, reflective of this essential distinction, have a different and distinct role within the Church and in society from that accorded to men, can no more be priests than men can be mothers.

The quasi-Marxist origins of contemporary feminist or women's liberationist ideology must be made clear . . . . It is particularly appropriate and necessary at this moment in history for lay Catholic women to continue to take a leading role in this "New Cold War."

Not only is WFF against abortion, it is equally against contraception, although not against natural family planning. Any WFF member who is unable or unwilling to avoid going against Church law—such as marriage to someone who has been validly married before—must follow another Church law and abstain from receiving Communion. They are particularly upset that Catholic schools (i.e., feminist nuns) have generally *not* faithfully taught Catholic dogma since the early 1970s.

WFF board member Sherry Tyree does not speak in anything like the strident voice of the printed material she sent me. Yet she admits she is angry at the many women (and men) who claim to be representatives of the Church yet do not believe, nor teach, all of what the magesterium (teaching authority) of the Catholic church has traditionally taught and stood for.

"We have a terrible, terrible injustice being done to kids and adults who have a right to be taught authentic Catholic doctrine," she tells me. "I am very angry personally with individuals whose upbringing is Catholic but who no longer believe what the Catholic church teaches, who insist on imposing whatever they do believe on anyone who will listen."

She considers that the only honest thing for people who do not believe everything that the Church teaches to do is for them to admit that they are no longer Catholics. "If you have thought seriously about what the Church teaches and have really looked into it, and still disagree, then for your own soul and your own intellectual integrity, you ought to look elsewhere. Besides," Sherry continues, "each Catholic represents Catholicism to everyone who is not a Catholic, and it is simply not right to claim to be a Catholic and not be a Catholic at the same time."

Among the women WFF particularly take issue with are those who are involved with feminist spirituality and feminist theology. Their literature claims that these women are radically opposed to even the most fundamental dogmas of Christianity and "have become pervasive within the Catholic church itself, and their influence seriously threatens the faith of all, in particular that of Catholic women."

ADVOCATES OF FEMINIST OR CREATION SPIRITUALITY

Contrary to some TV and newspaper reports that were especially prevalent during the 1992 presidential election, most advocates of feminist spirituality do not call themselves witches, nor are they forming covens or resurrecting ancient female goddesses to worship. Almost all of them have expanded their viewpoint of God to include the feminine, but they have not thrown away the male images that they previously held.

Years ago, Catherine was a nun and a traditional Catholic. But today her religious views have changed substantially. She explains her new beliefs very well: "It is like having a house of four rooms, and you were only living in two of them, and now you have opened the doors and are suddenly living in all four. And that kind of liberation is caused by a willingness to risk to expand your meaning of God. We girls got it that God was masculine, but the great discovery is that God is also feminine. And we are feminine, so we finally have an incredible, infinite knowledge and participation in the divine which we didn't have before."

Many of these women still actively participate in regular Catholic liturgies where a male priest is the central celebrant. Others attend feminist liturgies, which, while rarely if ever called Mass, enjoy a very similar format, but without the benefit of a male priest as central celebrant.

Another group is those involved with Women-Church, a coalition of some 40 local, regional, and national feminist religious organizations. Although begun primarily by Catholic women (many nuns), Women-Church now attempts to be so inclusive of different religions and ethnic groups that some may call it post-Christian.

Almost 2,500 women, from 48 states and 16 countries, took part in its most recent conference, held in Albuquerque in April 1993. Although women's spirituality was often discussed, the majority of the workshops and presentations were about some aspect of social justice, ecology, or multiculturalism. Conference rhetoric was particularly powerful. The following quote, in both English and Spanish, graced the cover of the program for the three-day event: "Weaving a revolution, many women, many threads, and through our cultures and with our spirit, a healing power will rise from the earth, a healing power will rise . . . WOMEN-CHURCH!"

There have been three such Women-Church Convergence conferences within the last 15 years. Whether gathered at a national event or at a small local meeting, this ecumenical group of women uses many different kinds of rituals that spiritually speak to them as women. As Sandra Schneiders explains, "They are busy being Church, not trying to reform it. These women have bravely moved ahead and begun to live what they believe. They are not waiting for permission or until the rest of the Church is ready to move."[5]

As Catholic theologian Rosemary Radford Ruether explained at the 1993 conference, "We're always being asked whether we are staying in this church [Catholicism] or leaving this church—and this is not a question that's important to us. Rather, we should be concerned about being connected to the spirituality that brings life. And if the church wants to relate to us, then that's fine."[6]

Some Catholic women today participate comfortably in regular Catholic masses, feminist liturgies, and Women-Church events depending on their opportunities and their current social situation. At the present time, however, most women do not think it is appropriate to take their husbands or male teenage children to feminist or Women-Church liturgies.

Often these women also belong to, or at least are sympathetic to, the Women's Ordination Conference, which began in 1975. However, few advocate any "add women and stir" idea about the Catholic church. Sandra Schneiders reports that many of these women are also asking themselves "whether the God of Judeo-Christian revelation is the true God or just men-writ-large to legitimate their domination; whether Jesus, an historical male, is or can be messiah and savior for those who are not male; whether what the Church has called sacraments are really encounters with Christ or tools of male ritual abuse of women; and whether what we have called Church is a community of salvation or simply a male power structure."[7]

Schneiders contends that at no time in history, except perhaps at the time of the Protestant reformation, has the Church faced a crisis of such proportions, especially since more than 50% of the Church in every location in the world are women. She sees the feminism of Catholic women as both the Church's ultimate and most serious challenge and its best hope worthy of its gospel roots.

I believe that Schneiders is talking mainly about radical feminists. My personal experience is that only a small percentage of women who still consider themselves practicing Catholics have even thought about, let alone believe, what I have just quoted Schneiders as stating. On the contrary, many if not most Catholic women are attracted primarily to the loving Jesus of the New Testament whom they hear about in the Epistles and Gospels read at each Mass they attend, not to the avenging God that they think is found in the Old Testament, which they have barely read.

Although most of these women remain Christian, they are also creating a new kind of spirituality based on feminine ways of looking at reality and feminine ideas of inclusive, circular organization. This spirituality is changing the Catholic church from the bottom up. Even though most of these women may not be able to put any theological name on what they believe, many are actually advocates of creation spirituality, which preaches about the interconnectedness of everything in the world.

As Vivian tells me, "I no longer believe in a fall/redemption spirituality. Instead, I believe in the Cosmic Christ, and I try very hard to help this Cosmic Christ be present in every situation that I am in. I believe that creation spirituality is going to make all the difference in the world. Through it, the dualisms are being knocked down, those things that separate men from women, lay from clergy, the Catholic church from other churches, science from religion . . . . It is all coming tumbling down. And I really believe that we are working toward global cooperation."

According to Vivian, the idea of a Cosmic Christ comes right out of St. Paul. It has been present in the Church for centuries, especially during the time of women mystics in the Middle Ages. For Vivian, there is a pattern that connects, that is continually moving in the direction of wholeness. It is moving in the direction that God wants it to move in, even when it doesn't seem to be doing so. She sees Vatican II and all that it has taught us as one giant example of how the Holy Spirit works.

Diane is an artist specializing in interior design who is studying for a certificate in liturgy from her local diocese. She faithfully decorates her parish church each week. She sends me a poem she has written about this ministry and her beliefs. Its final paragraph lets us experience rather than intellectualize much of what feminist and creation spirituality offers the average woman:

> My Art sings alleluia and amen . . . . It expresses God's invitation:
> Come and I am with you through it all.
> Come, trust me in your experience, in happiness or pain.
> Come, you are my child: as much a part of my plan as
>   was Moses, Mary or Jesus.
> Come, you are as much a part of my plan as the
>   flowers, the fruit, the butterflies or the black soil.
> Come with the life I have blessed you with.
> Come be renewed. Then go forth. Go forth to preserve
>   life, to be its care-taker. Become a co-creator in my
>   kingdom. Know that I am with you.

TRADITIONALISTS

Although many were slower than other women to jump on the Vatican II bandwagon, traditionalists now enthusiastically accept most but not all of the official liturgical and operational changes in the Church over the last 25 years. Although most would insist that they are not feminists, few have escaped being influenced by the women's movement. But instead of being angry, they have become more open and less judgmental through their limited exposure to new philosophies.

Those who never considered any form of contraception for themselves usually support their daughters' decisions to practice artificial birth control. Many of them would never miss Mass on Sunday but do not try to force their young adult children or grandchildren to attend. Few could be called scrupulous by anyone, but they believe in the formal teachings of the Catholic church and adhere to as many as they possibly can.

Although many complain about the quality of preaching at Sunday Mass and wish that their parishes were run more democratically, most are happy, at least in principle, with the spiritual nourishment and moral direction they receive from the Catholic church. While sharing many doctrinal beliefs with the fundamentalists, they are as upset with these strident voices as they are with those of the intense feminists. All are against abortion, but few support the tactics of groups such as Operation Rescue.

Their relationship to the Church is spiritual rather than political, personal rather than universal. They take on faith whatever the Church teaches. Their questions are to enhance their understanding, not to disprove or alter what for them are century-old truths. Their religion is a source of comfort rather than conflict. For most, it is an emotional, not an intellectual, experience. Many are beginning to like and approve of nonsexist, inclusive language but have never thought of God other than as Father or Lord.

Those who oppose the ordination of women—and by no means do they all—do so mainly because the idea is strange and makes them feel uncomfortable. Many of these women have been very active in their parishes since their teenage years, and happily continue to do whatever is necessary to keep their parish running smoothly.

Colleen is one such woman, and she hesitated to be interviewed for this book. "I'm tired of all the Catholic bashing in books and on TV," she explains. "I'm fed up with all the jokes about Catholics, all the sex talk on TV. There are very few things that you can watch with your grandchildren these days, or even by yourself. I do not wish to be associated in any way, shape, or form with any publication that will liberalize my views."

When I assure her that I will let her preview any quotes attributed to her, she continues, "The Church is going to survive, come hell or high water, no matter what any of us do, no matter what the Pope does, or how many priests are entering, or how many sisters there are left. The Church has gone through much worse times than this in its time, and I am sure it is going to come out on top of the heap, as it always has. We just have to have faith and we have to live our lives now as best we can in accord to what we know is right and wrong."

Dolores Leckey, writer, lecturer, and director of the U.S. Bishops Secretariat for Family, Laity, Women and Youth, tells me much the same thing when I ask her to explain her faith and how it has changed over the years. "I realize more and more," she explains softly, "that I can't control the world or a lot around me. I think I am learning to trust God more. I think that is the major thing I have learned. That I am dying, and I am not the master planner. That the beauty of life is very important, and it doesn't take money. It takes being quiet and rearranging things. The human soul does long for God. We need to acknowledge a willingness to serve God and others. Probably the hardest thing in the world to say and really mean is, 'God's will be done.'"

You do not have to be middle-aged or older to be a traditionalist. Laura, who is in her late twenties, finds she is becoming more traditional as she grows older. Once a radical feminist, Laura is working on her Ph.D. in theology at Notre Dame. I contacted her because I had heard that at one time she had seriously considered leaving the Catholic church and becoming an Episcopalian so she could be ordained a priest.

She writes: "As an undergraduate college student, I felt a great deal of pain and anger at the Catholic hierarchy over women's issues. I was pro-choice and I took it for granted that the Church's official positions on questions of sexual ethics and birth control were misguided. At the same time I found the liturgy and the Christian spiritual tradition a source of deep strength and I seriously contemplated entering religious life."

In the six years since then, Laura received her M.A. in theology, spent several years in social justice work with the Catholic Worker Movement, and acted as a counselor at a pregnancy crisis center. She met and married her husband, and later buried their young daughter, who was killed in a tragic auto accident. Though she is still a strong advocate for women's ordination, Laura's views about many other Church issues have changed.

"Slowly but relentlessly," she explains, "personal experience and that of the women I have ministered to have convinced me that traditional Christian teaching on sexuality has a deep wisdom. As my views have changed, I have come to the uncomfortable realization that the hierarchy of the Catholic church is the only group in our society that is maintaining these important values from the Christian tradition. They may not always express them well, but the Pope and the bishops have tirelessly defended principles which, if put into practice, would preserve people from a great amount of suffering.

"And the American bishops have also backed up their commitment with a massive financial investment in helping the poor, especially single mothers and their children, through the work of Catholic charities."

Laura articulately sums up what most traditional Catholic women believe but few are able to express verbally: "There is something to the idea of an authoritative magisterium. Ideally, it serves as a means of testing and discerning which cultural and theological changes are in the spirit of the Gospel and which are not."

In other words, if the hierarchy of the Catholic church is teaching it, it probably is true, regardless of what current popular opinion might say to the contrary. Most traditional Catholic women believe this "softly," and spend little, if any, time worrying about their beliefs or preaching them with capital letters and exclamation points like the fundamentalists do. They generally assume that most people, both women and men, are acting out of conviction and good will, regardless of what they say they believe. "Live and let live" could be their motto, "but please don't take my Catholic faith away from me, because it is a treasured source of comfort and support."

THE AVERAGE WOMAN
IN THE PEW

By now it should be clear that there is no such thing as an "average" Catholic woman. Her views depend on how and when she received her education as a Catholic, her age and life experiences, her personality and way of looking at life and its problems, her exposure to and opinion of the women's movement.

For some, religion and spirituality is the center of life. For others, it is a casual, one-hour-a-week Sunday morning habit. The political religious viewpoint of the majority of Catholic women probably lies somewhere between that of the traditionalists and that of the moderate feminists. The only way you can really know the views of the woman sitting next to you at church on Sunday is to engage her in an in-depth conversation about her life and her spirituality. The only group of women that may not be equally represented at Mass each Sunday are the radical feminists.

Few, if any, of the average women in the pew are in complete agreement with the "official" Catholic church on all issues. Many are particularly upset about how a specific priest, usually their pastor, manages "their" parish, especially when his actions show that he thinks of it more as "his" parish. All want their efforts—and the contributions of all women—to be appreciated and accepted.

"We can't be a 50% church," Sister Mary Glennon explains, convinced that she represents many women. "We have to be a 100% church. But being angry doesn't get the job done. I am not going to sit back and do nothing, but I am not going to go out and carry a banner either."

Linda, a single woman in her early fifties who attends Mass almost daily and enthusiastically studies the Bible, is not sure that anyone can be thought of as an average woman in the pew anymore. An enthusiastic leader in her inner-city parish, she tries to be honest yet loving with its priests, whom she patiently tries to help grow into mature, aware, responsible and caring men, a task she admits is sometimes difficult. "Life has changed tremendously since the 1950s," she remarks. "We can't put people into boxes anymore. There's room for everyone in the Church, for every woman to grow. Everyone will do it differently, depending on her time and interests. But women can't allow the males in their lives to think for them anymore. We women have come just a little too far for that."

Most women who participate in the Catholic church on a regular basis want to experience peace and inspiration. Even more, they are looking for a way to connect with God, to center and ground themselves spiritually, and to feel a sense of loving community. What they specifically do *not* want is to feel angry, uptight, and judgmental.

"Most things are a lovely shade of gray," Jane B. reminds me. "What makes me angry is people who judge other people, whether it be the pastor they judge because of his sermon, the school principal, their next-door neighbor, or the Pope. The idea that your information is the only source of reality is what really angers me."

Sister Sean Patrice agrees. "I hate extremists on either side. There is a circular continuum, and the two extremes end up backing into each other. I think there are more things that unite us than separate us."

Many women insist they appreciate the Church's carefully reasoned out approaches to morality. Martha explains, "It is not muddy. It gives you a way to develop a conscience without becoming scrupulous. It has a very carefully thought out process, which I think is important to the world. Most people agree with 90% of what the Church teaches, but most of us don't have the time or education to figure it all out for ourselves from scratch."

The average woman in the pew sees the teachings of the Catholic church as a firm foundation on which to build her own personal beliefs. But most prefer that big, sweeping philosophies be offered, rather than a detailed list written down in indelible ink or carved in stone. And many believe that much, but not necessarily all, of what they hear from the pulpit each Sunday makes sense. "I feel that I am fighting a lot of myths about what the Catholic church teaches," Jennifer relates. "I was pleasantly surprised when I picked up this book about the Church after Vatican II, and I found it more open-minded and reasonable than what my anti-Catholic friends were accusing it of being."

Probably far more women than the hierarchy realizes sadly claim that the Church, as an institution, discriminates against women. Many of them, however, also consider the Church their family, albeit one that may not always act in a charitable manner. And they realize that there is often the same kind of dichotomy within their relationships with other people: husbands, children, and parents. They do not expect life, even spiritual life, to be always perfect or easy.

"To me and to a lot of my friends, there seem to be two ways: Either you live within the Church and you try to make changes because you love the Church and you work through the Church, or you leave the Church," says Christi, a woman in her early twenties. Fortunately for all of us still in the Church, she and many of her friends are hanging in there, refusing to abandon it.

But average women in the pew also fear that as young women continue to assume more equal roles in other institutions within society, it may be increasingly hard to convince them that it is in their best interests to remain enthusiastic members of a Church that will not take them seriously, that often has poor management skills, that categorically refuses them a leadership position or even a real voice just because of their sex.

Indifference rather than anger is by far the more potent poison the Church could face. Despite what one may think when viewing the breakdown of our society as it is portrayed on television, in movies, and in newspapers, many women are as interested today in organized religion, personal spirituality, and a well-thought-out normative morality as they have ever been.

If one is willing to consider the spirit rather than the letter of moral laws, and is open to truly listening to women explain their beliefs and practices, it is possible to conclude that there is an amazing amount of support among every kind of Catholic woman for the large, life-giving, and life-sustaining philosophies of Christianity. And it is reassuring to discover that these same women have an equally amazing ability to sift carefully and critically through old teachings of both the Church and society in order to weed out specific rules that they consider flawed and unjust or impossible to apply indiscriminately to one's daily life. Thoughtfully, prayerfully, but persistently, the Catholic women today are coming of age in a changing Church.

In the next chapter we'll look at how some of these women deal with many of the crucial issues of the 1990s.

CHAPTER THREE

Catholic Women and the Issues of the 1990s

Some Catholics who grew up before Vatican II claim they remember being taught about the primacy of conscience. They insist they have always known that the bottom line for all their moral decisions is their own internal belief about whether the action they are contemplating is right or wrong.

THE INDISPENSABLE ROLE OF CONSCIENCE

Sister Mary Luke Tobin tells me a story about John Henry Cardinal Newman, an Anglican who converted to Catholicism in 1845 and became a Catholic priest. He was invited to a dinner after he had been made Cardinal, and another guest at the dinner proposed a toast to the Pope. Cardinal Newman answered the toast by saying, "To the Pope yes, but to Conscience first."

That was more than a hundred years ago. Regardless of what theologians taught, however, before the 1960s practicing Catholics were much more likely to consider the Church's teachings correct and binding than they are today. Those who could not live up to these teachings believed they were committing a sin. Although they might have felt their reasons for the forbidden action were compelling enough that God would understand and not condemn them to hell, few would have risked compounding their sin by receiving Holy Communion until they had been to confession and had agreed to avoid that particular sin.

I know a woman who had a child born out of wedlock in the early 1940s. She continued seeing the father of the child—who was married to another woman—off and on until he died more than 40 years later. Although she went to Mass every Sunday, she did not receive Communion until after his funeral. I do not think this was a big issue with her. It made her sad, I assume, not to receive Communion at various family religious celebrations, but she never considered that she had any other choice.

Most Catholic women today think much differently. Almost every woman I interviewed for this book told me of at least one Church rule that she either was no longer willing to keep or did not consider a "real" rule. Yet only one woman admitted that she did not go to Communion because of this.

There are several reasons for this dramatic change in religious behavior. Most Catholics today have an entirely different idea about receiving Holy Communion than they once had. Previously, the emphasis was on "being in the state of grace" in order to be worthy to receive the body and blood of Christ (the bread and wine). Not only could you not have even a drink of water since midnight, but many people considered that they could not receive Communion unless they had been to confession. Often only a small portion of the Church would approach the Communion rail.

Today, almost everyone who is at Mass goes to Communion. As one traditional woman I interviewed remarked, "When you read about the percentage of Catholics who practice contraception and then you see how many people go to Communion each Sunday, you start to wonder what's going on!"

What's going on is two things. First, people receive Communion in order to feel united to God and to heal their brokenness, not because they are already perfect. Second, few Catholics believe that contraception is a sin, regardless of what the official Church teaches. And they don't consider it a sin to break—or disregard—other Church rules either.

Vatican II emphasized both freedom of conscience and the fact that *all* the people who are baptized Catholics *are* the Church. Once the ordinary person in the pew starts believing that she is an integral and important member of the Church, she also begins to believe that the ideas that come out of her lived experience are also both important and valid.

According to Donna Tiernan Mahoney, this is how it should be. "We have a long-held teaching in the Church called the *sensus fidelium,* or the sense of the faithful, which holds that each of us has a sense of what is good, right, holy, and true. Wisdom resides within each one of us, not only within our clergy or hierarchy, because God resides within each of us. Therefore we have a responsibility to reflect back to our Church what God speaks to us [our conscience]. This is what it means to be part of the Body of Christ." [1]

My brother, a Dominican priest, points out that *sensus fidelium* and Cardinal Newman's toast are not speaking of some isolated, individual opinion, but rather of an informed consensus of a community of people in which each person has a chance to contribute his or her thoughts and experiences. Accelerated by the new ease of worldwide communication, that is exactly what is happening in the Catholic church today.

Jackie, who is in her early sixties, is a good example of how many Catholic women are changing as they begin to listen to their informed consciences in the modern world. The 1990s are moving Jackie from fundamentalist to traditionalist. She started to give me quick, pat answers during our interview, but more than once she caught herself, stopped, smiled shyly, and confessed: "I'll have to think about this."

Jackie claims she is thinking more and more about important issues these days, particularly since many of her co-workers are much younger and more liberal than she is. "If I take a stand, I have to prove my stand. I can't just say, 'Well, that's how it is' anymore. It's not 'That's how it is!' I have to *prove* how it is. You believe something for a reason! And you have to be able to hold up what you say."

In the complex and confusing 1990s, few people believe that it is possible for anyone—the Pope included—to have all the answers. Sister Hortense explains, "Before Vatican II, I believed that there was a list of dos and don'ts that everyone had to follow. Since then, because I have been fortunate to have good teachers, I realize that the right answers are not the issue. It is asking the right questions that is the issue."

Betty agrees with her. A teacher of both nursing and ethics, she often lectures about end-of-life issues. According to her, there is a danger of becoming so rigid about rules that the concepts are lost. "But Christ came to say, 'Don't make the rules God, make love God.' I get calls from all over the state. And people get so frustrated because I can't give them the answer to every question. Instead, I tell them the questions that they need to ask. And they say, 'Well, so-and-so said you would help us.' And I say, 'Well, I can help you with the process.'"

Marriage and family counselor Toni does much the same thing with her clients. She tries to help women use their ability to think and examine their feelings and expectations. "This is a huge, huge area, your whole spiritual life," Toni says. "I try to help them deal with teachings that they absolutely, in good conscience, can't agree with."

She tries to get her clients first to acknowledge their feelings, then to step back from the problem, bring in their own opinions, and work out solutions that may be compromises. Toni wishes that more teachers in the Church would be like Betty and openly state that they and the Church don't have all the answers about how to handle every problem that may occur during a lifetime. "The people I work with are a pretty good representation of the people in the pews," she says. "They don't realize there is confusion, they just sense it. To a great extent they think that they are the only ones struggling with the problem, whether it be birth control or abortion. So what we need, as paradoxical as it sounds, is institutional flexibility."

Another big problem is that often the women she is counseling have distorted and negative ideas about what the Church actually does teach. Most likely these women were brought up in the old, pre–Vatican II Church, because few of the women who are recent converts to Catholicism that I have talked to know about or even care about many of the old, very specific Church laws.

Sara converted to Catholicism in the early 1980s. She went through several years of RCIA meetings (RCIA stands for Rite of Christian Initiation for Adults; it was recently changed to OCIA, Order of Christian Initiation for Adults). Class discussions covered one's relationship to Jesus and God, and there was no emphasis on rules. Yet before she would agree to become a Catholic, Sara had several questions. "I spoke to one of the priests and listed all the things I disagreed with in the Catholic church, and he said, 'What we are looking for is if you believe in the Nicene and the Apostles Creed.' And I said, 'Oh yes, I do believe, with all my heart.' And the priest said, 'I'm not here to judge you. God is making all of these moves in you anyway. So the stirring is there. You come and join us and know that God is pointing you in the right direction.'"

Since then, Sara has become very interested in liturgy and is in an Advance Liturgical Formation class in her diocese. She first had to take the level-one class. Before joining, she was afraid it would be very conservative. "But it was all the new way!" she exclaims. "There was no talk about rules, laws, regulations, or sin. Every week we had a different topic. Once we had a discussion about the different sides of God. Another time we talked about what is Church. And almost everything they were teaching I agreed with. It was wonderful."

This, of course, is exactly what the fundamentalist women are complaining about. It certainly was easier to have a list that would tell you all the answers about how to save your soul. But as Rose Marciano Lucey explains, "At the end of life, we stand alone. I cannot point to a bishop or a priest or the Pope and say, 'He told me to do that.' I have to decide what I am going to do in the context of my conscience."

Rose had her CFM community to help her develop a sound conscience. "We were taught to look at a situation, to analyze it, and then to make a decision. And the decisions were usually the result of a long process."

Without years of study and a community of friends with more or less the same moral values, it is very difficult to feel confident that your conscience is telling you the truth about an action. Taking everything on faith like we used to do made us feel more secure. But Sidney Callahan, a teacher at Mercy College in New York, writing in an official Catholic magazine published by the National Pastoral Life Center in New York, shares how she copes with a conscience that disagrees with 10 or 15% of the moral guidance given by the Vatican.

"I obey all Church rules of life and practice," she states, "unless I have a very serious reservation of conscience. In the meantime, I work for reform and the collegial changes in the Church I think are necessary for fidelity to the Gospel."

She goes on to explain: "My dissent from our community's teaching authorities—the 10 to 15% divergence having to do with issues of pacifism,

sexuality, gender, reproduction, and the exercise of authority—must be justi-
fied and held in good conscience. As a protection against self-deception, I do
not feel it right to challenge the moral guidance of present teaching authorities unless I am morally convinced and know that many Roman Catholic theologians, some bishops, and many other exemplary faithful Roman Catholics
agree with my interpretation of the implications of the faith. My dissent rests
on my intellectual study and life experience and is reached after much prayer
and reflection.

"Since I believe we will all be judged [upon death], I always test my dis-
senting conscience by imagining the coming conversation with the Lord,
face-to-face. I would not dissent from a currently proclaimed teaching unless
I believed that in the future the Church will be guided by the Spirit to accept
the positions I now hold as God's will for us as a community."[2]

"Sidney Callahan's words," my brother assures me, "are exactly what *'sensus
fidelium'* really means."

My research in gathering information for this book tells me that many
Catholic women today agree with Sidney Callahan and are also following
her advice. Margaret, a longtime worker in her parish and a traditionalist in
most areas of her Catholic faith, concurs. "It is wonderful. I see more and
more now, particularly in the 1990s, people taking an ownership role, an
adult stand, expecting to have their opinions listened to, and taking responsibility for their own spiritual needs."

There is no doubt that the higher educational level of women and men
and mass communication are making all kinds of information—even the
many different ideas about morals and religious practices—accessible to the
average person. Knowing "official" Church teachings is no longer an accurate
way to predict what you, your husband, or the person sitting next to you at
Mass believes about many moral issues. In a 1992 Gallup poll, 81% of the re-
spondents said that it was possible to be a good Catholic and *publicly* disagree with church teaching. Most likely a higher percentage thought one
could disagree privately. The WFF insists that the order in which the questions were asked slanted the results.

What most Catholic women interviewed openly disagree with is narrow
and specific Church rules and policies. Contrary to the impression often given
out by the popular media, there is an inspiring amount of agreement among
most of these women about the broad, underlying principles of morality.

SANCTITY-OF-LIFE ISSUES

There are few, if any, women who disagree with the Catholic church's teaching that all life is sacred. Many Catholic women support the "seamless garment" analogy, which claims that each and every life issue is equally important. Many resent the attention given to the fight against abortion by people who do not equally support other pro-life issues that would rid the world of capital punishment, war, poverty, and child abuse.

Abortion

"I've been on phone lines for pro-choice and for the homeless, and collected food for the poor," one woman tells me. "Why is so much time and money spent waging a war against abortion when there are so many things that need the money more?"

Ellen Reuter is even more emphatic. "At the end of the U.S. bishops' Peace Pastoral, they say everybody should make up their own mind, that this is just a discussion, but when the bishops write about abortion, there's no room for discussion. So when you're talking about blowing up the earth and killing five billion people, that's for individual conscience to decide. But if you're talking about having an abortion, that's not for an individual conscience to decide. Now, either they're both wrong, or they're both for individual conscience to decide."[3]

Jane Redmont, who interviewed a wide variety of Catholic women during the 1980s, claims that there was more consensus about capital punishment than about abortion, though it was not as strong as the consensus on disarmament. Only a small minority of the women she talked to were not ambivalent about abortion.[4]

Sheila, who volunteers for the Catholic Worker Movement, complains, "With all the social issues that there are, why do people pick this one issue? What bothers me the most is that all of these pro-life people are the very same people who don't think that it is wrong to kill people with the death penalty and they don't think it is wrong to kill all those peasants in Central America. So I have a little difficulty with this pro-life thing."

Yet the WFF, which is obviously against abortion, does not have any official viewpoint on capital punishment. Spokeswoman Sherry Tyree tells me, "It has never even come up in a discussion. It is a red herring that those who favor abortion want to use to get us off the subject. But abortion is the moral subject of the day, and it will be for many years." WFF literature also does not take any stand on many other social justice issues that are important to many Catholic women today.

Of all the women I have talked to, only one, a recent convert, said she was "for" abortion, and that was because she works in a mental health facility. "I see what happens where mothers are substance abusers," she explains sadly, "and their children are born with serious physical and mental problems."

Almost every other woman was against abortion in principle, and almost all said that they personally did not think that they could have an abortion themselves. There was close to unanimous opinion that the widespread use of abortion is a serious evil in today's society and that abortion should not ever be considered a normal method of birth control.

However, most women volunteered that life was full of difficult choices, and that they would not dream of judging another woman who did decide that, in her situation, having an abortion was the lesser of two evils. Many think that the Church *has* to teach that abortion is wrong, but that there can be extenuating circumstances, which can make the abortion the more moral of the actions available. Very few women advocated civil laws that would completely outlaw all abortions for any reason. Many would second the remarks of Jesuit Father Avery Dulles in a lecture at Fordham University: "The church's primary task regarding abortion is to change public opinion, not to get a law prohibiting abortion passed. Even if pro-life organizations succeed in getting all abortion in the entire nation outlawed . . . in all probability the police and the courts would not enforce the law, or abortion will be simply driven underground. Laws that run against the consensus of the people will generally be ineffective."[5]

Lawyer Carolyn claims that "The Church recognizes that abortion is appropriate to save the life of the mother. What about if it is her psychological life? The emphasis now is on the fetus, and not how the individual sees it. We talk about rights and we should talk about power. It is always the power of the mother to make that decision. Instead, we are focusing on whether the government is going to make that decision, or the Pope is going to make it. It is also a decision to say, 'Yes, I am going to have this child.' And we don't help her before she makes this decision. We tell her what she has to do.

"My sister has four children, and we were talking to someone the other day who had a fit and said, 'Four children! Are you going to stop now?' And this woman claims she is pro-choice, but obviously she is not! Pro-choice often doesn't mean *your* choice, but *my* choice. So I think that all sides are concentrating on the wrong thing."

"I'm pro-life," 18-year-old Rebecca tells me. "But I've never been pregnant, so I don't know what I would do if that happened to me and I wasn't married. I think it would be really selfish to have an abortion, but then, being pregnant might be so traumatic for you that the circumstances make you feel like you have no choice . . . . But I don't think it is something that I could do."

Stacey, 31 years old, has similar thoughts. "I could never have an abortion. I think it is killing," she says. "But I've never been 13 and raped by my father, so it is easy for me to say it is always wrong."

Although identifying herself as pro-choice, Sheila's words are almost identical. "I don't think I could personally ever have an abortion," she admits. "But I don't think it is right for me to dictate to all these other people. I've never been 15 and alone and pregnant...or in my first year of college and pregnant. And I think it is especially wrong for the Church to say you can't have birth control and you can't have abortion. What are people supposed to do?"

"Could I have an abortion? No," Cassandra insists. "But I have no right to prevent another woman from having one. But I do have every right to work hard for the women who have had children and who need my help. Maybe there would not be so many abortions if women and children weren't seen as expendable property. I think the abortion issue would be much less of an issue if we took care of those who are born, who live in hunger and pain and need medical care and education. Then abortion would not be so attractive!"

Most women believe there is a vast difference between having an abortion early in the pregnancy—say the first 12 or 14 weeks—and later on. The problem is that serious birth defects usually cannot be determined until late in the pregnancy. The majority of women refuse to even think about that possibility until it actually happens to them. Then, for most, their response would not be automatic but would require much prayer and thoughtful discussion.

Nancy talks about her experience in medical school in the early 1970s. "In spite of all that I had studied, I didn't really have a working knowledge of what size a fetus was when it was four or five months old. I was in the pediatrics ward, where I saw all sorts of terrible tragedies, and the doctor would point out that it is possible to diagnose these problems in utero, and asked us what we thought about abortion. And we all said, 'Great!'

"But you couldn't diagnose these problems before late mid-trimester [five months or so]. And by then these were big kids, kids with feelings, and it was a terrible, horrible thing to do," Nancy says. "Then it expanded and it was not that you could abort a kid with some weird abnormality, but you could abort it for a social reason. Just like that, it changed overnight. I don't think abortion is right at any time, but there is obviously a difference between an abortion at six weeks and one at six months!"

It is much easier to be pro-choice about abortion in the very early stages of a pregnancy. Diane, who was very active in the right-to-life movement during the 1970s and a pregnancy counselor for three years, writes me, "In the nineties, as a result of my involvement with the peace movement, I am less inclined to force my opinion on others, and I am wondering more about when the soul enters the fetus . . . when there is a brainwave, perhaps?"

Many assume that it is normal medical practice to have a D & C (a very common gynecological procedure in which the endometrium of a woman's uterus is scraped) performed immediately after a rape, "just in case." But most also said that if they found out their daughter was three or four months pregnant, even by rape, they would encourage her to have the baby and give it up for adoption or help her raise the child. "I can't see stopping life once it is started," Jackie says. "It is like denying a genius to be born. And no matter how tough it would be, I told my children that if they ever had a problem like that, we would have to help them."

Six women I interviewed told me that they had participated in an anti-abortion protest. But at least half of them now claim they can no longer be active because of their repulsion to the tactics of Operation Rescue.

Sean Patrice is a very traditional nun who teaches elementary school and still wears a habit. "I went to a pro-life demonstration a long time ago," she tells me. "It was very nonthreatening. All we did was pray the rosary. I couldn't protest the way people are doing it now. I am not convinced enough on this subject to risk being arrested for civil disobedience."

"I think Operation Rescue has caused more problems than it has helped," Jackie explains. "They have polarized people. A lot of good people who should be elected to a public office may not be just because they have been identified as pro-life" (anti-abortion).

Others, equally against abortion, agree. "I think that they are sick," insists Sara. "They are trying to play God. I think they are doing it for themselves. It has nothing to do with saving babies. Anyone who is that fanatical is saving some part of themselves, working out of fear and guilt. It's heavy-duty judgmental! When people are holier than thou, that is what is sinful."

Another woman, one of only two I interviewed who volunteered that she once had had an abortion, explains her current position. "I have a problem with people who call themselves Christians who are blocking the abortion clinics," she tells me softly. "Before you accuse someone of being a murderer, look at yourself before you throw the first stone. Instead, offer that young woman a home. Help her care for her baby. Teach her how to be a mother to her child. And number one, give her back her self-esteem."

Jamie, a recent convert in her twenties, brings her very precocious and obviously much loved six-year-old to my interview. When he is not listening, she tells me about the pressure her family put on her to have an abortion when they discovered that she was pregnant and unmarried.

"My whole family wanted me to kill my child, and I couldn't," Jamie confesses. "His father wanted him to be dead, everyone did. And I would look up at God and say, 'Please do whatever you can to help me get through this, because no one is going to like me,' and they didn't until after he was born. And now he is the love of everyone's life. My brother would tell me through my pregnancy that he hoped my baby would die, and that I'd have a horrible labor. And I went through absolute hell, but I never lost my faith that I was pregnant for a reason. And I knew that Justin was going to be a special child, and he is. He is an incredible child in so many ways."

From her own experience, Jamie continues to be horrified at even the idea of abortion. "I think birth control is a family thing, private, it belongs in the home. But abortion definitely belongs in the Church. And I thank God that the Church is so actively against abortion."

Laura, another young woman Jamie's age, totally supports Jamie's viewpoint. When Jamie was pregnant, Laura was in college and very pro-choice. Since then, she has changed radically. Still a feminist on many issues, Laura explains: "I have learned the truth about abortion, that it ends the life of innocent children and physically and psychologically wounds women," she writes me. "It is an abandonment of the search for true equality and justice between the sexes. We need to transform society to make it possible for women to combine parenting and career, and to demand that men bear their full share of family responsibility, both financial and emotional.

"Instead, the abortion mentality continues the patriarchal assumption that women's ability to give birth to and nurse children makes them inferior to men. It demands that we sacrifice our own children, and part of our own womanhood, as the price of full participation in society."

Most, if not all, of the women interviewed, even those willing to be labeled pro-choice, agree with her.

Birth Control

If most Catholic women are ambivalent, at least in practice, about the issue of abortion, they unanimously agree that birth control is a necessity. Granted, a few advocate the use of Church-approved natural family planning methods, often for reasons that have little to do with official Church rules. But all agree that, at least in the United States, the age of extremely large Catholic families has long ended.

"People out of necessity have to limit their families. It is a financial situation. You just can't raise 14 children anymore like I did," Colleen explains. "But what do you use in order to not become pregnant? It is a very personal question between you, your husband, and your priest. I don't know the answer to that question. Do you use the Catholic-approved methods? If you do, are you gambling on the chance? You will always find a nickel for another kid, believe me." Now that she is 70, Colleen feels fortunate that the answer to that question is no longer any of her business.

Artificial Contraception

For most Catholic women today, however, the question of contraception is irrelevant, for very few women see any moral difference between using some form of artificial contraception and a calendar, even if the calendar is reading the natural signs of the woman's body rather than the squares of some poster on the wall. They agree with Franz Konig, the retired archbishop of Vienna, who has been quoted as denying the distinction between birth control that is natural (approved) and artificial (condemned) by refusing to believe that "from the moral viewpoint what is important is the 'trick' of cheating nature."[6]

Many Catholic women resent being told to "trick" nature. They agree with me that a child should be considered much more than only the result of a physical activity that can take five minutes or less. Instead, a child should be considered the result of a family.

"We always tell ours that we deliberately had them because we wanted them," Margaret explains. "I don't know how many people can say that when they are hitting and missing with rhythm or whatever. All three of ours were planned. We had wine before and celebrated. And it was the result of a family."

Another woman, an ex-nun and now mother of a large family, who teaches marriage and family life classes in a Catholic girls' high school, volunteers: "The Church's waffling around on artificial birth control bugs me. If you read the documents carefully, they really say, 'Strive for a natural way to regulate the births of your children, but ultimately you must make your own decision.' So the way I read it, a married couple can make their own decision to use artificial means if they think it is necessary. I don't see any difference between practicing rhythm and artificial birth control, except that one way is easier and more reliable for most people."

Gerry Dunphy agrees with her. "With 87% of the church community disregarding the church's position on birth control, surely it is time for a clear, logical argument outlining the fallacy behind the church's position. The world is full of man-made interventions, be it the rearranging of chemicals to make many products, the cutting down of a tree (that God evidently wants to grow), cutting your hair or nails, or organ transplanting."[7]

For most Catholics, the birth control debate is a nonissue. "There were five of us priests sitting around the dinner table one night talking," my brother tells me. "We agreed that, among us, we represented about 80 years of hearing confessions. And we concluded that all five of us together, over all this time, have had fewer than 40 people bring up birth control in the confessional."

Only two pages out of 116 of the U.S. bishops' very inspirational and well written 1991 teaching guide, *Human Sexuality*, are about contraception. It has become a subject that almost all parish priests—and many of the hierarchy—would just as soon forget. Sister Mary Luke Tobin insists that it is now high time for the official Church to simply say, "Catholics, make up your own minds and stop bothering us about this!"

Pope John Paul II does not seem to agree. At the 20th anniversary of *Humanae Vitae* (the encyclical outlawing contraception), he told hundreds of theologians that the Church's teaching was "written by the creative hand of God in the nature of the human person" and confirmed by God in revelation, and that disputing it is "equal to refusing to God himself the obedience of our intelligence." He told them that Catholics must take into account the "sure teaching of the magisterium" when preparing their consciences rather than following their "own opinion or that of theologians." [8] Five more years have passed, and he has not changed his mind about the *sinfulness* of contraception.

However, most Catholic women don't hear the Pope on this subject. Some of them even think the Church's teachings about artificial birth control are immoral. Several pointed out the massive and accelerating worldwide problem of overpopulation. According to World Bank estimates, 700 million people lived in absolute poverty in 1980 and 1,100 billion in 1990. [9]

"Why is the Church wasting all this time and energy on the subject of contraception?" Betty asks. "Christ said we had to use the earth, but he didn't say we should abuse the earth, and by overpopulating, we are abusing the earth."

Others believe the Church's teachings on artificial birth control are wrong—immoral—because of what they have learned about sex in their own marriages.

"*Humanae Vitae* is a beautiful document," Cynthia asserts, "except for the few pages about artificial contraception that don't make sense. The rest is beautiful. They almost have it. The Church teaches beautiful things about sex and marriage and I use it so much in my life. And it is very useful when I try to explain the meaning of sex to my children.

"But then they negate what they are saying by adding, 'But we still believe that men and women should not practice artificial contraception.'" Cindy continues, "And I say, 'But you just spent 20 pages telling me why we should!' They have almost grasped that having sex with another person is a sacrament. With it, I get healing, but I give healing also. God makes us capable of that together. And my husband can feel that, and I can feel that. And we can say 'Wow! This is powerful.' But until the Church can hear women, they aren't going to get it."

My brother Don, therapist and priest, concurs with Cynthia. "Sex is a portal of entry into the self, another, new life, and the presence of God," he explains. "The problem is how to coalesce these four values effectively and how to teach the coalescence. And for many theologians, another core issue is the nature of 'sacrament' as a state of being versus 'sacrament' as an event."

Obviously, not every instance of intercourse is sacramental, even in marriage, but it sometimes is, and the times that it will be cannot always be predicted, particularly not by a calendar. Many Catholic women may agree that abstaining from sex within their marriage because it is the "wrong time of the month" is not much different from abstaining from receiving Holy Communion at Mass for the same reason. Both activities can unite them in a particularly powerful way with God and with another human (humans, in the case of Communion), both can heal them, grant them forgiveness, and give them the strength they need to face the day-to-day problems of their lives.

Theologian Maria Pilar Aquino explains, "The Roman Catholic church has played a fundamental role in the private lives of women, particularly sexuality and moral norms and values. But today things are changing. Women are able to distinguish what the institutional Church is teaching and what they need. The criterion for women to decide what they will take from the institutional Church and what they won't take is their experience in life, their own physical and spiritual needs. No matter what the Church says about birth control, if they need birth control, they use it. No matter how the Church says that sexual relationships have to be performed, if they love their husband, they do what they think is right. The Church no longer is the owner of this private sphere of women's lives."

Humanae Vitae is not only the Church of today's most controversial document, it is the Church's most ineffective document. It is probably almost singlehandedly responsible for the rapid shift that Catholics made from obediently listening to Church authority to obediently listening to their own consciences, which occurred during the 1960s and 1970s. Unfortunately, when the Church insists on dogmatically restating advice that goes against most people's lived experiences, some of its other much-needed advice loses its credibility also.

Noted sociologist and prolific writer Father Andrew Greeley spends quite some time on this discussion in his book *The Catholic Myth.* He states that when he was in the seminary, moral theology books said that a spouse (usually Catholic) could consent to contraceptive intercourse if the other partner (usually non-Catholic) insisted and the sex was essential to prevent the marriage from breaking up and the unwilling partner remained "passive." He believes that few priests (as confessors) used this "escape hatch" until the mid-sixties, when many priests and laypeople were beginning to ask, "What does the Vatican know about married love?" According to Greeley, two factors were working in the lives of Catholics which caused them to question the Church's teaching on birth control: the increase in education and social status of Catholics and the development of the birth control pill.[10]

Catholic women could not stay isolated from other forces of the 1960s either. They were quickly assimilating the ideas of both the sexual revolution and the women's movement and were coming to believe that personal sexual satisfaction was both a possible and worthwhile goal, and that they, as women, needed to take charge of their own lives.

"The feminist movement and things I was reading started to make a difference in my life," Ann Z. tells me. "I started feeling that maybe I could—and maybe I should—make some decisions for myself. The feminists were marvelous. They talked about all sorts of things, like sexuality, things that I thought were supposed to be secrets. And I thought, *Well, if they aren't blushing, maybe I ought to form my own opinions on these subjects too.*"

"Pope John the 23rd had established a commission to investigate the problem of birth control, most likely with the intent to change the teaching," Greeley writes. "To keep birth control off the floor of the Vatican Council, Pope Paul VI expanded the commission and seemed, in his vacillating, to also be leaning toward a change."[11]

Pat and Patty Crowley, president-couple of the Christian Family Movement, were one of the three couples appointed to the commission. The commission widely distributed a questionnaire to married people asking for their experiences using the rhythm method of birth control.

The Crowleys were inundated by letters, most of them from women who unloaded burdens that they had carried for many years. Shaken by what they were reading, Pat and Patty sent copies of the letters to the commission secretary in the hope that they would eventually reach the Pope. After several years of research, the commission prepared a majority and a minority report.

The majority (80%) believed that artificial contraception was not intrinsi-cally evil and that the teaching of the Church should be changed. In 1966, the commission disbanded and members returned home, assuming that the majority of the report would be honored.[12]

The whole discussion in the 1960s about birth control was hardly done in private, and the majority report was leaked to the press. Very conservative Catholics, already upset with the many changes that Vatican II was making, had another reason for anger. "During the sixties, I did think that the Church's teaching might be changed on birth control, and it made me mad at that time, because I hadn't been able to use birth control, so why should other people?" Jackie remembers.

But for most Catholics, especially those who had already switched to the Pill, the subject was quickly considered closed. People—particularly the Crowleys and the majority of the commission members—were shocked when the encyclical *Humanae Vitae* was issued in July of 1968, rejecting the advice of the majority opinion. In the United States, more than 600 theolo-gians signed a statement disagreeing with the encyclical.

Humanae Vitae really didn't upset too many laypeople in 1968. They had already made their decision. "In the sixties, the Church was considering the new Pill as a moral alternative form of birth control," Diane recalls. "My hus-band and I began to use it. Then Pope Paul VI issued his decree against it. Our parish priest told us to follow our conscience. It was the beginning of making my own decisions about morality, of taking responsibility for my soul, and of developing a grown-up approach to the Church."

Since then, most Catholics consider the contraception issue their own personal and private business and few pass this "burden" on to their priests in the confessional. "The more serious impact was on the clergy and the reli-gious [nuns]," Greeley writes. "It was a shocking disappointment."

It told them that the forces of reaction were back in power in Rome. The permanent moral crisis of the clergy had begun. The Catholic church had deprived itself of any ability to respond to the so-called sexual revolution of the 1970s. No one took it seriously on sexual matters anymore, not even its own members, not even the devout ones. In 1963, half the Catholic popula-tion had accepted the Church's teaching against artificial birth control. In 1974, only 12% accepted it.[13]

According to Greeley, most American bishops are very well aware that their laity do not observe the birth control encyclical and that their clergy make no attempt to enforce it. Nevertheless, in order to keep the Vatican happy, they must pretend for public record that the encyclical is accepted and that Pope John Paul II's attempts to reinforce it during the last decade have been successful.

For most devout Catholic laity, this was the first time they deliberately disobeyed Church teaching. The fact that they did so and were not greatly troubled afterward prepared them for a future in which they would increasingly make their own decisions on moral and religious matters and yet continue to participate as active Catholics. At the present time, Catholics are even more likely than Protestants to insist on conscience as the ultimate norm of moral action. The birth control encyclical was the emancipation for the most devout of American Catholics—exactly the opposite of Pope Paul VI's intention.[14]

Natural Family Planning

The rhythm method of birth control is based on the principle that a woman is only fertile during certain days in the middle of her menstrual cycle. Assuming that your cycle is 28 days and you are always regular (a big assumption for many women), this means that your most fertile period is approximately from the 10th to the 16th day of your cycle. How badly you don't want to get pregnant usually determines if you abstain from sex for only those 7 days each month, or if you throw in a few more days on either side, just to be safe.

I kept a small calendar in the top drawer of our dresser and every time I had my period, I would count ahead 28 days and circle the date my next period should begin, and then count back to the middle of the month and cross out the days when we shouldn't have sex. It required almost zero verbal communication or discussion.

Between 1962 and 1969, my husband and I used this method of birth control. As long as we didn't have sex on any of these middle days of my cycle, which was pretty regular, I did not get pregnant. Every time we did (four times—at least two of them on purpose because we had mutually decided to have another child), I got pregnant. We were one of the lucky couples for whom the rhythm method of birth control worked like it was supposed to. But I was still a nervous wreck whenever my period started a day or two late.

Since then science, with lots of encouragement from the Catholic church, has refined the rhythm method so that it depends on the woman being able to recognize physical changes in her body—a mucus discharge for one—which signal that fertility is about to begin. Both partners, of course, must be willing to refrain from sex during these periods. The instructions usually followed today by couples deciding to use natural family planning (NFP) are called the Billings method. It is taught by many hospitals in the country.

Both the reliability and the desirability of this method vary among the few women I interviewed who use or have used this method. Sharon was particularly pleased with this method of birth control, although she adds that if getting pregnant is the worst thing that can happen to you (which it never was with her), it might be a problem. After the birth of their third child, she looked into the research that was being done on NFP and found it interesting.

"I loved three things about it," she tells me enthusiastically. "It was natural and couldn't do my body any harm; it gave me a way to learn about my own body and take control of it; and it demanded that my husband also respect my body and my cycle. I used this method because I thought it was the best method. It was not just a Catholic faith activity. The two times that I did get pregnant were because we had sex anyway, even though we knew it was the wrong time of the month. I kept the charts for years, and I could tell when my ovulation was. We both had to work it out together, to explain our needs to each other, and I think it was very positive for our marriage most of the time."

Now in her fifties, Sharon admits she no longer cares about this issue anymore and doesn't know what she would tell her children about it. "The Church teaches that you have a duty to find out as much as you can about yourself—not conquering your body and keeping it down, but getting to know how it works and appreciating it. The problem with the Church's stand on birth control is that it is another 'thou shalt not.' Usually they don't help you do anything else either. But, at least in the last 20 years, the Church has taken a real leadership role in natural family planning."

One mother I interviewed, a woman in her late twenties, says that she used NFP because she was looking for a natural method (she could not use the Pill for health reasons); because a close relative was a teacher and an advocate of the method; and because of the teachings of the Church. She did get pregnant "accidentally" using this method, but it was only after four years of marriage. She confirms that it means about one week per month of abstinence. "During the four years we used NFP, there were a lot of times when we wished that we could just run down to the drugstore and buy a contraceptive," she admits.

Now, with a brand-new baby, this young woman and her husband are using artificial contraception because they have concluded that their friends who use only NFP seem to have their babies very, very close together. "But it is a viable alternative to other forms of birth control," she insists, "and it is a method that the Church recognizes as OK."

"When I think of natural family planning, I think of my neighbor," Betty relates. "Every time you look at her she's pregnant! They wanted me to teach NFP when I was working at the hospital. I taught it once, and then I said, 'This is crazy. This should not be called natural family planning. It should be called abstinence!'"

Psychiatrist Nancy had the greatest reservations against artificial contraception, primarily because she claims that even the best method is only 96% effective (which means the other methods are far less effective) and, therefore, pregnancy can occur, which means that abortion could be a possibility—something that she is very much against. "The procreative and the erotic aspect of sexuality cannot be separated," she insists. "The Church is very accurate about that. Human life can always be the result. If they are going to sell us sexuality as a sensation in order to keep us busy while they perpetuate whatever it is they want to on us, they have to try to separate sexuality from procreativity, which they are trying to do, but it can't be done. So you can see what is happening: massive, widespread abortion.

"I do think people need to behave as sexually conservative as they can. And there are ways, natural clues, to tell whether you are ovulating or not. I always test my positions with the Church, because I do feel that the Holy Spirit is working through the Church, and no matter what we think, our perspective is so limited."

Although Nancy was married once for a short period of time, she is not married now, nor does she have children. Despite what she says above, she maintains that "if I were in an ongoing, sexual relationship, I would definitely contracept with something that wasn't going to damage my body, like a barrier method. But I would also accept any children I conceived. I would never abort for any reason."

Sterilization

Sterilization is against official Church teachings also, but it is not talked about much since it affects fewer people. I remember making a documentary in Ecuador about peasant cooperatives. I was in a small village, bunking in the rectory of a Catholic church high above the treeline in the middle of nowhere. I overheard the pastor talking to the doctor about how they would explain to a young woman, who was mentally retarded and kept having defective babies, that she needed to be sterilized.

Sterilization was not on my list of questions for this book, but two women volunteered their experiences. One, who had four children in about as many years, remembers being very upset when her husband had a vasectomy without telling her. She had taken the Pill for four or five days after the birth of her fourth child in the mid-sixties, and had gotten deathly ill. "I wanted to have lots of kids, but my husband did it for me, to take care of me," she explains. "He thought I was having a difficult time, which I was, but not because of the kids. My problem was with my marriage. I had never practiced rhythm. I wanted to have kids. So I had said to my husband, 'Why don't we practice the rhythm system? It really enhances your marriage in many ways.' But by then it was too late."

She admits she has never used any method of birth control herself and never told her girls anything about it. "It is a very personal thing in everyone's lives," she insists. "And now 13- and 14-year-old girls can go to a clinic, without their parents' knowledge, and ask for a pill, which infuriates me."

Another woman's experience was just the opposite. I do not use her name here because she is a very active, well-known pro-family Catholic lecturer. "After four children, the doctor didn't think I should get pregnant anymore. I was mixed on whether or not to have a tubal ligation, like he was suggesting, because I had four boys and really wanted a girl. I never even thought of discussing this with a priest. We went ahead and did it, and I remember praying when I went into the hospital to have it done, 'OK, God, if you really don't want this done, don't make it successful!'"

She laughs, saying, "I did end up getting pregnant again, so I started joking to everyone that if a Catholic has a tubal ligation, it just won't work. I did not know I was pregnant, and I was breast feeding one of my other children at the time. I was four months into the pregnancy when I found out. I had a miscarriage the next day."

After that, they used conventional contraception, and later they did decide to try to get pregnant on purpose. "We both got the courage at the same time, and the next morning I said, 'Oh, I've lost my nerve again,' and my husband said, 'Too bad, I just know you got pregnant last night.'" And of course I had, and when they did the cesarean, the doctor said the tubal ligation looked fine to him and he had no idea how I had gotten pregnant!"

Happily they got their girl!

Other Beginning-of-Life Issues

Human Sexuality, published by the U.S. Catholic bishops, tells us the official Church teachings on modern-day reproductive technologies: artificial insemination, in vitro fertilization, surrogate motherhood, and so forth. The distinction is made between what is technically possible (what one can do) and what is morally admissible (what one ought to do). "The Church's approach to artificial aids to procreation is grounded in two fundamental values: (1) protecting the life and dignity of the human being so created; and (2) the conviction that the transmission of life ought to occur through marital intercourse. For this reason, one cannot use means and follow methods which could be licit in the transmission of the life of plants and animals." [15]

There is no doubt that medical technology is creating more and more moral problems to be solved, and many women are very happy for the Church's leadership in urging caution. Fortunately, most women have not yet had to face many of these decisions, and few women brought up these subjects in their interviews with me. Many people, not just Catholics, look to the Church for guidance on these subjects. However, I believe most women think what is needed is broad moral teachings about the sanctity and dignity of life, rather than minute, point-by-point specific rules on each new issue.

Jennifer is close to completing a Ph.D. in biology. Her emphasis is on genetics. "I don't have any idea about what the Catholic church teaches on genetics, genetic engineering, and so on, but I think they are against some of them, and these things scare me a little too. I think that often science steps in and does things without thinking about the moral consequences, but fortunately my research is with tiny worms you see under a microscope, so I don't have to worry about all of this. I've always thought that for religious reasons it would be very hard for me to go into human genetics, and it would be difficult for me to give out information to parents who were trying to decide whether or not to terminate a pregnancy, so I have chosen not to deal with this issue."

Many average women in the pews have not had enough personal exposure to these issues to have come to an educated, informed opinion on many of them. Probably in vitro fertilization, using the married couple's own sperm and ovum, is the most common area in which they are least likely to agree with the Church's official teachings. Ann Z. brings it up in our phone conversation. "I went to Mass not too long ago, where they talked against in vitro fertilization, and I thought that what the priest said was just insane," Ann fumes. "How dare he, in one breath, talk about how life is sacred, and then talk about how we are not allowed to use the free will and intelligence that same God gave us to create life."

Euthanasia

A member of her diocese's Life Issues Commission, Betty is the chairperson of the End of Life Committee. One of the few married women on the commission, she insists that the Catholic church should be spending most of its time on the medical issues of the future, such as "genetic engineering, in vitro fertilization, euthanasia," rather than worrying about issues such as contraception, which should be considered dead and buried. But Betty realizes that these issues are very difficult.

"There aren't any easy answers," she explains. "The Church can come out and say that this is the way it is, but that doesn't mean anyone is going to believe it. We found that out with *Humanae Vitae.* So the question now is how to give guidance to the Catholic people, to all people, in a way that will help them make these decisions."

Most women realize that these subjects are much more complicated than they may seem. Linda reflects, "I certainly don't want to be hooked up to some machine. I don't think I could take a person's life, but for those who feel that they have to, I can totally understand, because they don't want to see their husbands and wives, their mothers, their brothers and sisters suffering. When I was caring for my neighbor with AIDS, there were times when, if I hadn't been who I am—I don't know if that is cowardly or what—that I might have given him enough medication to let him go."

At the moment, even the bishops can't agree on what to tell people. "The bishops are writing all these conflicting articles about withdrawing food and fluid, and it puzzles me terribly," Betty remarks. "Why are we fighting over this? Why don't we see that there are so many hungry people in the world who need food, who need vaccinations? Instead we are spending all our energy talking about prolonging a dead person's life."

Betty realizes that it is a problem that requires informed decisions, and ultimately each decision will have to be made by the individuals involved. Carolyn agrees. "We will almost all be in the position, at some time in our life, to have to choose to end someone's life, or at least to allow it to end," she insists. "It used to be that someone died, and that was it. Now the chances are that you are going to have to make that choice, even about yourself!"

Arthur Caplan, director of the University of Minnesota's Center for Biomedical Ethics, confirms Carolyn's opinion. "The decision to withhold some form of medical treatment is not rare, but one the majority of Americans can expect to face. Today 1.7 million of the 2.1 million annual U.S. deaths occur in hospitals, nursing homes, and similar institutions. Seventy percent of those deaths in institutions are preceded by a decision not to do something."[16]

Carolyn does not believe the government, the Church, or anyone else can make absolute, abstract judgments on these issues. "The Church is looking to the government to control these life issues," she explains, "instead of looking at the individual whose life is being withdrawn . . . the fetus, the comatose person, and so forth . . . instead of looking at how to teach the individuals who are having to make these decisions how to make them. So I think they are taking the completely wrong approach. The only way you can make a decision in any of these issues is in the context of the faith, in the context of a moral system of your belief in the Gospel."

Carolyn does not believe that the government or the Church can tell you whether to pull the plug on your dying mother, or exactly when to do it. Once again, she confirms that women today expect their Church to help them by enthusiastically and inspirationally giving them broad, moral philosophies to use as guides for the difficult decisions they have to make at different stages of their lives, rather than specific "thou shalt nots" on each and every one of these issues.

UNTIL DEATH DO US PART: MARRIAGE AND SEXUALITY ISSUES

Despite the more or less mainstream ideas of most Catholic women today about abortion and artificial contraception, many are concerned about the blatant commercialism and proliferation of recreational sex, the increasing amount of pornography, the spread of sexual diseases, the younger and younger age at which children are becoming sexually active, and the ever-increasing number of poverty-ridden single-parent homes. Many women interviewed were glad that someone (e.g., the Catholic church) was attempting to preserve what used to be considered conventional sexual morality.

Interestingly, it was the young women in their twenties who most often brought up the necessity for a "hard line" from the Catholic church and were the most vocal about protecting their younger siblings from the temptation of becoming sexually active too soon.

Stacey echos what several young women told me. "I think that the Church has to be against premarital sex. Otherwise, even more teenagers, who are not responsible adults, would become sexually active. One of the big reasons I didn't have sex was because the Catholic church told me not to. And high school students are not at the right age."

Several women also mentioned that the fear of AIDS could turn out to be a 1990s blessing in disguise. When it comes to their own personal behavior, however, and not that of their children, most women want their Church to paint broad and inspirational strokes about morality, including sexual morality, and leave the dotting of each *i* and the crossing of each *t* up to each individual adult. This is particularly true on such subjects as divorce and remarriage.

Premarital Sex

Current studies contend that only 25% of American girls and 15% of American boys are still virgins by the time they are 18 or 19 years old.[17]

Teenagers have always had sex, but certainly not as many and not as openly as they do today. "I was a teenager in the sixties," one woman tells me, "and I believed, as I had been taught, that God was the angry God out there who kept score. To keep my wicked, sinful self on his side, I had to go to confession a lot. Of course, I was always sinning anyway, and when I was 16, I got pregnant, got married, and then quickly had another baby, thanks to the rhythm method."

Today, as then, one large preoccupation of most parents is how to keep teenagers from thinking that it is OK to have sex. For many of us who are middle-aged or older, and who were married at least by our early twenties, not engaging in premarital sex was not much of an issue, because most of our friends were not sexually active, at least not openly, and it was just something that you didn't do. A lot of us were "making out" and often feeling very guilty about it, but actually having intercourse was not something "nice girls" did. Before the 1960s, living together, even with your fiancé, was usually not an option. So for many of us, remaining virgins until our wedding night really was not much of a problem.

But nowadays, the media make it seem as if every teenager is having sex with someone on a nightly basis—which is hard to believe, since we all know teenagers who rarely go out alone with a date and who find it difficult to find someone to go with them to the prom. Regardless, there is little doubt that more and more children are engaging in sex today at younger and younger ages.

Seventeen-year-old Rebecca, who went to a private school where many of the girls board, tells me, "High school is a kind of eye-opening experience. I know that a lot of girls are sleeping with their boyfriends. I go to a Catholic school, but it seems it is very easy for girls to just 'slip over' that little rule. I know very few girls who say that they won't have sex before they get married. I think religious reasons might prevent me from having sex. So maybe it is just that the people who are having sex talk about it more than those who don't. I think it is about 50-50. Also, a lot of the sexual experiences have a lot to do with having had too much too drink."

Her sister, Christi, who has just graduated from a Catholic college, confirms Rebecca's remarks. "I don't think being a Catholic makes a big difference for most kids on whether they are going to have sex before marriage. I don't want to say that premarital sex is rampant on college campuses, but I saw a lot more of it than I thought I would. I was a little unprepared. For a lot of kids, it isn't an issue. It is just what you do."

But Christi did not find it hard to maintain her own sexual values. "Wherever you go, you can find like-minded people. It depends on who you hang around with. And in college there are other issues. I don't think there was any pressure to do it. It was pretty much your own choice."

Laurie, a graduate of another Catholic college who did wait until she was married to have sex, agrees that teenage celibacy is still possible. "All of my friends who did have sex before marriage were very responsible. They all went on the Pill. But it was after college. I don't know anyone who was sleeping with her boyfriend in college."

None of these three girls thought they were strange because they were not involved in a sexual relationship at a young age. Christi volunteers, "I was just reading an article that boggles my mind. It was about a teenager who tested positive for AIDS, and the doctor asked her to write down the names of all of her partners in the last two years so they could get tested. And she said, 'It wasn't hard to come up with a list, but when I got to 24, I had to think, *Oh gosh!*'" Christi found the article shocking. "That has to be a completely different perception of sexuality than I can imagine!" she exclaims.

While Andrew Greeley's statistics say that only 18% of Catholics consider premarital sex always wrong,[18] most women who consider themselves practicing Catholics firmly believe the many beautiful things that their Church teaches them about sexual relations and believe that sex should be reserved for adults in a committed relationship.

Terry left the Catholic church during her early twenties for a fundamentalist church, but the sexual values that she had grown up with stayed with her. "I moved in with this guy, and we were sleeping together, of course, and here we were both born-again Christians, and it suddenly occurred to me that the whole situation was weird. Here he was talking about the Lord all the time, and we were supposed to be such good Christians. But I knew what we were doing was wrong and so I decided that everything had to change." So she left both him and that church.

Nancy remembers that sexuality was the number-one issue for her as a young adult Catholic. Starting right from high school in the 1960s, "it was just about impossible to date and not get involved with things I should not have been doing."

As a psychiatrist, Nancy explains: "There is a tremendous struggle between your body at those ages. It is like stopping water from flowing downhill. One act leads to another. You either inhibit the act entirely, or the pleasure associated with it. You have to do something to stop that cascading effect. There are tremendous conflicts, even today, with the whole business of sexuality being so loose and so familiar. We see it on TV and in the movies, and we are bombarded with it. It is a big problem."

Several mothers interviewed insist that they have talked at length with their teenagers and they believe them when they say they are committed to wait until marriage to engage in sex. Margaret assures me, "I don't think my girls are in the minority because of the AIDS scare, at least not with their group of friends. They are all dedicated to making sure that the man clears his HIV test before he touches them."

Other women are hopeful but realistic that they can get the message across about premarital sex. "I can talk about these things with my older kids," one woman explains, "but my younger teenagers are very defensive."

Jamie, a single mother in college and now happily married, is pretty pragmatic. "I don't think that 16-year-olds should be put in the position of having to decide between having a child and having an abortion. If I have a daughter, I'll pray that I can teach her not to have sex before marriage, but if I can't, I would want to know that there is something I can do. Peer pressure is so hard; each year it gets harder. I would want to know that I could give my child birth control pills and not be ostracized for it."

Most women agree with her and do not see giving birth control advice as sending a double message. "I tell my teenagers, 'Don't drink or do drugs,' and they know I mean it," one mother explains. "But I also tell them that if they do drink, don't drive, and I promise that I will always come to pick them up, with no lecture, if they need me to. That's basically the same message I give about having sex. 'Don't do it, but if you do, be sure both of you are protected.'"

She also allows her 23-year-old to sleep with his girlfriend in the guest room when they come to visit. "They are going to do it anyway, and I don't like them having sex in the back of the car on some dark hillside," she adds.

But many other mothers are equally insistent that their unmarried children do not sleep with their girlfriends or boyfriends in the family home. "They know I have very strict standards, and they don't even ask," one mother tells me.

Psychologist Patricia Miller was one of the consultants to the bishops for their 1991 book *Human Sexuality*. Her field is sexuality, and she specializes in counseling teenagers. "In teaching marriage and family classes, all the kids want to talk about sexual questions," she relates. "Yet most of them feel they can't ask their parents almost anything without upsetting them. Kids will only talk to you about sex if they think you are comfortable talking about the subject, that you will be truthful and honest with your answers, and not judge them for what they are asking."

Pat tells them that as a mother, a teacher, and a psychologist, she does not think teenagers should have sex. She finds that the best way to talk to teenagers is to ask them thought-provoking questions, like "Why does your mother not want you to have sex?" She turns the question about having or not having sex into a broader discussion.

"You don't make their decisions for them. Telling them what to do does not work. You have to realize that ultimately they will make their own decisions. I tell them to pray about it, to educate themselves as much as possible, and to be responsible for their own actions. I try to give them the tools to use to make a good decision. I ask them to make a list of the advantages and the disadvantages, of all the possibilities that could happen. I explain that intercourse should not 'just happen.' It is too beautiful not to be a conscious, thought-out decision. I don't tell them to just say no. I tell them to just say later."

Extramarital Sex

Andrew Greeley reports that in 1986, 45% of American Catholics thought that premarital sex was never wrong, and 71% thought that extramarital sex was always wrong. He claims that by the time they are 25, most Americans are monogamous most of the time.

"Jesus was much less interested in problems of sex than contemporary religious leaders," Greeley contends. "His major intervention in the matter was to declare the equality of men and women. Before his time, men did not commit adultery against their wives when they were unfaithful. Their offense, if there was any, was against the husband of the other woman. Jesus said that men and women who are unfaithful to each other *both* commit adultery."[19]

In the 1990s, fear of AIDS has definitely thrown another consideration into this question. One woman, an African-American who has always been single, tells me, "Anyone who has sex outside of marriage these days is crazy." She considers extramarital sex a sin and explains that although she has never been married, she has had sexual relationships and has been pregnant.

"I know how these things have affected me spiritually," she relates. "I know that sex is very dangerous outside of marriage, very risky. I'm not going to die because I masturbate, but it definitely tears you down spiritually. And so there are good reasons against doing all these things that have little to do with Church laws. If the Church were a little more honest and open and explained how extramarital sex affected you spiritually, more people would listen to it. The Church needs to teach why abstinence is important, not just tell you it is a sin."

No other woman I interviewed brought up extramarital sex and so I assume that all, or at least almost all, Catholic women are against having an affair when they are married to someone else. In my own experience, any Catholic woman I have ever known, including myself, who was even tempted to have an affair outside her marriage has been besieged with heavy and long-lasting feelings of guilt, even if they didn't go through with it. This was particularly so if the man they were interested in was also married.

Assuming that AIDS is not a worry, sex between unmarried committed adults is another subject altogether. One woman tells me that after her divorce she was committed to the standard that sex should happen only in marriage. "What I discovered," she admits, "is that I stayed away from men. Which was OK, because I didn't really meet anyone I was interested in."

Five years later, she met someone at a weekend conference. Everything clicked, and before she knew it, "I had hopped right into the sack with him. When I returned home, full of guilt, I was positive that I had ruptured my relationship with God. I was very, very upset."

The man convinced her to talk to her priest and get herself straightened out. She says, "The priest told me, 'It is mainly the Protestants who are holding out for this hard line business of sex outside of marriage. Catholicism has always understood that it has to flex with the times.' And it was such a relief," she sighs. "It put me right back into the Church. I had been away for a time, but I started going to Mass all the time and everything. He made me really feel that I belonged."

I remember reading an article in *Redbook* in late 1967 when I was pregnant with my third child. A young woman had written to explain why she believed in sex before marriage. She had only had sex with the man she eventually married, however, which I thought made her argument pretty innocuous. However, I wrote a rebuttal to her article. I kept a copy of the rebuttal with the idea of giving it to my children when they were teenagers. I remember wondering at the time if my opinion on this subject would substantially change 20 years later.

It has, and it hasn't. My point then—as it was when I talked to my teenagers—is that it is very important to have a special bond between you and your spouse that you have never had with another person. I have also come to the opinion, however, that one of the main reasons many of us got married was that we wanted to have sex. And most of us who had sex without waiting equated the act itself with being in love. For many, marriage to the man involved was then no longer a choice, it was a given. So one way or the other, sex led many of us into marriage, and I now know, especially after talking to hundreds of women, that as exciting as that can be, it is neither a good reason nor a sound basis on which to build a marriage.

As we talk, one young woman confesses, "We only had sex a few times before we were married, and we made it into this great big thing and were disappointed. When you are in a relationship, I think sex should not be such a focus. It should be just a part of your life. I definitely don't think you should wait until the honeymoon night. It is just another way to get to know the person. I think that premarital sex between two responsible adults who are able to deal with the consequences of their action can be good to do."

Patricia Miller tells me, "I don't think that many Catholic couples are going into marriage virgins. Some are, but not many. And never before have we asked couples to wait so long to get married and have sex. Before, puberty began around 16 or 17, and people got married around 20. Now puberty begins at 12 for girls, and many women are waiting until they are 28 or 30 to get married. So the generation [parents] which is faulting young people today for having sex before marriage is not the generation that waited for 15 or more years to have sex. They were abstinent at the most for 4 or 5 years. If you look at sexuality, and consider what we know now, that it is part of our holistic development, it makes one ask: Is it possible to put that part of our development on hold, while the rest of us is growing in other ways? I don't know the answer, but I have to acknowledge that it is a legitimate question."

Thirty-one-year-old Stacey, who has been a very devout Catholic all her life but is recently divorced, confides that she is dating a 38-year-old man who has never been married. Their relationship has not yet turned sexual, but Stacey explains, "If he were still a virgin, I'd be very concerned. He has not been promiscuous but he was in a three-year relationship with a girl, and for the Catholic church to think that someone is going to wait until their late thirties and still be celibate is pretty farfetched. It is not going to happen."

Stacey wishes she could remember the exact words of a priest at her college. "He gave us a list of questions that we should be able to answer yes to before we could consider having sex with a person. They were questions about commitment, respect and love, honesty, willingness to accept a child if that should happen. My friends and I have used it as a guide ever since."

She then quickly assures me that only mature adults, not high school students, in a monogamous relationship could answer yes to all these questions.

Divorce

As far as I know, the Catholic church has never taught that it is a sin to get a divorce. However, many people think that it does, and even some who intellectually know it doesn't still feel uncomfortable going to Communion after they have been divorced. Most Catholic women work hard to keep their marriages intact and many look to their Church for spiritual and psychological help in doing so.

Maria, talking about a difficult time in her marriage, speaks for many Catholic women: "I told my husband I wanted a divorce, but then I started thinking about the children, and my Catholic faith. And I found I just couldn't do it. Not because I was going to hell if I did, but that divorce isn't the solution. Staying and improving things is the solution. I could picture my wedding day at the altar, for better or for worse, and so I ended up staying, and it is the best decision I ever made in my life. Thank God for my Catholic training!"

But few people today—even Catholics—think that a marriage should be preserved at all cost. The bishops themselves are energetically tackling the topic of wives who have been abused—both physically and mentally—and have recently published a booklet on the topic that is receiving wide distribution. Their first word of advice for anyone caught in a dangerous marital situation is "leave."

In Catholic circles as well as nationwide, divorce has lost much of its stigma and is considered unfortunate but sometimes necessary. "I used to feel that there should be no such thing as divorce," Sister Sean Patrice remarks. "But my family is divorced all over the place, and what I am seeing is that each person does deserve some happiness. I don't say anything to my family about remarriage. I wish them well. I pray for them and hope that they will be happy. When I find out about reality, I see that what is black and white on the books turns out to be gray."

Remarriage

The real moral problem for Catholics is not divorce but remarriage. Since the Catholic church considers the sacrament of marriage indissoluble, if your first marriage was a valid sacrament, you cannot get married again in the Catholic church. If you are remarried, but not in a Catholic ceremony, you are not allowed to receive the sacraments. However, since 1975, you are not considered excommunicated and you are entitled to pastoral care on the part of the Church and full participation in parish life.

Ellen Reuter is a little more graphic and a lot more personal in her summary of this new interpretation of an old Church law. She says it feels to her like "You can come to the family reunion, but you can't eat any of the food!"[20]

If you wish to receive the sacraments of the Catholic church, you must have your first marriage annulled so that you can get married in the Catholic church.

"In granting an annulment, the institutional Church is not declaring that the marriage never took place, but that the marriage was never sacramental in the full Catholic understanding of sacrament because of one or the other partner's incapacity for full relationship or his or her lack of commitment to the permanency of marriage. An annulment does not deny that there was a human marriage or have any bearing on the legitimacy of the children of this marriage."[21]

Andrew Greeley explains that the new annulment norms make use of the notion of psychic incapacity, which means that although the two partners were legally married, they lacked sufficient emotional maturity to contract a permanent bond that is sacramental, "that is to say a reflection of the binding passion between Jesus and His Church; God and her people."[22]

Sofia tells me that when she came back to the Church 10 years ago she went through the process of having her first marriage annulled. For her the procedure was healing. Stacey, who is just now going through the process, is not as positive. Stacey and her ex-husband remain friends, and she is finding the annulment procedure both long and threatening. "You have to answer 53 very personal questions, not just about yourself, but about your ex-spouse," she explains. "And the last thing I want to do is drag out all the dirt that he has had in his life. There are questions about abuse in his family, what his relationship to his parents was like, and so forth. On my side, things were fine, so I don't have horrible things to say. But for him, I really feel badly making him go through all this. To have to go and rehash all his life to prove that he has a psychological problem is terrible. And the priest is saying to me things like, 'I didn't realize that he was on antidepressant medicine, we can use that.' And I don't want to have to use information against anyone."

Living in a state with no-fault divorce laws, Stacey finds the Catholic annulment process psychologically disruptive, even though she has the complete agreement and support of her ex-husband. A friend of hers had to have three witnesses and a psychiatric evaluation. That thought horrifies her. Besides, she is anxious to get on with her life. "The last thing I need is to drag this out for another three years," she explains.

Rather bitterly, Stacey tells me the story of young man she recently met at her parish church. "He is going to RCIA to become a Catholic. And he used to be a biker, was into drugs and everything—a mother's nightmare—and he has been married twice. But if he ever wants to get married again he can, because neither of his first two marriages was in the Church. And it really makes me angry. I did everything right the first time, and now he can get married in the Church and I can't!"

However, a priest has told her just to get married civilly—not that she has another wedding on her mind at the moment!—and then when her annulment goes through, she can get married in the Church. "That's fine," Stacey says. "But then what do I do? Sit in the back of the Church, an outcast who can't participate?"

Stacey claims that if she were not remarried in the Catholic church, she would not go to Communion because she would feel so guilty. "I even feel funny now, being divorced, going to church and Communion," she confesses. "If I got remarried, I would probably switch parishes, but even then I wouldn't feel I could get involved, because what if anyone found out that I wasn't remarried in the Church? I couldn't live worrying like that."

Stacey grew up after Vatican II, but many of her moral judgments are the same as those of pre–Vatican II Catholics. Another woman, who has received national prominence as a very active but conservative Catholic, confides that she received similar advice from the priest helping her. She had been positive that her husband would shortly receive an annulment of his first marriage when she married him in a civil ceremony, with the plan of getting married in the Church as soon as they could. His first wife would not cooperate, however, and the annulment process was halted.

"We did go to Communion, like the priest told us we could do," she says, "but after a while, I couldn't stand it anymore, because I thought in my heart I was doing something very wrong. It was very hard on my husband, who felt completely betrayed by his first wife, and to this day he still thinks he should be able to go to Communion. But he understands why I think we shouldn't. I love the Church and not going to Communion has not been a problem for me."

When most people think about an annulment, they think of a long and scary encounter with the Church's marriage tribunal. However, Jane Redmont discusses an alternative that sounds quite accessible. "In cases where the divorced Catholics and the clergy determine that seeking an annulment would be either dehumanizing or discriminatory . . . the return to the Sacraments follows the divorced person's ongoing conversation with the priest and consultation with his or her conscience." [23]

Andrew Greeley calls this the Pastoral Solution. He explains, "If the priest concludes that the person believes in good faith that he or she is free to marry, then he notes that while the Church cannot grant permission and can not publicly validate the marriage, the person nonetheless has the right to receive the Sacraments." [24]

In actuality, today many Catholic women see no reason why they should not receive Holy Communion (the only sacrament that Catholics receive often) if they are not married in the Church. Many young women or new converts don't even realize that this is, or at least has been, a very important and usually followed commandment of the Church.

Terry thought she shouldn't go to Communion because she was divorced, but it never occurred to her to not go to Communion because the marriage had not been in the Church. She was surprised when I told her that, according to Church law, she and her husband (both baptized Catholics) hadn't been in a valid marriage in the first place, so her divorce was irrelevant as far as Church laws were concerned.

Jamie, a convert, was told by several priests that she could not get married in the Church because her husband-to-be had been married before in a Catholic ceremony. So they looked around until they found a Protestant minister who would use all the Catholic prayers in the marriage ceremony.

"We really wanted to get married in the Church, but we couldn't," Jamie says. "But that doesn't mean we can't practice our faith. And no one ever said we couldn't. We wanted to get married in the Church because we wanted to, not because it would have made us better Catholics." She claims her husband wouldn't go to Communion until he had gone to confession and had talked to a priest, because he had been away from the Church for a long time. "But I don't even think he brought up being remarried," she adds.

Another woman, who admits she does not volunteer this information in the many Catholic groups she is involved with, tells me that she and her husband (a Catholic since birth) were married in a Protestant service. When she converted to Catholicism she refused to be remarried in the Catholic church. "They told me that we should be, but I said we were already married and that Christ was certainly at our wedding," she explains. "And that this was just a Church rule, an institutional rule, that I don't buy. To say I'm not really married . . . that's the stuff that drives me nuts about the Catholic church."

She claims that if they decide to renew their marriage vows sometime, it will definitely be in a Catholic church, "because that's our religion now." But until then, her Protestant marriage is perfectly fine.

Sharon tells me a similar story. "My younger sister is remarried, without an annulment from her first marriage. And she goes to Mass and Communion every Sunday and has no problem with it. Her idea is that institutional

Church rules haven't caught up with her needs yet. But now her husband is studying to be a Catholic and she is afraid that if he gets baptized and wants to receive Communion, the fact that they are not married in the Church could become a problem."

Judging by what many women have told me, Sharon's sister is worrying without cause, for probably no one will say anything. As we are seeing, the Catholic church in practice is flexible, despite its reputation to the contrary.

Sheila agrees with my assessment and offers the following explanation: "If you ask some bureaucrat, he will just say no, but if you just go ahead and do it, its OK. As long as you are not sticking it under the bishop's nose, he's not going to do anything. And they're not going to kick everyone out who's been divorced and remarried. In the first place, there would go all their money."

Although I realize that the Church is going through a huge financial crunch these days, like every other segment of society, somehow I am not as cynical as Sheila and several other women who made similar comments. The Catholic church has managed to survive all these centuries because it is equally dogmatic, understanding, and forgiving. The only sin the Church does not seem to forgive easily is scandal, which means unrepentant, willful, very loud, and very public acts of defiance and disobedience.

It seems to me that the Church operates out of a dual personality. One side is very legalistic, rigid, with specific laws for almost every situation, which is the side the institution most often presents to the general public. The other side is compassionate, understanding, and easily able to compromise, which is the side many of its priests and members most often present to one another. It is hard to know if the hierarchy—which many of us see as a group of old men gathered in some large room in the Vatican writing page after page of catechism question and answers—really believe that all their members should faithfully follow each and every rule. Perhaps they, too, simply see their work as the necessary cement for a foundation that is strong enough to allow the creative and diverse spiritual structure built on top of it to sway and bend in the wind without ever breaking or falling apart.

Regardless, only people who are very spiritually mature, who have highly developed personal beliefs and self-esteem, and who are able to differentiate between the letter and the spirit of the law are comfortable operating within the ambivalence and confusion that this dual personality of the Church creates. Others either leave the Church entirely or, guilt ridden, cope as best they can. It is these women who go to therapists like Toni for help. Toni finds most of them shockingly ill-informed, and the Church itself shockingly confused. "Inherently, confusion is bad," she explains. "I think a lot of the confusion is because the Church doesn't publicly acknowledge that there is room for individual conscience, for differences of opinion, or for a morality that is also determined by one's circumstances."

One solution might be for the institutional Catholic church to permit publicly what is fast becoming accepted by many priests as well as the people in the pews, regardless of official teachings. The reception of Holy Communion should no longer be considered a litmus test for orthodoxy. Rather, it should—officially and legally—be said to depend only on one's faith and desire to be united with God.

CONTROVERSIAL SEXUAL TOPICS

Catholic women today are no longer hesitant to talk about any number of sexual issues—perhaps they never were. At first glance many of them appear both candid and sexually liberal. In fact, the only part of the sexual revolution that most of them have bought into is the belief that sexual activity has a far greater purpose and reward than just procreation. They approve of sex that is committed, monogamous, and caring. Many have elevated sex to lofty heights, but even those who are not that idealistic condemn casual encounters and anything that threatens to commercialize or cheapen sexuality. They are particularly concerned that their children are growing up in a world that has made sex into an easily available and disposable toy.

Homosexuality

Although I have met other Catholic lesbians, only one woman I interviewed volunteered that she had been in a long-term lesbian relationship. No one else seemed uncomfortable about talking about homosexuality, however, and several women mentioned that their views on this subject were slowly changing.

Although these rules are no longer in effect, almost every nun will tell you about the rules against "particular friendships" during their early years in the convent. They now know that this is a euphemism for lesbian relationships. Before the 1960s, however, most of them, and many of the rest of us, did not know that women could be homosexuals. We thought that only men were gay.

So I was surprised at the number of nuns and ex-nuns that brought up the topic of homosexuality in the convent. Upon closer examination it appears that few, if any, were talking about anything close to genital sexuality. But that doesn't mean that they didn't feel just as guilty. Kathy's story is highly representative. "In looking back," Kathy tells me, "I was just a troubled, starved-for-affection person. When I was in the relationship, it felt like I was flirting with mortal sin. But homosexuality was never talked about in the convent. We didn't think women could do it . . . be homosexual. I thought this even when I was in the relationship. Then it suddenly hit me one day, and I was so surprised at my thought. And it made me consider myself not a very good person."

She found herself anxiously waiting for her friend to come home from school to their convent every night, and planning to be together every minute that they could. Eventually, filled with guilt, she managed to get herself transferred to another state and away from the temptation.

"These kinds of relationships were physical to a certain degree," Kathy continues. "But now, looking back, I can only think of four different pairs of nuns who probably either had a lesbian or a borderline lesbian relationship. But we didn't even talk about these things, or know that they could happen. It was just that we had no other sexual choice, and it was like we were all on a starvation diet of affection deprivation."

When she brought this up in confession, the wise priest told her, "It sounds to me like you want to marry and have children. And you just don't have the courage right now." The last time Kathy saw him he told her, "The Church is learning a lot. You're not meant to be here. God has planted this other desire in you, and you have to learn how to let yourself go and leave."

Today, happily married with five children, Kathy says that she still doesn't look on homosexuality as just another lifestyle choice. "I really think that it comes from a deficit in your family background. But I don't think of it as a sin. Promiscuity is, but not committed homosexual relationship."

More than age or education, whether or not she actually knows a homosexual seems to play the biggest role in a woman's beliefs. Many of the Catholic women who disapprove of homosexuality in principle suddenly become tolerant once they have a friend who is homosexual.

"I have two women friends I grew up with who just adopted a child," Sister Sean Patrice remarks. "I just found out they were lesbians, and I was shocked. But knowing them on a human level makes me much more tolerant, yet I don't condone their behavior."

Another woman tells me passionately, "In theory, I think it is an abomination and should not happen. On a personal basis, my brother is in a homosexual relationship, and I could not be happier that he has found someone that he can really love and care for. And I know that he is a good Christian man who is honest, moral, decent. And it makes me very angry if someone claims that he is not."

She claims that she has friends who are "torn to shreds about how to be a good Catholic and still be homosexual." She wishes that the Church was more articulate on this issue, but she has no idea about what she wants the Church to say.

Many thinking and caring women are beginning to believe that homosexuality is part of a person's makeup and is not a choice. My mother, Marian Bramble, who is an extreme sexual conservative at least in regard to any sexual activity outside of marriage, used to cry and say, "Oh, it is so sad!" on the rare times that anything about homosexuality came up. However, in interviewing her for this book, she surprised me by saying, "If it is part of your biological makeup, it can't be wrong. It can't be a sin as long as it is a caring relationship."

Jane Redmont claims that the heterosexual women she interviewed were almost equally divided between complete condemnation and complete acceptance of homosexuality. However, her research is several years older than mine, and opinion on this subject is changing rapidly. Stacey articulated the majority response that I received: "Between two consenting adults, as long as they aren't hurting anyone, their sex life is their own business."

Many Catholic women believe sex is a holy activity that connects people with one another. They believe almost all of the spiritual values about sex that the Church teaches and are slowly but surely beginning to transfer these positive viewpoints to committed sex between monogamous and caring people everywhere, and to consider all sex that is not committed and caring as immoral, regardless of where and between whom it is practiced, even in marriage.

"There is one gay man in my office who comes in and brags about the number of dates he has each weekend," Stacey tells me. "I would think it wrong if he were talking about five different girls in a weekend. Yet we have another man in our office who is in a monogamous relationship with a man, and that's entirely different."

Cassandra is even more specific. "I think the Church has done a terrible disservice by what I call 'pelvic theology' at the expense of justice for all. These are nonissues for the Church to consider. If you are living the Gospel challenge, you are living a life of justice, and care for all. Everything then is motivated by love for another and God, and that's the two sides of the same coin. Homosexuality is not a choice, so there is no inherent evil in homosexual behavior."

Even very traditional women did not feel that discrimination against homosexuals was legitimate, unless they specifically were found to be trying to "teach and spread" their lifestyle. Many women, particularly feminists, were very upset with the June 1992 Vatican statement which, while acknowledging Catholic social teachings that "the intrinsic dignity of each person must always be respected in word, in action, and in law," at the same time claimed that there were situations, such as teaching, athletic coaching, adoptive parenting, and military recruitment, in which discrimination against homosexuals could be practiced.

"To say that it is just to discriminate tears me apart," insists Jo'Ann. "Discrimination is unjust. There cannot be just discrimination." The Sisters of Loretto unanimously approved a rebuttal to the Vatican statement, which they sent to the Vatican.

"I think the Church's new doctrine on homosexuality is immoral," Cynthia tells me. "We are in a city and a nation where the number-one hate crime is against gay people. How do you preach that they are an abnormal group of people, but that we should still accept them as long as they don't do all those evil things? You can't teach that! It is too inconsistent. And for men in the Church who say that they are so logical, it is too illogical. It is very immoral. It is a sinful doctrine."

Lawyer Carolyn is less passionate but equally insistent. "The Church uses archaic language without explaining the meaning, words like *disordered existence*. That is a theological term, but when you use it in a modern context, it sounds terrible. I wish the Church would be more cognizant of its public relations aspect, and also not take the attitude that it has to force office holders who are Catholic to try and enact the Church's moral teachings into secular life. I don't think it is necessary and I think it is counterproductive."

What makes the Church look particularly hypocritical on the issue of homosexuality is that many people believe that a large number of Catholic priests are homosexuals themselves. A friend of mine, who is a priest and gives many retreats for both men and women religious, tells me that as many as 40% of priests may be homosexual, or if they are not, they are at least concerned that they might be. He also says that the lack of women being ordained into the system encourages male priests to act out their homosexuality because it is easy for everyone to overlook it.

Andrew Greeley claims that perhaps a quarter of priests under 35 are gay, and perhaps half of that group is sexually active, sometimes blatantly so. In the past, priests were not as aware of their own sexuality, and homosexuality was rarely suspected, even if perhaps it showed up in a propensity to dislike women. However, today priests are more likely to understand their sexual orientation and to act on it, particularly if it involves an easy-to-conceal man rather than a woman. "It would appear," Greeley claims, "that sexual acts with men are not as bad as sexual acts with women." Greeley contends that since Church leadership has no idea how to respond to the problem, it engages in denial, a psychological mechanism that screens out evidence that everyone else sees. [25]

Pedophilia and Sexual Misconduct of Catholic Priests

This is such a hot topic in the news that many women brought it up in our interviews. Although cases of sexual abuse were swept under the rug in the past and denied by the hierarchy, today the pendulum may be swinging too far in the other direction. Over the last three years I personally know of two cases where sexual misconduct charges were used as a political weapon in an attempt to "do someone in."

Regardless, many insist that pedophilia is the sexual issue of the 1990s for the institutional Catholic church. Jason Berry's book, *Lead Us Not into Temptation*, claims that 400 U.S. and Canadian Catholic clerics have been accused of child molestation, costing the Church roughly $400 million in damage payments and other expenses as of 1992.[26]

Tom Fox, editor of the *National Catholic Reporter*, talks about an October 1992 conference he attended sponsored by Victims of Clergy Abuse Linkup (VOCAL). He claims that this issue has received far greater national media attention and may be causing more lay Catholics to question the health of their Church leadership than any of the earlier sex-based or related issues.[27]

This is all old news to Cynthia. When she was a campus minister, she was officially interviewed concerning two pedophilia cases. "I heard about it all over the place from young men I was helping," she tells me sadly. "It was either that they were involved as young boys with a priest, or that they fought off advances from a priest . . . . This was not gay sex, this was pedophilia, and the Church has to deal with it."

Psychotherapist Richard Sipe has probably studied the sexual abuse phenomenon longer than any other Catholic professional. He claims that the celibate/sexual system that surrounds clerical culture fosters, and often rewards, psychosexual immaturity. "The homosocial system of the hierarchy that excludes women categorically from decision making and power at the same time that it glorifies exclusively the roles of virgin and mother creates a psychological structure that reinforces male psychosexual immaturity and malformation."[28] Snipes claims that as difficult as it is to accept, child abuse by clergy is made possible by the hierarchical and power structures of the Church.

Sister Hortense told me the same thing. "The hierarchy is cutting off important services because they need the money for huge pedophilia payoff lawsuits that are the result of the patriarchal Church making incredibly bad decisions concerning who they decide to ordain," she contends.

Some women, like Linda, relate that they feel compassion for the priests involved. "All human beings have problems," she tells me, "and instead of sending them from parish to parish, the Church must get them help and not become embarrassed because someone has a problem."

This issue is getting such national attention not only because it is sensational and emotional, but also because it may be the only moral subject in the Catholic church today about which there is absolutely no ambiguity among the people in the pews!

Sex Education

A 1990 national study found that of the 500,000 babies born to teenage girls in one year, 30,000 were born to girls under age 15.[29] Another report claims that more than 1 million teenagers become pregnant and that 2.5 million teenagers contract a sexually transmitted disease each year. Most Catholic women do not doubt that sex education is desperately needed by their children as well as by many adults. However, some have reservations about how this topic is being presented in the schools, and they fear that the nation's children are being forced into premature sexuality by the press, TV, and movies. "It scares me to realize what my grandchildren are faced with," Colleen tells me solemnly. "They are losing their childhood."

Terry is a college professor who has been the moderator for a Catholic group at a fundamentalist university. "My kids get very angry about the Church marching against abortion clinics," she maintains, "but they don't understand the whole picture. One of the things we need to do so badly is to teach kids about sexuality, instead of hiding it in the closet."

No one denies that children are being faced with more and more choices and problems at younger and younger ages. Sexual issues are only a part of it. "I do appreciate the difficulties of parenting all the way around," Nancy comments, "and the difficulty of instilling your values when you have a society that breaks down your values any time it can. It is not Catholicism or spirituality. The question is, how do you get your children to identify with *your* set of values?"

If they were honest, most parents would admit that they often want their teenagers to have better values and behave more morally than they themselves do. Sex education specialist Patricia Miller agrees. "I am so angry at the way the Church and society ignore teenagers and are always willing to criticize and put them down without having good programs for them. It is very easy for adults to preach abstinence or complain about teenagers' sex lives, but that doesn't mean that the adults are living the way they are preaching. The youth only reflect adult culture. If we don't like the way they are behaving, we have to look at our own behavior and see what they are reflecting. What they actually experience at home is what forms them."

My interview with Patricia was most inspiring, and I only wish there was room here to transcribe it word for word.[30] "Society has made sex equal intercourse," she claims, "but sex education is lots more than just 'how to do it.' What we are really talking about is the spiritual, psychological, intellectual, and social dimensions, as well as the physical." She is particularly enthusiastic about the U.S. bishops' booklet, *Human Sexuality*. "It says that sex education should not be act centered. It should be about the whole person," she says. She claims the document makes a very important contribution and should be considered a threshold document.

I got the booklet, and I agree with Patricia that it is inspirational and sensitively and beautifully written. Unfortunately, the few pages on birth control are like a red flag to someone like myself who considers these teachings immoral. I urge readers who may share my prejudice not to let the contraception debate turn them off without first reading the many beautiful and worthwhile comments in the book. It makes me both sad and angry that the inspiration and moral direction that is so needed by most of us personally, and certainly by society at large, on the subject of sex automatically gets "written off" because it is accompanied by this now no more than academic discussion about artificial contraception.

Talking to Patricia Miller sends up no such red flags, however. She makes you want to rush all your kids to any class that she teaches, then sneak in with your spouse to hear her yourselves. "What we need to do is try to find a way for people to know as much about sexuality and marriage as they do about anything else. We live in a culture where we have orientation for people on how to make hamburgers at McDonald's, but no training for marriage or parenthood," she maintains.

Instead of wasting valuable time discussing whether we should teach sex education, Patricia contends that we should realize that our children are getting sex education every time they turn on the TV or go to a movie. "What we need now is to say together as a Church that we are going to figure out the best possible way to teach what it means to be a Christian sexual person, and sink money into that rather than spend time at meetings fighting with the 9% of Catholics who want to keep us from teaching these things in the Catholic or public schools."

If she has any concern, it is that there are many areas of the country that are allowing the 9% to dictate that there will not be a sexuality program in the schools. "The bishops say that if the majority of parents want this education, then they should have it, and others have a right to keep their kids out of the program. But some schools take that to mean if one loud and very aggressive parent is against it, the program just doesn't happen."

Listening to her, I am once again reminded, as I have been so many times while doing research for this book, of the necessity for each Catholic woman today, including myself, to gather her own resources together and accept the sometimes time-consuming responsibility of making the Church, society, and especially our own families and our own souls come ever closer to the potential that God has in mind for all of us.

AIDS

Many, many Catholic women are impressed with the work that is being done by Catholics to help people with AIDS. I was impressed by the number of women who are volunteering or have volunteered to work directly with AIDS patients. The active compassion of the Church for sufferers of AIDS was noted time and time again by different women, who represent many different kinds of Catholics and different political points of view.

"I am very moved by the Church's response to AIDS and to people with AIDS," Kathy tells me. "I know a priest who works full-time at an AIDS hospice. And I am very proud to be in a Church which reaches out in compassion to people in a nonjudgmental, very loving way. I think lots of what we read about the Vatican responses on subjects about AIDS are quoted out of context. In fact, most of what they say is very compassionate about people. I have heard noncompassionate, judgmental things about homosexuals, but never about people who have AIDS."

I think Patricia Miller speaks for most women when she says, "The topic of AIDS is a medical issue. It is not a moral issue. We have to stop equating condoms with birth control, and start seeing condoms as a medical tool to prevent disease. We do that in other ways. The Church teaches that we can save the mother's life if there is a problem, even if it should mean the death of the unborn child, as long as that is not the intent. And the bishops said in their 1987 document called *The Many Faces of AIDS* that education about condoms as disease control could be a part of a total program of sexuality education based on abstinence."

She claims that the majority of high school teachers know that the topic of condoms is going to come up. "It is disease prevention. It is a medical issue...and we have to teach the whole truth, which is that condoms don't always work."

She insists that there is a lot more to teaching about sexuality than talking about condoms. "One of the mistakes that people make is they think that if you talk about sex or condoms, that means you are going to be doing it every day of the year, rather than just as a small part of a total holistic program."

It cannot be denied that some Catholic women would rather pretend that neither they nor their children are living in the often confusing and very tempting 1990s, in which all kinds of behavior are not only possible but often depicted as desirable. However, I believe that most parents who are willing to realistically appraise the society in which they and their children live are giving out this message: Casual sex is both physically and spiritually dangerous. Don't do it! If you refuse to believe what I am telling you and insist on learning all of these things from your own experience, at the very least protect yourself and your partner physically as much as possible.

OPTIONAL CELIBACY FOR PRIESTS

The most adamant and vocal voice I have heard against optional celibacy for Catholic priests was that of a wife of a Methodist minister as she began to describe the unrealistic expectations of her husband's congregation about her own behavior and participation in his church. Most Catholic women, however, are not thinking about the problems of being a priest's wife when they bring up the subject of married priests. Of all the proposed changes women suggest for the Church, letting priests marry is the most frequent and comes from every kind of Catholic woman.

To most women, the idea of married priests is much less a sexual issue than a balance and education issue. Many women believe that priests would be better off in their own physical and psychological lives if they were allowed to marry, as well as better equipped from practical experience to understand and advise their parishioners.

In a June 1992 Gallup poll, 75% of all Catholics surveyed supported married priests. Jane Redmont found close to the same percentage. "Well over half the women I interviewed favored a change in celibacy for priests. Their strongest rationale for the change was relational maturity, capacity for intimacy, and the ability to understand the daily lives of their parishioners."[31] The women I interviewed agreed.

"The priests don't have anyone," Maria says sadly. "No one to say, 'Honey, you've had enough to drink.' They are so lonely, and that's why they have problems. Some are compulsive gamblers, alcoholics . . . . A man needs a woman."

Cassandra remarks that as the married laity grows older, it learns new skills. "But the man in isolation doesn't," she says. "You can read every book in the world, but until you spend day after day in an intimate relationship with another person, you don't know diddly."

While both the official Church and many priests talk about the spiritual value of celibacy, it is actually just an operational Church rule. Many of the Apostles were married, and it was not until the 12th century that the Church universally attempted to enforce celibacy. Even today, there are married Catholic priests with full religious faculties, for the Church has welcomed married Episcopalian and Lutheran priests who convert, and allowed them to remain priests and keep their wivess.

This angers many of the 19,000 or so U.S. priests who, by marrying in the last 20 or 30 years, have been forced to give up their altars and their vestments. According to one study, in the United States half of the men who have been ordained priests and are under age 60 are now married. By the mid-1990s, the number of ordained men with wives is expected to equal or surpass the 26,000 unmarried active parish priests. At the very least, not allowing these men to practice their profession represents a huge drain of talent and training and is particularly considered tragic by many who know that 45% of the world's parishes and 10% of the U.S. parishes no longer have priests. [32]

Donna Tiernan Mahoney, in her book *Touching the Face of God*, writes that one reason the hierarchy of the Catholic church is against married priests is that once a priest is allowed to live a normal family life, it will be harder to "control" him. For her, the issue of celibacy is also an issue about power.

Some women suggest that if priests were married, the parishioners would get two people for the price of one. "My brother-in-law is an Episcopalian priest," Jane B. remarks. "It has not been easy for my sister to be the wife of a priest, and they have problems, like everyone, but it also gives him strengths as well. He certainly understands the problems of married couples and of parents. And my sister is a wonderful help to him, almost like an assistant priest."

"If there were married priests, there would be more priests in general and each priest would have less responsibilities," hypothesizes Laurie. "They might be better at marriage and family counseling if they were married. It seems funny to take premarital counseling from a man who has never been married."

Sharon tells me, "The majority of people have a more adult relationship with the Church now than they used to. Many of the priests have gotten very burned out because they don't feel the support of the Church anymore. And the priests we lose are the good ones, who need to be affirmed. Priests may be more accessible if they are celibate, but I think a loving couple, both working together, would be very good. The possibilities are limitless. It is stupid that we don't explore all options."

Despite the large percentage of Catholic women who think that priests and all of us in the Church would be better off if priests could marry, several women brought up practical reasons against optional celibacy. For them, expense—both financial and time—was the major problem.

Carolyn insists that all of those people advocating optional celibacy are not thinking clearly about the financial ramifications. She claims that married priests would need a decent wage, not the $600 or so a month they get now, and they'd have to maintain separate houses and not all live together like the present system. "They couldn't be on call 24 hours a day anymore," she says, "and they'd all have a huge number of kids just to prove that they were not practicing birth control. Married priests would mean an enormous number of changes."

Although many Catholics assume that optional celibacy for male priests will happen first, most likely within their own lifetimes, many women and some men believe that it would be much simpler and require fewer financial and logistical adjustments to just begin ordaining women.

That many women are so enthusiastic about the idea of married priests says as much about their ideas on marriage as it does about their opinions on the priesthood. The jokes and cartoons about women refusing to consider that an unmarried man could be happy may be true. All of the arguments for optional celibacy have to do with the advantage of a priest having a wife, not the advantage of a woman having a priest for a husband.

But upon examination of how many Catholic women view the sacrament of marriage, we see that there is something deeper behind this discussion than the hope that there may be a whole group of men in need of a match-maker soon.

THE SACRAMENT OF MARRIAGE

The Similarity Between Marriage and Religion

This is a favorite topic of mine—not that my own marital or spiritual activities are always perfect and satisfying, but that when both of them are, I find them very similar.

In 1957 my sister Joanna, in a long white wedding dress and veil, walked down a church aisle with 67 other young women in the ceremony that would make them each a nun. They were acting out the idea of being a bride of Christ, although my sister insists that the symbolism meant nothing more to her personally than just dressing up and looking pretty for one last time. If so, I feel relatively sure that she was in the minority. Many of the nuns who tell their stories in *Whatever Happened to the Good Sisters?* talk about being a bride of Christ. And, in a convoluted way, this very idea is partially what's behind the institutional Church's refusal to consider women for ordination.

Nuns are not the only women who make Jesus into the perfect husband. I remember praying to Jesus—before I was married, and also as a young wife—and thinking how nice it was that I could make God—Jesus—into whomever and whatever I wanted him to be or needed at the time. That is something that obviously cannot be said about a spouse!

Andrew Greeley likes to compare the romantic novels that he writes to essays on spirituality:

> God does passionately desire us in a way similar to how an attractive member of the opposite sex might desire us. And we desire God in a way similar to the way we might desire an appealing member of the opposite sex. Catholicism will discover that the adequate response to the sexual revolution is not continued repression of sex, but its sacramentalization, or more properly, its resacramentalization.
>
> If God is the lover, and if human love is a valid metaphor for divine love, then does it not follow that human sexual arousal is potentially a metaphor for God, a hint of what God is like, of the power and the need and vulnerability and the beauty of God? Despite Augustine and the Roman Curia of the present, Catholics still picture the erotic lover as a metaphor for God. The Curia will never change that, so perhaps it ought to try to understand it.[33]

Demetria Martinez agrees with Greeley and claims that this is one of feminism's key insights: that sensual enjoyment may reveal more about the nature of the divine than abstract, doctrinal truths do.

"In the past 20 years," she writes, "a body of feminist literature has emerged identifying the erotic not only with what happens in bed, but with the ability to understand the world through feeling. As such, the erotic is a source of power distinct from patriarchal definitions of power that pit reason against emotion, equating the latter with dark, mysterious forces (epitomized in the feminine archetype) that must be controlled, not honored."[34]

When I bring up this topic, one young woman reminisces about a former boyfriend. "I was very much in love with him. At Mass one evening, the sermon was about the Eucharist and the realization struck me that I love this person so much, I want to take a part of him and have him as part of me, to give myself entirely to him. Then I thought that maybe Jesus loves us so much this way that he gives us his body and his blood to make him part of ourselves. And that made the Eucharist a lot more real to me. It made me realize our need for this kind of love. Even in sex, we are still two separate people trying to fuse ourselves. In some way, our relationship with Jesus through the Eucharist is symbolic to that."

Catherine has been a nun and is now a wife. A filmmaker, she has created many documentaries about spiritual and social issues. She tells me, "When I got married, the big surprise was how much I ended up learning about myself because of the relationship. Before, dealing with world hunger or liturgies for children involved mostly putting out a product. It didn't come back at me. I didn't engage with it like I do my husband. When I say or do something, and he says or does something in response, it makes something rise in me that I have to deal with, right now."

She contends that her ministry as a nun was a total pouring out, but because there was rarely any immediate feedback, it was also like making love to someone who was paralyzed. Her marriage gives her more opportunity for spiritual development because it helps her focus and discover more about herself each day. "The more I know who I am, the more opportunity I have to create who I want to be. By changing responses, I continue to work with the dark side of myself. This insight gives me the opportunity to change into what I want to become. And I pray constantly that I will be able to look at my husband without judging him, and allow him to be who he is."

She maintains that although sometimes they don't make love, they just have sex, often making love is a grace-filled moment. "The preparation for it is to pray every morning, and to listen to my husband without judging."

For many of us, the dynamics are the same whether we are talking about religion and our relationship with the institutional Church, or our relationship with our spouse. In her best-selling book, *You Just Don't Understand*, Deborah Tannen explains that men (often unconsciously) look for winners and losers—for a hierarchical status—in most situations, while women (also often unconsciously) look for connection.

Family therapist Toni says, "There are some real differences between men and women, and one of them has to do with power and competition. For men, wherever there is a winner, there is a loser, while for most women, cooperation is the mode."

One woman explains it to me this way: "When you talk about the Pope and the hierarchy, the big problem is they don't want to look foolish, like they have lost control. They can't let it be known that so many people have a different opinion than they have, or even that there really is room for lots of different, sometimes even conflicting, opinions. It is the same kind of problem my husband and I—in fact my boss and I—often have."

And so women have learned how to manipulate situations with roundabout and zigzag tactics in order to allow men to cooperate with them without losing face. For example, a woman will make a man believe that her idea really originated with him. Time and time again, it appears that women react to the hierarchical leadership in the Catholic church today the way they react to their husbands when they are being equally dominating. In truth, some women (and not only intense, radical feminists) are getting very tired of doing so.

One woman, who is acting as pastor of a Catholic church, explains her frustrations: "I live in a relationship with the other half of humankind: my husband. We are equal. Somewhere around the 10th year of our marriage, it was either we had this equality or we couldn't have a marriage, and we are happier now . . . so it is very frustrating to go from this kind of situation into the direct opposite (with my job for the Church)." [35]

In the 1990s, most women believe that men have something to learn from the feminine experience of reality, just as men are beginning to realize that women, too, are able to learn much from the male experience. The struggle to integrate the male and the female sides of each personality often takes an entire lifetime and can be the source of both conflict and joy within a marriage, just as it is currently the source of both repression and enlightenment within the Catholic church. Even those men who have problems understanding that both experiences are equally valid and important when confronted by their wives, suddenly understand when they begin to relate to their daughters.

Some women instinctively feel that the imbalance that is often so evident within the power structure of the Catholic church might be well on its way to dissappearing once priests are allowed to marry.

Cassandra explains it this way: "I have a sense that what is drastically wrong with the Roman Catholic church is enforced celibacy. I think part of the training of clerics—and they will deny this to a man—is subtle and not-so-subtle misogynist attitudes. There is such a fear of women that the fear turns into hatred. And it comes out in different ways in different personalities. In other ministries, where the minister is married, the wife quickly dispels this."

What a big burden for the poor wife! Cassandra's words make me immediately understand why the wife of that Methodist minister was so against optional celibacy for Catholic priests.

THE FORBIDDEN SUBJECT: THE ORDINATION OF WOMEN

With the exceptions of the topics of married priests and perhaps remarriage after divorce, in this chapter we have discussed general moral issues that pertain to all humanity, not just Catholics, and certainly not just women. While groups may differ on the exact details about how to live a good and holy life (for example, many African Muslims practice polygamy), many of the broad moral philosophies behind different religions are the same.

I remember writing the narration for the program that the Hindus, Buddhists, Muslims, and Jews put on for Pope John Paul II during his 1987 visit to Los Angeles. Each group, including the Catholics, presented what they considered to be a core reading from their sacred literature, along with a musical sample from their culture. I was amazed to discover the basic moral similarities among them, and found myself contrasting how beautiful it all sounded with how many people had been killed throughout history by wars waged against each other by the followers of each of these five religions.

This section, however, has to do with Catholic women in particular, because it is about an organizational as well as spiritual issue that primarily concerns them today, although many other denominations, both Christian and non-Christian, are finding themselves faced with similar challenges and new ways of thinking by their women members as well.

The Sacrament of Ordination

One of the definitions of the Catholic church is that it is a "sacramental church." We learned years ago, in the Baltimore catechism, that a "sacrament is an outward sign instituted by Christ to give grace."

Some sacraments (special signs of God's presence in our lives) we give each other (e.g., marriage, where the priest really is only a witness). A valid baptism can be performed by anyone who pours the water over the head of a person and says the right words. While priests and deacons normally perform this act, in an emergency (e.g., danger of death) anyone else (even a woman!) will do. For example, Protestants who convert to Catholicism are not rebaptized.

Although more and more people, particularly women, are beginning to talk about "sacramental moments," the Catholic church has only seven official sacraments. Four of these sacraments, which both males and females generally receive only once in their lifetime, mark a passage in a person's life cycle. They are baptism, confirmation, marriage, and anointing the sick (called the last rites by most people, this sacrament used to be known as Extreme Unction).

Two sacraments unite us to the supernatural, spiritual world on an ongoing basis. Today one of these is received often, sometimes daily or at least weekly, by most practicing Catholics and is called Eucharist (Holy Communion). Another, reconciliation (confession), used to be received often but is becoming rarer, at least in the United States.

There is one sacrament, however, that the official Catholic church teaches can be received only by men. That is ordination: the sacrament which bestows the necessary "power" on a man to make him able to bring God's grace to the rest of us in the special, organized, and institutional ways of the other six sacraments.

The Catholic church also teaches that an unbroken line can be traced from each validly ordained priest living today back to Christ, who ordained the first priests (the 12 Apostles) and made Peter the first bishop and first Pope. (Peter never called himself bishop, or Pope for that matter, but that is another story.) This tradition of unbroken continuity is one of the mystical and spiritual qualities, not to mention temporal and political dimensions, that the Church is so proud of and which many women bring up when bragging about why they like being Catholic.

To become a priest, a man must be ordained by a bishop who can trace his ordination back to Peter. Although the Roman Catholic church believes that some Protestant priests (primarily Episcopalians, but maybe some Lutherans) and certainly Eastern Rite priests also may make the same claim, it is only in the Roman Catholic tradition that one can be sure.

While I doubt that there really is anything close to an actual paper trail about all of these ordinations, it is not something I, nor many Catholics, spend much time researching or worrying about. I am perfectly willing to believe that this unbroken line of succession is at least philosophically and metaphorically true and important for the identity and spiritual power of priests in the Catholic church today.

Some people (mostly priests high up in the hierarchy, and even some women like the fundamentalist members of the WFF) claim that a woman can no more be a priest than a man can be a mother. However, most women think that the only reason women cannot be priests is because no Roman Catholic bishop will ordain one. (Episcopalian and Anglican bishops have ordained women.) Regardless, most Catholic women really are not interested in the job (we'll see why later).

There are two main reasons why a woman might want to be ordained a priest.

Spiritual Reasons

The first and most important reason is spiritual (although many men as well as fundamentalist women may not believe me) and has nothing to do with women's liberation, Church politics, status, power, control, or even justice.

The most important act that the official Church says only an ordained priest can do is to be able to say Mass, which means changing the bread and wine into the actual body and blood of Christ. This is the very core of the Catholic religion and for centuries has been considered its most important spiritual activity. Yet the number of people allowed to perform this most important act—ordained priests—gets smaller each day, and few predict there will be any improvement in these statistics by the coming century.

In the meantime there are many good and holy Catholic women throughout the world today, many with the same or better education and spirituality as male priests, who find themselves in situations where the institutional Church needs an ordained priest, yet none is available. While particularly true in the Third World, this is becoming more prevalent in developed countries as the number of priestless parishes grows in Europe and the United States.

The problem of a male-only priesthood is also graphically apparent at Eucharistic celebrations of Religious Orders of Women who have to search for a priest to "import" to say Mass for their churchful of women. For many of the assembled nuns, almost all of whom are educated and spiritual women, this feels something like a woman celebrating a special birthday party but then being told that a man, a stranger to the group, will have to be brought in to blow out her candles.

Catholic women who remain steadfast in the belief that only a male ordained priest can consecrate the bread and wine often are like a doctor who has had to leave her medicine bag behind. They consider the sacraments important; they have a specific occasion when they have use for the sacraments; yet they are not allowed to help themselves or the faithful they serve tap into these important spiritual resources only because they happen to have been born female.

Political Reasons

However, many women who are not in immediate need of the tools that ordination could give them are upset by the Church's policy as well. Not only are they not able to use all of their very needed spiritual talents, they feel like they can be the secretary but never the boss. In the 1990s this type of job discrimination is not only considered immoral but illegal in the United States.

Not being able to be ordained categorically relegates all women to second-class status in the Catholic church, regardless of how compassionate, understanding, or even inclusive some male members of the Church may be. This is because the most important spiritual activity (Eucharist) and all real power (the making of ultimate decisions on moral as well as temporal rules) are in the hands of ordained men. As Donna Mahoney writes, "All the interaction, writing, and sharing between priests and women notwithstanding, women will not be accepted as equal within Church structures until they can be ordained." [36]

Pope John Paul II and many of his friends claim that the topic of ordination for women cannot even be brought up because women cannot "image" Christ. According to them, because Christ was a man, only men can be Roman Catholic priests. Furthermore, they say, "If Christ had wanted women to be priests, he would have chosen a woman for at least one of his 12 apostles." Tradition and sex organs are the two main reasons the Catholic church refuses to consider ordaining women.

There are several standard answers to both of these remarks. Not only does no one know what Christ looked like (my mother is convinced he actually may have been black), no one seriously suggests that in order to "image" Christ, all priests should be Jewish, thirtysomething men. Even the New Testament talks about women who were close friends and companions (e.g., disciples, if not apostles) of Jesus.

European theologian and writer Uta Ranke-Heinemann gives a fascinating and detailed history of the fear and oppression of women by religious men (both in the Catholic and Jewish faiths and almost since the beginning of time) in her enlightening book *Eunuchs for the Kingdom of Heaven*. She is a world-renowned scholar and each page of her book is full of more facts than most of us ordinary women in the pews can remember, let alone comprehend. But she gives scholarly proof to what almost all Catholic women today either feel intuitively or have discovered by reading their Bibles. She writes:

> Jesus was a friend of women, the first and practically the last friend women had in the Church. He caused a stir by the fact that he had dealings with women, that he was surrounded by 'many women' (Luke 8:3) which, for a rabbi and teacher of Jewish law, was absolutely inappropriate and unprecedented for his day and age. We all know that he had twelve male disciples, but he also had many female disciples, including society ladies such as Joanna, the wife of a high official under Herod Antipas. Nowadays, these women would be called 'liberated,' because they did not accept traditional female roles, but on the contrary, financed Jesus and his group 'out of their means.'
>
> In Jesus' day, the general practice was that if a woman so much as spoke with a man on the street, she could be repudiated by her husband without repayment of the marriage portion—roughly equivalent to our alimony. And conversely, it was considered outrageous for the student of a rabbi (= disciple), not to mention for the rabbi himself, to speak with a woman on the street. These women gathered around Jesus, his female disciples, were not a passive audience. Women were the first to announce the resurrection of Jesus.[37]

In other words, Jesus regularly broke many "good ol' boy" rules. He not only considered women his close friends, he also took women very seriously.

Knowing all of this, most Catholic women today dismiss as ridiculous the stated reasons that the institutional Catholic church gives for not allowing women to be ordained. Even conservative women, who have a history of unquestioning acceptance of Church teachings, are beginning to have their doubts.

Laurie, still in her twenties, tells me that the idea of women priests "is so against what I have been raised with. We just went to a Bible study the other night, and they were talking about how in Jesus' time there were no women apostles. It was really a discussion group and different people were citing passages in the Bible where it shows that Jesus didn't have women priests...and that most of his followers were men." She hesitates, then adds, completely uncoached by me, "But I don't know if this is really true. Women probably just didn't get written about as much."

More than a few scholars agree. "Evidence clearly exists, and has been documented, that women were priests in the early church. An Italian (male) scholar, an editor of a scholarly journal on Christian antiquity, *Vetera Christianorum*, provided the cogent literary and epigraphical evidence that women were indeed being ordained into the priesthood of the Christian church from the second to the fifth century." [38] Artwork in the catacombs also indicates that women took an active part in the celebration of the Eucharist.

Modern-day Women Priests

Several leaders of the U.S. Women's Ordination Conference insist that, on a trip to Eastern Europe, they actually met with women who had been ordained during the Communist era in Czechoslovakia so that they could work, as priests, in the Catholic underground. So much secrecy was needed that often the women's own families did not know that they were ordained priests. Today these women priests believe they still must stay hidden in order not to be condemned by the Vatican.

As more Christian denominations begin to ordain women, the Catholic position looks even more suspect. The subject is a relatively new one, however. Before the 1960s it was rarely brought up, and then only by naive elementary-school girls who happened to wonder out loud why they couldn't be altar boys. During her interview with me, Mary Anne remembers that in 1967 a study of nuns showed that only 15% of them had ever thought about the ordination of women for themselves or for any other woman. Thirteen years later, the percentage of nuns who wanted, or knew someone who wanted, to be ordained had risen to 50%. According to Gallup polls, in 1974 only 29% of all Catholics (men and women combined) favored the ordination of women. In 1985 this had climbed to 47%, and by 1992 the figure was 67%.[39]

The only reason that the issue of women's ordination is not a bigger, more passionate subject in the Catholic church among laywomen is because, unlike doctrines on birth control, abortion, divorce and remarriage, it does not intimately affect very many people in the pews, since hardly any of them (either women or men) want to be priests anyway. But that doesn't mean that the subject doesn't anger many women who bother to think about it. And, in fact, there are hundreds, if not thousands, of Catholic women today who have graduated from universities and seminaries with all of the credentials for ordination except male genitalia.

Eighteen-year-old Rebecca explains, "My perfect church would have women priests. It would be open to having women as much involved as they can be. I don't know if there are a lot of girls who would want to be priests, but there is the idea that you don't want to be told that you can't. You want it to be an option, even if you don't think you are going to choose it. But they are saying we can't even think about it . . . that it is not even possible, just because you are a woman, which is a real turn-off. I think they will have women priests in my lifetime. If it doesn't happen eventually, there aren't going to be many priests left."

Many men in the Catholic church today agree with Rebecca. Father Richard McCormick, a Jesuit priest and ethics professor at Notre Dame University, claims that before Vatican II, "I would have viewed the ordination of women as forever impossible. Not so now. I have come to see it as not only possible but desirable and inevitable." Part of what has changed his mind is "the privilege of experiencing personally the ministry of women. This has dissolved emotional obstacles that were far more formidable than any theological analysis."[40]

I don't mean to imply that all Catholic women are in favor of women's ordination. Some, like Sherry Tyree, find radical feminists—the kind of woman they think wants to be ordained—so strident and obnoxious that they wouldn't consider going to a Mass that one of them was saying. Although in the 1960s Sherry thought that it was just a matter of time before women were ordained, today she is glad she was wrong. "I first started changing because I saw that the women I knew who really wanted to be priests were women I didn't particularly like. They didn't have a sense of humor. They took it all too seriously. My first reaction was purely personal. I didn't like these people, and I didn't want to see them on an altar. I wouldn't go to Mass if they were the ones saying it."

Other women, even those with reasonably modern viewpoints about other issues, simply find the idea of women priests "weird" and hard to get used to. Many of them are women who still feel uncomfortable with the idea of their personal physician being a woman. Margaret is even more specific. "The people I know," she says, "are violently against women's ordination. Traditionally women have not been priests, and we have to acknowledge that if the spirit has never moved people into wanting women to be priests, there is a reason for it."

Although Sister Sean Patrice agrees with Margaret, she finds her resolve softening. "I am not in favor of women's ordination," she explains, "but I have mitigated my absoluteness against it. If the Pope said tomorrow that it was allowed, that would be fine. It would mean that the Church has looked at it and agreed, but I still think it could be pretty hard to get used to. I don't have any problem with women lectors or women Eucharistic ministers anymore, however."

Jackie is even more honest and probably speaks for the majority of people who claim to be against women's ordination. "I know it is just a tradition," she tells me. "I'm just not ready to give up that tradition. I don't think the world is ready for a woman leader. We aren't there yet, not that we aren't going to be there, but we aren't there yet." And we laugh, for we realize that while I (the supposed liberal in this conversation) am only talking about women priests, Jackie (the supposed conservative) is talking about a woman Pope!

Two of the most highly educated of the women that I interviewed who do not travel in Catholic feminist circles and therefore have not been involved in the discussion of women priests before (they had never heard official Church arguments) have some very interesting sexual speculations about the issue which probably come closer to the truth than they realize.

"There must be some deep philosophical, symbolic reason for it," Jennifer muses, "that you think of the Church as the bride and Jesus as the bridegroom and there is some sexual reason tied to that for only having men as ministers. However, if tradition is their reason, or if it is only because women don't look like Jesus, I'd say, 'Welcome to the nineties, guys!'"

Psychiatrist Nancy carries Jennifer's thoughts to their logical conclusion.

"The only way I can understand it is the yin and yang thing . . . because the feminine is evil and male is good, just like the feminine is dark and male is light. I think the Church must believe that. It must go back to something basic, like it is impossible for two women to have intercourse."

However, the stated reason that the Vatican gives against ordaining women is a lot less complicated. Rosemary Chinnici quotes a late 1970s Vatican declaration on the subject in her book *Can Women Reimage the Church?*:

> The Christian priesthood is therefore of a sacramental nature: The priest is a sign, the supernatural effectiveness of which comes from the ordination received, but a sign that must be perceptive and which the faithful must be able to recognize with ease.
>
> The same natural resemblance is required for persons as for things: When Christ's role in the Eucharist is to be expressed sacramentally, there would not be this 'natural resemblance' which must exist between Christ and his minister if the role of Christ were not taken by a man. In such a case, it would be difficult to see in the minister the image of Christ. For Christ himself was and remains a man.[41]

Interestingly, the official Church seems to believe that Jesus said, "Pretend to be me as you do this," rather than "Do this in remembrance of me." Several women remarked that this Vatican declaration is what turned them into intense feminists. At the time, Silvia was in a master's program in pastoral ministry at her local seminary, which she loved until she read the above document. "I became furious," she fumes. "That was my radicalization. I began to question everything from then on. And I had a really hard time finishing the program, but my husband urged me to do so and get my degree."

Emily had a similar reaction:

> My initial response was one of disbelief. It seemed impossible to me that the leadership of the Church had reduced 'imaging Christ' in such a crass way as being physically masculine. I felt naive, duped, betrayed, lost. I had the distinct sense that now everything in my life had a different meaning. And I knew, with my whole self, that what I had just read was not the truth. These words contradicted everything I had ever been taught and believed about myself, about Jesus, about my Christian vocation.
>
> I knew that I had experienced the living Christ in many women who bore no 'natural resemblance' to Christ but who had in so many ways made Christ incarnate for me. I knew that there was much in me

that blocked others from seeing Christ, but I knew from the depths of me that my female body was no obstacle.

I knew that I had been led on by a male clerical magisterium who flattered me by telling me that I was created in God's image, shared in Christ's mission, while all the while believing that I was basically inferior and would never be a 'perceptible' sign of Christ's presence. I had never wanted to be ordained. I still don't. But that had nothing to do with being united to Christ. I knew that the document was false, and from that moment on, that I could never presume truth from an institution that had denied my own truth.[42]

Silvia's and Emily's emotional words were echoed by many women who read the Vatican declaration, so many that by now Catherine Mowry LaCugna, associate professor of systematic theology at Notre Dame, suspects that the authors of the document may wish they had never printed it.

As a theologian, she considers that the argument against women's ordination because of tradition is legitimate and worthy of serious scrutiny and debate. But this new reason for rejecting the ordination of women "was so offensive, so patently without precedent or foundation, and so inconsistent with the Church's own sacramental theology and previous tradition, that the arguments against ordaining women now seemed specious as well as deeply sexist."[43]

Regardless of Vatican pronouncements about the subject, and the fact that it is thought to administer a deathblow to the career of any priest who disagrees with the Pope on this subject, supposedly 30 U.S. bishops now favor women's ordination and as many as one hundred would express sympathy for the idea were it not for Pope John Paul's strong insistence that the subject remain closed.[44]

There is another reason against women's ordination that many women (particularly older women) give me, even those who are feminists in every other way and personally have nothing against a woman being able to be a priest. And that is that once women are allowed to do something, most men will stop. That is certainly what has happened and is happening in many other fields (education, for example) when they are opened up to women. Many women believe this would be equally true about priesthood.

"If women could do it," Jane H. insists, "the men would all drop out. It would suddenly be seen as having no value."

"It is partly the male ego," Marian B. explains. "For example, it appears to me that now that they have women on the altar in our church [to give the readings as lectors and to distribute Communion as Eucharistic ministers], there are no men doing these things anymore. I am afraid—and I don't think that this is the fault of the Church—that if they have women priests, pretty soon there will be no more male priests."

Margaret is probably 40 or more years younger than Jane and Marian but her reasoning is similar. "I have a fear that men who go to Church because their wives tell them to will not appreciate some woman in the pulpit telling them what they have to do the rest of the week. There are so many countries where men barely get in the front door of the Church now, that they would just not go at all if there were women on the altar. Men by nature would rather stay home and watch football, or even cartoons, on television. [Including her husband, she confessed, even though he once was in the seminary, is very active in their parish, and once considered becoming a deacon.] If you took the priesthood away from men, I don't know if you would get any men in the Church. My mother says that men have their moms yell at them when they are little kids. They have their wives yell at them when they are grown men. If they go to Church and have a woman yell at them there too, they won't even bother to go."

On hearing Margaret's comments, my sister Joanna suggests, "Perhaps yelling at the congregation is something that needs to be changed and should no longer be a definition of a priest!"

I am sure she and many other women have plenty of ideas for more creative ways to "cheerlead" people into heaven than to scream threats at them.

All of the above are sad but probably true commentaries about the state of organized religion in the world, especially the Western world, today. In the 1990s women usually make up about 80% of churchgoers and maybe 85% of the lower echelons of church workers. So for the most part, saying Mass is something that clerical men do for women.

"If 85% of the churchgoers are women, why shouldn't 85% of the priests be women?" a male friend suggests and then adds, rather sheepishly, "That's an interesting idea, but somehow it is slightly offensive to me anyway."

All of this proves that the whole discussion against women priests is culturally sanctioned discrimination and has nothing to do with religion or the spiritual.

The Controversy Continues

Whether one likes the idea of married or women priests, today's refusal by the official Church to consider either deprives 65% of its members throughout the world the opportunity to celebrate regularly what those same leaders declared in the Vatican II document on the liturgy as "the peak toward which all church activity is directed and the summit from which all its power flows."[45]

The act of consecration of the bread and wine has always been considered the central part of any Mass. But the rapidly growing lack of priests is changing both this belief and practice. More often, congregations are not actually participating in a Mass but a Eucharistic prayer service, in which preconsecrated Communion hosts are distributed in a ritual that closely resembles an ordinary Mass to anyone who is either not an informed Catholic or not paying close attention.

I was on a writing assignment in Ecuador a few years ago. One Sunday, several of us accompanied a priest on a two-hour ride over barely passable dirt roads to a Church in a far-off village. It was packed with both men and women, many of whom were catechists who were given boxes of consecrated hosts during the Mass. They then set off on foot to other small churches in the mountains, where over the coming weeks they would hold prayer services and distribute Communion.

Despite Church teachings to the contrary, I believe that these Eucharistic prayer services are beginning to be looked upon by most of the people in the pews as the same as Mass and that, for most of these congregations, the subject of women's ordination is no longer of much interest, if it ever was.

My sister Joanna tells me about her recent sabbatical. Part of it was at a farm in the country, and there were eight nuns in attendance, most more conservative than she. They all went to town for Mass each Sunday, but the rest of the time they had a morning prayer service that they each took turns to plan, which was usually very parallel to Mass. In it, preconsecrated hosts were distributed. Although all of them knew in detail the difference between a Communion service and a Mass, within a few days they began to say to one another, "What time is Mass this morning?" And these women were highly educated and for the most part conservative nuns. They, of course, knew they weren't actually having Mass, but the similarities to Mass stood out more than the differences.

Margaret tells me angrily about a similar situation. "My father and mother-in-law moved into a parish in Oregon where there was a woman administrator who did the Eucharistic celebrations. She didn't explain the difference to people between a Mass and a Eucharistic prayer service and acted as if she were a real priest saying Mass," Margaret relates.

"My father-in-law is an ordained deacon, and when he moved into the parish, he took it upon himself to educate the people of the parish about what she was doing," she continues. "And so the people went to the bishop and told him, 'Get rid of this woman, and get us a priest once a month if that's at all possible, but remove her.' And all it took was someone educating the people to the truth."

Although there is probably much more to this story than I was told, it not only proves my point about what Eucharistic prayer services are quickly becoming, it also emphasizes some of the difficulties that the ever-increasing number of unordained women who are given parishes to administrate are coming up against. It is no wonder that many women feel angry and frustrated.

It is not only younger, feminist women who are feeling this way. A year or so ago, my sister's community of nuns had their yearly gathering in their Mother House, which was once where all the young girls who just entered lived and has now been turned into a residence for retired nuns. A special Mass had been planned for this celebration and their very large chapel was packed with sisters.

For some reason, the priest never came. As time went by, the assembly became more and more restless. Finally, one of the nuns, who has a master's degree in liturgy and is the associate director of the Office for Worship of her diocese, came forward and led a Liturgy of the Word, which included the reading of the Gospel and other Mass prayers. It, of course, stopped short of the consecration of the Communion bread and wine. Since there were not enough preconsecrated hosts in reserve, and also because the sister leading the service does not believe in Communion services anyway, no hosts were given out.

My sister wrote an article about the reactions of the older nuns to this event for her community's newsmagazine, which she shares with me. In it, Sister Agnes Joseph, who entered in 1924, explains, "I felt very disappointed. I came to receive Jesus and I couldn't, so I felt like I was deprived of something I wanted very much. And we have so many beautiful sisters who would make wonderful priests. I hope the time comes soon when one of our sisters can celebrate the Eucharist for us."

Sister Anne Terese, a relative "youngster" who entered in 1934, exclaims in the same article, "I was in the choir loft, and I heard all the diversity in what our sisters were saying [at the meeting]. At the same time, I saw clearly our great unity, and I felt very proud of our community. Then when Father didn't come for Mass, I felt sorrow that none of these sisters whom I was so proud of could celebrate the Eucharist. This is a great change of heart for me. Before this event, I never thought that any sister should be able to celebrate Mass. Now I pray that day may come, even if it does not come in my lifetime."

My sister Joanna reflects on her reaction to this event. "I felt angry that the head of our order, who was sitting in front of me, could not get up and celebrate the Eucharist; angry that any of our sisters well trained in liturgy, theology, and spirituality could not say Mass," she confesses. "Angry at the Church that we are all committed to, but which does not permit full use of our gifts, and which seems to value 'maleness' over availability of the Eucharist.

"I also felt powerless and frustrated. I like to do something to solve the injustices I see in the world, and with this injustice I am at a loss to know what to do. But I also felt proud of our Sister who got up and led the service, aware that a previous year, when the priest did not come, we all sat in the chapel and did not even celebrate the Liturgy of the Word. And I felt excited that so many of us were having a common experience that day which would lead to much reflection and discussion about the ordination of women."

One would think that in a world which so obviously and so desperately needs spiritual comfort and direction, any person interested in providing or participating in religious experiences would be thanked, not censored. And that, at the very least, people who believe in the power of prayer, and more specifically the power of the special connection with God and one another that the Eucharist provides, would be actively campaigning for women's ordination.

In a letter to the editor that was published in the December 28, 1984, edition of the *National Catholic Reporter,* I wrote: "I propose that all of us, either as lectors or as participants in the pews, add this prayer to the 'Prayers of the

Faithful' during Mass: 'That the Church extend the power of full sacramental ministry to all who are called by the Holy Spirit, we pray to the Lord.' As innocuous as this statement is, I am too chicken to say this aloud in my church. Every Sunday I promise myself, 'next week,' but I am afraid of being labeled a radical and a nut, of feeling embarrassed."

Almost 10 years have passed since I wrote that letter, and I have not had the nerve to pray my prayer out loud even once.

Holy Thursday is the day that commemorates the Last Supper, which was when the first "Mass" was said by Christ. One Holy Thursday, Terry (knowing nothing of my views or my letter) tells me, she forced herself to be brave.

"The sermon was about vocations," she confides, "and so it suddenly occurred to me that this was the big day for ordinations. I remembered all the things that the Women's Ordination Conference had said in their last newsletter about praying for women's ordination at the Prayer of the Faithful. And I started shaking all over. I was sure my voice would shake, and that the students sitting next to me would be upset. But I made myself say it out loud: 'Let us pray that any woman who feels called to be a priest can someday be ordained,' and immediately a hush came over the Church, everyone was so shocked at what I had said. But the college kids who were with me claimed I sounded fine. In fact they were very proud of me!"

I had already heard about this instance from Jamie, another young woman in the same parish. "Last Easter, some woman actually said something out loud about 'I pray that someday women can become priests,' and I think that 90% of the church gasped. I was one of them," she says, "because to me, a priest and a nun are as much like a man is a man and a woman is a woman. It is just more comfortable for me."

Many women don't agree with her privately, but most of the "average women in the pews" are, like me, too cowardly to make a public fuss. And for some of them, as well as for the majority of nuns and other feminists, the subject may be fast becoming one of only academic or political interest. As difficult as it is for many Catholics to believe, the subject of women's ordination may be on the way to becoming the same kind of "nonissue" spiritually that the subject of artificial contraception has become sexually for almost all Catholic women.

WHAT DO CATHOLIC WOMEN WANT? A DISCIPLESHIP OF EQUALS AND A RENEWED PRIESTLY MINISTRY

Today, women are becoming better educated about religious matters because many seminaries and universities, in order to survive financially, have welcomed their participation and tuition checks. As they study, they not only keep abreast of the newest theological and spiritual theories, they help form these ideas as researchers, authors, and lecturers. As they gain more confidence in the validity of their own lived experiences and insights, they begin to feel free to share their new talents with one another and the world at large.

Despite being forbidden from entering into the actual power structure of the institutional Church, women are beginning to take charge of their own spiritual lives and to help other men and women come closer to the supernatural and one another. Foremost on many of their agendas is the call for a "discipleship of equals and a renewed priestly ministry."

Fundamental Change in Some Beliefs

In the last 15 years or so, there have been two very slow changes in the way many women—and some men, even a few priests—are beginning to think about the subject of ordination and the priesthood, and even the sacrament of the Eucharist.

The first shift is a growing pressure for a democratic church made up of a community of equals, rather than one which installs one class of people (e.g. male priests) permanently over all the rest of its members. The second shift is that some people suggest that ordination is not actually necessary for anyone, because it is the *entire* congregation that calls forth Jesus' presence at each Mass, not just the magic powers of the priest.

Let's examine what these two changes actually mean.

This first shift should be obvious to anyone who is reading this book or has read any of the literature in both the popular and the religious press on women and the Catholic church. As Sherry Tyree of Women for Faith and the Family puts it, not only does she find these feminist women who want to be priests strident and abrasive, but "these women are not just talking about ordination . . . . They are trying to change the entire structure of the Church!"

Sherry is very correct. She might also add, "and change the entire structure of society as well."

The majority of women who might want to be priests refuse to consider being part of the clerical, hierarchical system that presently exists. They are praying and working for a democratic, circular model of Church, rather than the pyramid-shaped model that is currently in effect.

Let's listen to Bridget, who just entered the convent, went to the Graduate Theological Union in Berkeley during the 1980s, and has a master's in theological studies.

"I used to think I wanted to be ordained," she explains. "But I tend to think so less, because of the chaos and the mess that everything is in. If ordination came the way it is right now, no. Because of the way that parish priests aren't supported at all by the hierarchy. And also because of the structure. I think until we get away from expecting parish priests to be everything: financial director, playground director, liturgist, presider, etc., and this is going to take a change in Canon Law." Until parish councils really have authority, and laypeople are consulted as equal humans, unless the Catholic church becomes inclusive and democratic, Bridget would rather not be ordained.

Even the Women's Ordination Conference (WOC) itself does not have a clear picture about the exact form that a "renewed priestly ministry" should take. But they are positive it should not be according to any "add women and stir" formula. WOC national coordinator Ruth McDonough Fitzpatrick has a far bigger agenda than that in mind.

"When—if—they promise us ordination provided we give up identifying with the poor and the oppressed, the gay and lesbian communities, the Women-Church movement, the controversial 'fringe groups' [the people Jesus called his friends and broke bread with], know that we'd rather die than be compromised. The clerical caste system tries to lure us to compromise our principles. We maintain our integrity," she writes in the October 1992 edition of the WOC newsletter. She contends that rather than being "anti-Church," like many conservatives accuse WOC of being, the Women's Conference Ordination and many other feminist grassroots organizations like it are keeping women in the Catholic church by giving them hope.

Often the average woman in the pew only vaguely understands or even cares about the polemics of the feminists regarding Church structure and women's ordination. But she does understand that, although laypeople (mostly women) are doing much of the work in her parish and providing all of the financial support, her opinions, formed out of her lived experience, are often neither asked for nor heeded in her parish and diocese.

However, there are so many other pressures and problems in her life that she does not have the energy nor the motivation to complain much about her Church, let alone hit her head against a wall trying to do anything about it.

So she makes use of what the Church offers that is helpful and important to her, and doesn't worry too much about the rest, unless some book or friend happens to stir up her emotions. Then she may be as likely to blame the messenger as the message.

What is particularly useful and comforting to her spiritual life is her personal relationship with Christ in the Blessed Sacrament (Eucharist) and the community of believers with whom she worships on a regular basis. Over and over again, that is what women told me keeps them in the Catholic church or brought them back after they had left for some other denomination.

"I like being around the tabernacle. It feels like a person to me. It is the one thing the Church has going for it. And at times when I have been distressed, I have gone and stood outside the church even if it was locked, almost like it was a person to comfort me," Nancy explains.

"There is something about the ritual that is comforting. The Eucharist is very special. It is much deeper than other religion's rituals," Terry insists. "When I started going back to the Church, I did it slowly. For the first year or so, I would just sit outside and come in for Communion. I was going back because I couldn't find the connection with God that I was looking for, and I had always found it in Communion in the Catholic church."

"When I was laid off from work," Linda tells me, "I started really wanting Holy Communion, and I thought, *Well, now I have the time, I can go every morning.*"

"The thing I like about the Eucharist," Sharon explains, "is that it is the focus on God that transcends all of our individual needs. We become one. It gives me spiritual nourishment and is also the sign of unity and togetherness."

My list of quotes could go on and on. Almost every women interviewed gave me a beautiful one. However, what is even more interesting and astonishing is that there has been a second shift over the last 10 or 15 years about this very Eucharist, and this shift is coming about slowly and quietly, making its way down from the lofty writings of theologians (or up from the hearts of the Catholic populace) to the people in the pews so subconsciously that I hesitate to write about it because it will shock many who read it.

This radical switch, which is growing in strength, involves our ideas about what Eucharist is and how this change to the bread and wine at Mass actually comes about.

We used to believe (and many of us still believe today) that something magical happened to the hands and very self of the priest when he was ordained, so that, by some hocus-pocus of words and act, he and he alone changed what used to be only bread and wine into what became the body and blood of Christ . . . so that it was actually the physical Jesus sitting there on the altar disguised as a piece of bread and a cup of wine.

Communion was so holy, and we were so unworthy, that we could not touch it with our hands, and would break out in a cold sweat at the very thought that the host might fall out of our mouths and actually touch the ground. As children, we heard legends about St. Tarsicius, the young boy of the early Church who, when accosted by some "bad men," died rather than gave up the consecrated hosts that he was carrying to Christians who were imprisoned because of their beliefs. We spent hours in religion classes learning Church theory about Holy Communion, using impossible to really comprehend words like *substance* and *accidents* and *transubstantiation*, going through all sorts of intellectual exercises as we tried to dissect, explain, and prove the miracle of God's presence in the Eucharist.

But today, many Catholics are beginning to think about the Eucharist differently. A Gallup poll, conducted between December 1991 and January 1992, asked Catholics their beliefs about this central doctrine of the Catholic church. Thirty percent said that Communion brings them Christ's body and blood under the appearance of bread and wine (the "correct" answer); 29% agreed with the statement, "You are receiving bread and wine which symbolize the spirit and teachings of Jesus and in so doing are expressing your attachment to his person and his words"; 24% said they are receiving "the body and blood of Christ, which has become that because of your personal belief"; and 10% said they are receiving "bread and wine in which Jesus is really and truly present."

Kevin Haney, a board member of the St. Augustine Center in Richmond, Virginia, which commissioned the study, was shocked and said the results are a "severe indictment of Catholic education and of liturgy as practiced in the parishes."[46]

Theological nuances notwithstanding, most Catholics would consider all four answers correct. As our understanding about Eucharist changes, we are not taking away from but adding to its meaning and importance in our lives. And to say that this approach makes one not a real Catholic is like saying that someone who is bilingual is not a real American. For without knowing it, we are beginning to internalize the idea that saying Mass is something we all do together, and that the presence of Jesus in the Eucharist, while equally dynamic and mysterious, is much more than, as well as on a different plane from, what we once thought it to be.

Convert Sara especially appreciates this change. "I used to fight the idea of the real presence in the Eucharist, but having it explained as meal sharing, and looking at things in a different light than 'magic' makes sense. I fight the whole idea of lightning coming down. I am so grateful that I have met different people who have explained things to me in different ways. They have shifted the meaning for me, just like my idea of the sacrament of reconciliation (confession) has changed from penance for our sins to celebration that we are once again walking hand in hand with the Lord. I am comfortable in the Catholic church now, so I feel very happy."

Theologian Bernard Cooke adds scholarly words to Sara's new insights. He writes: "Christians are not meant to 'attend' the Eucharist; they are meant to 'do' it. We have become so accustomed to the notion that the ordained celebrant and he alone is the agent of the Mass, that we have forgotten that it is the community gathered as the body of Christ which enables the risen Lord to be present as the principal agent."[47]

He goes on to explain, "The principal agent of the Eucharist action is Christ himself, present as the risen Lord; it is he who, through the symbol of transformed bread and wine, speaks his gift of self to his friends. However, this word of self-gift can take place only because the Christians gathered for

Eucharist are acting as his body, situating his saving action in space and time, providing the agency for his communicating with those who believe in his risen presence."

Cooke concludes, "Can there be a different explanation of Christ's Eucharistic presence and of bread and wine become body and blood, an explanation that preserves authentic Catholic belief, without subscribing to a physical/miraculous understanding of the bread become body?

"Reflection on the eucharistic mystery by some of today's leading theologians points to such a 'new' understanding. This explanation stresses the sacramental nature of the Eucharist, that as sacrament it works as words do, that is, to establish communication and consequent presence of one person to another. Simply put, what is occurring is that the risen Lord, through the communicating sacramentalism of bread become body, is offering himself in saving friendship, and becomes lovingly present to those who believe and who profess their reciprocating love by word and by the action we call 'communion.'"[48]

What Do These Changes Mean to the Average Person?

Most of us women in the pew don't read much modern-day theology. I am sure my mother hasn't in years, if she ever did. Yet intuitively, during the April 1992 uprising in Los Angeles, where she and my father live, she acted out what Cooke is telling us.

My parents were civil rights activists for many years. My father encouraged his parish Knights of Columbus to invite the membership of African-Americans back in the 1950s. My mother held welcoming parties for new black neighbors as their inner-city parish changed its racial composition. They have considered it their moral duty to stay a member of the same parish for more than 50 years, even though they are one of the few white couples left in the neighborhood.

So my mother was heartbroken and in tears as she watched on TV, her bank, pharmacy, and grocery store burning to the ground during the L.A. riot. Fortunately my sister was with our parents, and she tells me this story. "Mother was so upset. All she could do was say, 'We need to pray for this city. We need to have Mass.' But when we called the rectory, they had already had Mass that morning, had locked up the church, and were not planning any additional service. So Mother said to me, 'That's OK, we'll have Mass at home. But we'll just tell Dad it is a prayer service, because he is pretty conservative and we don't want to upset him.'"

My mother got her church prayer book, brought out some wine and bread (asking my sister if it would be all right to use ordinary sandwich bread because that was all she had), and they proceeded to take turns reading all the prayers of Mass, including the words of the Consecration. "I didn't have the nerve to ask her what she thought was actually happening," my sister says.

When I interviewed my mom for this book, I asked her, "Do you think anything different happened at the table during the riots when you three read the prayers of Mass than what happens when your son—a priest—or your brother-in-law—another priest—says Mass at that very same table?"

She answered, "No. Christ is present where he wants to be present. There is no reason why my son can call Christ into our midst any more than my daughter can. When we did these prayers, we felt a relationship with each other, and with God, and happiness that we were all together. God is present where he wants to be present, and that is what I thought then . . . and what I have always thought."

Our mother is an intelligent and committed Catholic who probably has not read a feminist article (although she has been a feminist since the day of her birth!) nor a theological one in 30 or 40 years. But in a time of deep emotional crisis, she needed to reach out and connect with Jesus, with all the people in her city, and with her loved ones in her home. And she did it, instinctively, in the best way that she knew how.

I have told this story to many women during our interviews, always expecting someone to be shocked or even surprised (as my sister and I were). No one was, not even the traditional women that I talked to.

Anne Brotherton, a member of the Sisters for Christian Community, is an associate professor of sociology and ministry and the director of experiential education at the Jesuit School of Theology at Berkeley. When I tell her about my mother's Mass, she explains, "Nobody, even in theological circles, talks about things like transubstantiation anymore. I hear people describing Eucharist as the real presence of Christ which is brought about by the faith of the worshiping community. But," she adds, "this is a relatively new concept.

"I speak not as a theologian, but as a sociologist observing these things," she continues. "There is an emerging theology which will point to the ability, or the appropriateness, of any faith community celebrating Eucharist. We are quite a ways from that, however, but there are small groups who, when they meet, feel it is not appropriate to go out to the highways and the byways to find an ordained man, when they are a faith community themselves. Their ideas are not canonical, according to official Church law. But they are not doing this to defy the institution of the Church. They are simply doing it because that is what Catholics do when they pray together. It is not orthodox. But it is a valuing of the Eucharist as the primary sign of the worshiping Catholic community."

Kathy believes the idea of the people themselves saying Mass is not all that new. "In the late 1970s and early 1980s, I was teaching that it was the community who were making the Eucharist," she remembers, "not just the hocus-pocus from the priest."

"In high school we conjured up an image of a plastic Jesus that we thought was happening because a priest said magic words," Sister Hortense says. "And now it is a celebratory meal that we all participate in because of our presence, and because of the presence of all types of folks that make up the Church. It is the gathering of the community that brings the presence of Jesus. It just happens that the presider is helping us, as a community, focus on what is happening there."

Theresa often takes a Communion host from an earlier Mass to her mother in a rest home. "I get it, already consecrated, from the tabernacle," she tells me, "but one of these days I am going to just take it out of the box of hosts which is sitting in the sacristy. Whether I take it from the tabernacle or from the sacristy, I know that it is the moment that I am sharing it with my mother that it becomes Jesus. I just repeat the Gospel story when I give it to her, and I say, 'We remember when he took bread and broke it.' That's the time it becomes Jesus."

Once you have a medical problem, you keep running into everyone else who has had the same experience. Similarly, I keep hearing more and more stories about the Eucharist that are similar to the one about my parents during the riots.

"We cannot go into town because if we were to go and buy wine [for Communion] it would give us away," Rigoberta Menchu, Nobel Peace Prize winner and Guatemalan activist, explains how the women say Mass together when they are hiding from the military in the hills. "So we gather together, take tortillas and water, bless them, and share them. And that to me is the body and blood of Jesus Christ."[49]

My sister tells me about a Christmas Midnight Mass last year at her inner-city parish. "There were three male priests standing around the altar during Mass," she explains, "but the priest who was the main celebrant of the Mass asked the people in the pews to say *all* the priest's words of the liturgy, including the words of consecration, and he said the people's part during the entire Mass."

Father Michael Crosby writes about what he thinks is happening. "Above all, these recovering Catholics [who refuse to stay addicted to clericalism in a dysfunctional church] will celebrate in his memory the breaking of the bread and the sharing of the cup even if they may have to do so without an ordained cleric."[50]

"At a non-theoretical level, the very conduct of Christians today testifies to a new understanding," I read in another book. "When clerics are unavailable for servicing the needs of small communities that spring up, the laity preach to themselves and sometimes lead themselves in eucharistic praise without bothering to ask whether their eucharist is a Eucharist with a capital E."[51]

Jane Redmont concurs. "Catholic women are gathering together for prayer, study, service and celebration. Rather than asking to be let into the church, these women have decided to go about being church. By breaking the bread, reclaiming a simple gesture laden with centuries of religious meaning, they do not intend to desecrate, but to deepen and hallow the meaning of the sacrament. They mean to connect in a fresh way the gifts of the earth, the presence of God, and their daily lives."[52]

"People are beginning to believe that it is not just special, magic words of the priest that make Jesus present," my sister explains. "But that he is present all the time, most particularly in the gathering of the community who believes in him. And it is this community which both reminds us of his presence, and makes him even more present."

"Today people think of Eucharist more as bread and nourishment and being involved with community," Barbara tells me. "It is the symbol of being broken and then made whole again, of being shared. And that, in the sharing, there is enough for everyone. People of many diverse backgrounds are brought together. A Maryknoll priest came to our convent in the early eighties. He told us that people were entitled to a Eucharist that was nourishing to them, and suggested that maybe people had to create the rituals to do that."

Sharon relates that she especially likes going to Mass in a nearby Benedictine monastery, where the priest hands out the hosts ahead of time and has each person hold it up during the consecration as they all say the words together.

When almost everything you read and many people you talk to are saying the same thing, it is difficult to doubt that what is being said is really what many people are beginning to believe. This is especially true when you discover many of these new ideas almost accidentally, without either expecting them or looking for them.

A Respectful Hesitation to Verbalize New Ideas

These are new perceptions, however, and many average women in the pews will be shocked to read them. In fact, only a few of the women who are beginning to share this new view of the Eucharist have taken the time or have had the courage to put two and two together and articulate what is happening.

Despite how it might appear to someone reading this chapter, most of the Catholics I am quoting cannot in any way be considered radical feminists. They continue to respect, love, and honor the institutional Church. It is only because the ritual around the Eucharist means so much to them that they wish to pray this way whenever possible.

But that doesn't mean that they don't occasionally have some misgivings or at least an active ambivalence about activities, even holy ones, that at first glance look like they could harm the unity of the Catholic church. That is another reason why many Catholics are all but silent about this shift in their thinking about the Eucharist.

But what is being proposed, in a very quiet and respectful manner, is an entirely different way of thinking about the institutional Church and our relationship to it. And many are beginning to conclude that this new way of thinking will eventually take us back closer to the rituals and faith experiences of the early Church.

Let's have Sharon sum up the beliefs and conflicts within many of us who are starting to look at the sacrament of Eucharist in this expanded way. I have known Sharon since she was 13. Now a wife and mother, she is probably the holiest, most sincere, and most religiously together Catholic I have ever met. She is certainly one of the best educated, for although she is just now study-ing for her master's in theology, the Catholic church has been the center of her life since childhood, and she has attended almost every kind of religious seminar or workshop that anyone can mention. Her opinions are particularly valuable.

"But I also believe in the Church and the handed-down authority," she stresses. "And this question comes up for all of us: How do you guarantee that what we are talking about here is in the spirit? By what authority? In the anointing of a person (by a bishop) there is an earthly guarantee.

"That doesn't mean that you can't have an anointing by the spirit of a woman, or anyone. However, I love the structure of the Church too. I know we would start another Church if we got rid of this one. Just like if most of us got a divorce, we'd probably end up marrying someone else who is just the same as our ex-spouse anyway. So what most of us want, like most of us in our mar-riages, is to work out the problems in this Church, not to get a new Church."

Sharon goes on to explain what she means by problems. "Anything that separates each of us from each other, and from ourselves, and from God, is not of God and should be thrown out of the Church. And anything that builds unity and gets us to communicate with each other, to share ourselves with each other, to be bread to one another, is good. I think we are at the end of the age where we ask that step-by-step instructions be written down for us. Instead we are asking, 'What is God calling us to do?'

"The early apostles went out to break bread with the community," Sharon continues. "But it is not a magic thing. It is in the people, in sharing. It is in that oneness. I think ideally anyone could say Mass, but practically, on a human level, we have ordination so as to keep it so that anyone can trust, no matter what kind of a home they come from, that there is some stability. If we rush in late to Church, grab the host and run out to the car because we are in a hurry, we haven't received Jesus, even if an ordained priest conse-crated the host. Or if we receive the host without believing it, it isn't Com-munion either. It is the faith that is healing you, and the bread and wine are the outside symbol of it."

As she talks, a thought occurs to me: At the present time, having an ordained priest say Mass with us versus a group of us saying Mass together may
be like the difference between getting married and living together in a committed relationship. Perhaps the structure is helpful in making the act symbolic of something even bigger. But if this is true, then the structure needs to
be made accessible to all believers, regardless of their sex.

Until then, few women are advocating completely doing away with male
priests and bishops, or even with the Pope, the symbol of our unity. But that
does not deny that more and more people—at least women—are beginning
to believe that they, too, have priestly powers, even without ordination.

A New Meaning for the Word **Eucharist**

What is considered a "Eucharistic experience" is expanding rapidly as well.

One nun, who is one of the highest-ranking women in the hierarchy of
her diocese, speaks for many when she explains it this way: "I still have a reverence for Eucharist as we used to think of it, but for me, the House of Affirmation [a treatment center for women who have substance abuse problems]
is where I find Eucharist in their struggles and their brokenness. It is not that
Eucharist has changed, but that it has broadened from the narrow viewpoint
we had of it before."

For Sister Marguerite, this meaning of Eucharist is the most powerful. "I
find it next to impossible to participate in Eucharist separate from a context
that includes a relationship to others. Today I know many Eucharistic moments. I feel called and drawn into the brokenness of life of the ones I have
the privilege to serve."[53]

"When I was living in a shelter for homeless and abused women," Jo'Ann
recalls, "we all lived together and prayed together each morning. For me, that
was probably the closest thing to real Eucharist that I have ever experienced."

"Talking to you like this, and sharing our intimate thoughts about our
spiritual lives," a woman from Texas tells me, "is Eucharist to me."

For a long time, Christ was "locked away" in little gold tabernacles within ornate and awe-inspiring cathedrals. He came out only on special occasions, like
morning Mass, set free by the priest in his elaborate, long, flowing vestments.

Now, however, Jesus has been let out of the churches and allowed to walk through the streets of the world where we come face-to-face with him daily in Eucharistic moments in the strangest places. And this is happening to every person—woman or man—who strives to take his words literally: "I was hungry and you fed me, thirsty and you gave me a drink; I was a stranger and you received me in your homes, naked and you clothed me; I was sick and you took care of me, in prison and you visited me" (Matthew 25:35–36).

No one is suggesting that many, if any, of us come even close to this kind of idealism on a regular, or even frequent, basis. But when we do, we understand some of what the phrase "a renewed priestly ministry" is coming to mean.

TAKING CHARGE OF OUR OWN SPIRITUAL LIVES

Feminist Issues

In 1984 Joan Turner Beifuss examined religious feminism for the *National Catholic Reporter* and described it this way: "It identifies with the poor and hurting. It insists that liberation in one area must lead to liberation in all. It denies the split between spirit and matter. It honors sexuality and women's bodies. It calls for reintegration with nature rather than its subjection. It demands that women's experiences be regarded as valid and redemptive. It recognizes new spiritualities and theologies that grow out of these experiences. It attempts new ways of speaking of God. It incorporates dance, song, visual arts, and poetry into its worship and revelation." [54]

Ten years later, Beifuss's definition rings even more true. As these views and activities are passed down from radical feminists to moderate feminists, they begin to slowly percolate through the "political" ranks of women until, today, they are beginning to reach the average woman in the pew.

More and more women who are studying formerly male-dominated disciplines such as history, psychology, and religion are coming to new and interesting insights about what they find or, more correctly, don't find there. And what they notice is that it was not just radio and television that left out 50% of the human race before the 1960s, but almost every other document and information source as well.

As women become more educated and in touch with one another, they become excited about filling in the pages of "herstory" that are missing. They begin to try to create for themselves (or reclaim) the kind of experiences that they have read about—experiences that until recently were for the most part reserved for men.

Women begin by insisting that their names, even female pronouns like "she" and "her," be included in the annals of time. They start to suspect that, if they really have been made in the image of God like they have been told, then their feminine nature must also be found somewhere within God. They look for ways to come in contact with this God that particularly speak to their feminine hearts and souls.

One of the first ways that Catholic women begin to claim their own personal relationship with the supernatural is by creating spiritual rituals that echo and share their own inner truths.

Feminist Liturgies

Since the mid-sixties, women (often nuns) in charge of retreats and other gatherings that are primarily if not exclusively attended by women, have created beautiful rituals that unite the members of the group in prayer and friendship and help them feel the presence of God in their midst. Although blessing and sharing bread and wine is often part of these liturgies, participants are usually careful to never claim that Mass is being said, nor even verbally hint that this might be so. In fact, some of these rituals make no actual mention of the word *Jesus* or *Christ*, even at gatherings like those of Women-Church—so afraid are women that they will be accused of heresy or of "pretending" to say Mass.

Regardless, few women who have attended these services deny their spiritual and emotional power. JoAnne tells me about her first experience with such a liturgy while she was in law school at Notre Dame in the early 1980s. "I went on a silent retreat at St. Mary's across the street from Notre Dame," she says, "with a bunch of interesting Polish housewives. And they were upset because there were no priests to hear confessions. Nuns, who were still pretty conservative, were running the retreat.

"Anyway, one evening we sat in a circle and it was basically a prayer kind of thing. There was this gorgeous loaf of bread and some grapes. Then this nun gets up and reads the Eucharist story from Mark, but there was no attempt to reenact the Eucharist and make it a women's Eucharist at all. But it suddenly came to me that it absolutely was.

"We were busy singing 'Amazing Grace,'" JoAnne continues, "and on the last verse, out of nowhere, my voice rose, and it was on key, and I was singing loud, and I knew that was Jesus Christ we were passing around . . . just as much as when Father Mike said Mass. I didn't say anything to anyone, because the thought was just too outrageous. But I remember the moment. I have never forgotten that. I believe that it happens all the time."

JoAnne insists that no one else in the room understood what was happening, but she did. "It has nothing to do with theology," she says. "It is something you just know. And I believe that it happens again and again, and it is as if the Apostles were right there. Some of the Apostles probably sneezed, and they didn't have a clue about what was going on, but nevertheless, Jesus poured himself out and passed himself around, and the same thing happens. And it is not just a symbol, it is a sacrament. It is real."

I have been part of several such liturgical experiences myself, and they have all been spiritually wonderful and uplifting, and not in any way subversive or heretical. In order that readers may discover this for themselves, and perhaps adapt one such liturgy for their own use, I have included the script for such a prayer service in the Appendix.

Many of these liturgical experiences celebrated over the last 30 years have been created by the very same women who were also actively involved in creating meaningful liturgies for official Church services. If these women had been men, they would have been ordained priests saying Mass and no one would have thought a thing about it. It would simply have been business as usual.

And so perhaps women who have enjoyed these spiritual opportunities owe a debt of gratitude to the institutional Catholic church, because if it had been willing to ordain women, it is very likely that many of these women's liturgies might never have taken place. The very people organizing them would have been swallowed up by the system, and many would probably be desperately trying to prove that being a woman did not make them less able or less orthodox than men. By not ordaining women, the institutional Catholic church has caused the proliferation of these feminist liturgies by creating a vacuum that has been filled by women's spirituality and creativity. Strange are the workings of the Holy Spirit!

What's more, refusing ordination to women has caused a dramatic increase in feminist theologians teaching (one of the few jobs open to them) in universities and seminaries around the country. It is particularly ironic that the women the institutional Church finds "unfit" for ordination these days are often the very people preparing men for ordination!

Women-Church

These feminist liturgies are often simply part of a retreat or some other special celebration for women in which the participants go back to their regular lives and normal Sunday Masses feeling spiritually enriched.

However, there is a loose network of feminist organizations throughout the country as well as the world, called Women-Church. Their first conference was in Chicago in the early 1980s. In 1987 they assembled as a group in Cincinnati, and in April of 1993 in Albuquerque. Although every attempt is made to be ecumenical and inclusive, at the present time most of the women involved come from the Catholic tradition.

One of the movement's founders and coordinators, Mary Hunt, defines Women-Church for us: "It is not an organization with members, elected officials, or its own clergy. It is not a club from which men are excluded and in which children are tolerated if they keep quiet. It is not the women's auxiliary of the larger church. Nor is it simply a place where women who have been wounded by patriarchy can find comfort.

"My definition of Women-Church is that it is a global, ecumenical movement made up of local feminist base communities of justice-seeking friends who engage in sacrament and solidarity," she continues in the press release Women-Church sends me. "We do not demand unilateral allegiance to Women-Church. Nor do we make a practice of criticizing other churches. We are Church. Our primary attention is on being Church. The rest is detail. Women-

Church is not schismatic. It is a spiritual expression of the deepest aspects of the Christian tradition."

Some women are very happy to be able to worship together and to feel the solidarity of women without men around. However, other women, like Cynthia, who agrees that these feminist liturgies are powerful, are hoping and praying that the day will come when women and men—equal and united—can officially celebrate Mass together.

"I am much more at ease and more likely to feel that each participant is being valued and respected when women do Eucharist than I am at many official Catholic masses," Cindy explains. "But they both operate out of a feeling of exclusiveness. And what I am looking for is a union of all of us, men and women. Until there is a union, women are going to be doing their masses, and men are going to be doing their masses, and this is not Eucharist in either sense of the word for me. It isn't.

"What I mean is," she continues sadly, "I can't bring my male teenagers or my husband, because they aren't respected. They are the enemy, which they feel. And so where do I fit in? I am looking for union and I have two choices, both less than perfect. Fortunately, every once in a while, I find a really good Mass at a regular, male-priest led service, which holds me, and my family, for about six months."

One solution to Cynthia's problem is for the institutional Catholic church to recognize the gifts of all its members, even women. The other, perhaps more likely at least in the short run, is for feminist liturgies to go out of their way to welcome men and families.

Feminist Theology and Feminist Spirituality: Bringing New Insights to Women and Men

Women are not only finding feminist ways to pray to God, they are finding new ways to think and talk about God as well. In fact, the influence of feminist spirituality is growing, and slowly but surely it is not only reaching the average woman in the pew but sneaking into liturgical experiences and ideas held by society at large as well.

Most women today are beginning to take their own spiritual experiences seriously. They are starting to realize that what they read in the Bible, or in Church documents, often reflects only the experiences of men, who are not only psychologically and biologically different from women but whose life and ways of looking at things are also different. So women flock to Bible-study discussion classes, many ecumenical, as they attempt to claim the truths found in the Bible for themselves. Scores of other women are enrolled in theology classes or workshops.

Most of us believe that stories in the Bible were written not as TV documentaries (the creation story, for instance) but to pass down larger, human truths in a metaphorical way so that we can understand them, adopt them as our own, and make use of them in our own lives. Even so, there are some biblical stories that just don't make any sense to women. One that has never made sense to me is the story in which Abraham takes his son Isaac up to a mountaintop, where, according to God's command, he prepares his son to be sacrificed. Fortunately for both of them, at the last minute the Angel of the Lord intervenes and explains that God was just testing Abraham.

We were taught that this tale both foreshadows the sacrificial death of Christ and points out that humans should be prepared to follow God's commandments, even to the point of sacrificing their own child. But as a mother, there is no way this story speaks to me, except negatively. Any mother I know would equally fail the test and tell God no from the very beginning.

Feminist spirituality offers us a systematic method to solve these kinds of comprehension problems. Since it is based on experiences that are common to women, feminist theology offers new ways to look at spiritual truths that make sense to women and gives them the tools for spiritual growth. It unmasks the symbols or images that have excluded women and searches for alternative symbols that tell women's stories in a positive way.

A feminist theologian and marriage, family and child therapist, Rosemary Chinnici explains that women sin differently than men. According to her, women's sin is the "sin of hiding," choosing to be named from without by someone else, while pride is the sin of men.

"Traditionally, theology has understood the primary sin of humanity to be that of Pride . . . of turning from God toward oneself. But this is men's sin," she explains. "Women need to move from a sense of relatedness and connection to self-definition and uniqueness. Men need to move from a sense of separateness and self-definition to relatedness and connection. Each takes their original attribute with them so that maturity consists in the ability to be both related and self-identified at one and the same time."

Those of us who read these words know that what she is talking about is finding a balance in our lives.

"Religion has traditionally been examined and preached by men," Chinnici continues. "So it makes sense that the usual understanding of sin is pride. An awareness of pride keeps one from isolation and encourages relationship, a message that men developmentally need to hear. This message has disastrous effects on women, however. For a woman to be encouraged to always remain in relationships and never be selfish subverts her psychological development." Chinnici claims that the message women need to hear is one that stresses self-definition, separateness, and self-care.[55]

Chinnici helps her women students reimage old stories and come up with a new theology that speaks to them personally. For example, she suggests that the story of Martha and Mary in the New Testament (where Martha complains about having to do all the work while Mary listens to Jesus) might be reimaged by having Christ and Mary go into the kitchen and everyone sit around talking while they all work at getting dinner ready together. Lot's wife would be reimaged so that she is turned to stone not because she looked back, but because she shed tears of salt for the people she loved whom she had to leave behind.

"We simply do not realize the uniqueness of our prayer life, the value of our own stories, the truth of our own interior maps," Chinnici maintains. "Instead, we often mistake men's experiences for our own."

Many male theologians are beginning not only to thank female theologians for their contributions, but to agree with them. "It is now common for theologians in North America to embrace the fundamental critique and approach of feminist theology," Catherine Mowry LaCugna writes. "To affirm the importance of women's as well as men's experience of God; to acknowledge the extent to which the Christian tradition has been one-sided, to seek to correct these deficiencies in their own theological reflection while remaining in continuity with the past and rooted in the life of the church. Indeed, it would appear that the term *feminist theologian* now seems redundant if not outdated."[56]

LaCugna's statement should please all women who read it and make them realize that the 1990s version of religious feminism is *not* anti-men! The feminist theology of today not only helps women embrace their own lived experiences as also representative of common human truths, it offers to the world a new order in which men and women are really equal. It does *not* mean to *re-place* the oppression of women with the oppression of men.

Even so-called radical feminists confirm this point. They are not plotting to put women on top. They are only attempting to replace the patriarchal ladder of status with the circle of mutuality. "Only when women contribute equally with men to the definition of humanity will it be realized that what is normal for women is normal for humanity, just as what is normal for men is normal for humanity," Sandra Schneiders writes. She contends that we must embrace both individual rights and relational responsibilities for both men and women on the basis of self-definition and self-determination of both, "not the self-determination of men and the male definition of women."[57]

As inspirational as they probably sound to Schneiders and other radical feminists, it is her other remarks that frighten many "unliberated" women.

Schneiders defines feminism as "a worldwide movement that envisions nothing less than the radical transformation of human history." She claims that "women do not seek to participate as imitation males or on male terms in a male construction of reality. Rather they have undertaken a deconstruction of reality in more human terms."[58] According to her, this change will help save the race and the planet.

"Feminist spirituality is necessarily informed by a developed feminist consciousness," she continues, "which is the awareness of sexual oppression and involves a critique of patriarchy as the cause of that oppression, an alternative vision of a non-patriarchal future, and a commitment to structural change to realize that vision."[59]

The Fear of Feminist Rhetoric and the Feminist Movement

Schneiders' comments are all well and good if you don't happen to have to (or want to) live with a man. But the majority of women are in serious relationships with men. And although they often may complain about men in general, their husbands or boyfriends in particular, they resent other women (especially unmarried nuns) not only telling them how oppressed they are, but also telling them what to do about it.

Most laywomen have no idea about any of the conflicting ideologies and compromises that must be worked out inside the convent. They just assume that most nuns live in a large enough group where they can find other people who agree with them, no matter how radical their ideas may be, without having to leave the convent. That is a luxury that a wife does not have. The closer the feminist complaints come to the truth about women's lives, the more confused, as well as angrier, most "unliberated" women become.

"No, I don't approve of ordaining women," Colleen assures me. "Maybe because I am too old-fashioned to accept that. I just say no to that. I would go to a woman doctor, but not to a woman priest. I just don't feel it is a woman's place."

She hesitates, then says, "Yet that's not what I mean at all. The feminists would be all over me for saying that. I don't know why I don't feel right about it. I just feel that the figure of authority . . . " she pauses, then adds, "However, I certainly am a figure of authority in our family, not any more or any less than my husband is. Yet I don't feel right about a woman being a priest. Many of the things the feminists are teaching are fine, but they go too damned far. Let's leave some of this stuff alone . . . the master race. You are a man or you are a woman. You are equal." Obviously frustrated, she ends her thoughts by saying, "I don't know why feminists have to be so feminine."

Which is not what she means at all. What she really means is, why do they have to be so masculine? (i.e., think that they alone have the truth). Many women can handle being put down by a man. After all, that is something they expect, which they are used to handling. But being put down by a woman is something much, much harder to take. All of the women I interviewed who identified themselves as conservatives were angrier at intense, radical feminist women than they were at men.

Not only do they know from experience that being a "patriarchal man" isn't all it's cracked up to be, they don't like having to look over their shoulder all the time to see if someone—some male—is about to oppress them.

"There's a part of me that can get hooked into hatred, and I don't like that part of me because it's not good for me or for anybody around me," one woman explains. "I found that when I was with someone who identified very strongly with the women's movement, I didn't like what happened to me." [60]

I understand exactly where these women are coming from. Most of us sincerely want to keep the peace, and for many of us, feminist literature feels or used to feel almost pornographic, or at least like the "True Romance" comic books and magazines we used to read in the drugstore as teenagers or hide from our mothers at home. They made us, at least while we were reading them, physically yearn for something that we were sure we shouldn't or couldn't have.

As my sister became more liberated as a nun, she used to send me all sorts of feminist self-help books during the 1970s, with pertinent sentences underlined. One was titled, *I'm Running Away from Home but I'm Not Allowed to Cross the Street.* And, although I appreciated her love and concern, I remember telling both her and myself, "If I'm going to stay in this marriage, I can't read this stuff."

"We started a women's group at our parish," Cynthia relates. "It was called Bibles and Babies, and we were all diehard feminists, nursing our babies. And then we sort of split up, because it got very heavy. Women started asking questions about their relationship with their husbands, and that caused a real problem."

The very thought of having to recognize ourselves as oppressed and then having to change the entire way that men and women have related to one another over the centuries petrifies most women who have a hard enough time trying to make small changes in the way they and their husbands relate to one another as it is. Furthermore, many women are not completely convinced that the feminist, circular model of society and relationships is always the only way to go. For one thing, no one, not even the feminists, pretends that it is very efficient. What it usually means is hours of talk, trying to come to some consensus.

Even many modern and liberated women of the 1990s often try to distance themselves from the word *feminist,* when in truth they are actually feminists themselves. A professional and liberated friend of mine and her husband were over for dinner one night, and everything she said was prefaced with "I'm not a feminist, but . . ."

Frustrated but a little bemused, I finally asked her, "Valerie, what do you mean you're not a feminist?" and she immediately replied, "I mean I'm a humanist. I like men. I'm not a lesbian."

She is not alone in her opinion about what the word *feminist* implies. "I think of myself as a feminist only in that I subscribe to equal rights for women, but not as a strong anti-men sort of feminist," Jennifer assures me.

"I don't accept what some white, middle-class feminists are saying about us, that we Hispanics aren't feminist enough," Maria Pilar insists angrily. "I think they have to understand that it is one thing to be a white woman, and a very different thing to be an Indian American woman—a *mestiza*—in a highly racist society."

"I really try to keep away from things that are totally feminist," Betty claims. Another professional woman who by any definition has to be considered a feminist, Betty continues, "I don't believe in that any more than I do masculine superiority. I think it is wrong that a woman gets a job just because she is a woman, just as I think it's wrong that a black man gets a job just because he is black. I think it is wrong for me to want to be better than men, so no, I don't believe in the feminist movement."

The truth is, however, most women who call themselves feminists—even radical feminists—aren't lesbians and don't believe that women are better than men. They just want to be equal and to be able to define their own lives. Regardless of what they may say or call themselves, all of the women I interviewed for this book have been extremely influenced by the women's movement, both in society at large and religion in general, including those actively campaigning against feminist philosophies. Most of these women share much more in common with women who are proud to declare themselves feminists than they think.

Women at every place on the political spectrum can be called feminists because they are beginning to trust their own insights and they are refusing to let others, even other women, define their reality. Their main problem is with the word itself, which has had a bad reputation for many since the day it was first coined.

"I myself have never been able to find out precisely what feminism is," wrote Rebecca West in 1913. "I only know that people call me a feminist whenever I express sentiments that differentiate me from a doormat or a prostitute."[61]

This "bad reputation" is what caused 63% of women polled by *Time Magazine* in February 1992 to claim they are not feminists, yet 82% of these same women said they have more freedom than their mothers did; 57% said there is still a need for a strong women's movement; and 39% said that the women's movement has improved their lives.

Much of this reluctance is due to most women's intense fear and dislike of any kind of confrontation. Quite a few women of the 1990s are glad there are feminists, and many are even happy to be feminists—as long as no one calls them that!

The Shift Toward Inclusive Language

It has become politically incorrect to use generic male words when referring to any combination of people who are not all male. This dramatic change in the way most of us now speak has been brought about by two forces: the women's movement and the speech patterns of our children.

Since almost every kind of job is now open to women, children can't conceive of calling the women who do these jobs men, and are quick to correct you if you call the "mail person" or "mail lady" a "mailman." Nor does it even occur to them that the word *man* could mean "woman," too.

Although this new speech pattern has been influenced by teachers (and sometimes by mothers and older sisters), much of it comes automatically because of a new reality, out of visual logic, rather than out of any allegiance to the women's movement. Children simply find the whole topic ridiculous. The subject is not so ridiculous to those of us who were born before the 1960s. "I invite you to be open to the possibility of changing your language to be inclusive," writes Phyllis Willerscheidt, executive director for the Commission on Women in the Archdiocese of St. Paul and Minneapolis. "Even though I am aware that changing our habitual patterns of behavior is difficult." [62]

As a writer, getting rid of the generic *man* was indeed difficult and, at first, seemed silly to me too, until I had an Awareness Experience (which I have also included in the Appendix and urge you to read). All of a sudden there was an emotional "click" in my brain and the whole subject immediately made sense.

But for young women today, many of whom are keeping their own names or coming up with some hyphenate when they marry, and who have never seen a "women's" section in the classified ads of a newspaper, inclusive language is a given. It was the only topic where I found an opinion predictable by the age of the person interviewed. Almost all younger women, even the very traditional or fundamentalist ones, were offended if they personally were "lumped" into the generic "man." The older a woman was (unless she was a radical feminist) the less she cared about this topic, regardless of how liberal she was on every other subject.

While many women over 50 thought this discussion trivial, only one woman was actually angry about this newest change in English usage. English teacher Sherry Tyree complains that many times, not using the generic "he" forces us to choose between being politically correct or grammatically correct. "The conflict that arises is at what point do you stop being faithful to language because you don't want problems with someone out there?" she asks. She claims that the feminists' insistence on inclusive language is really part of a much larger attempt at social engineering, which she doesn't like.

Some of the hierarchy of the Catholic church share Sherry's viewpoint. Several different feminist nuns tell me about a letter (letters?) they have seen from Vatican sources which warns that the topic of inclusive language is only the tip of the iceberg and therefore "dangerous."

"The letter very clearly says to watch out for this desire for inclusive language . . . that they have to be very careful how they handle this because the issue is much bigger," Jo'Ann says, smiling. "And they are right."

However, regardless of whether the topic was influenced by political overtones, inclusive language is becoming such common practice that there is no way this trend will be reversed. The institutional Catholic church itself is studying how to change most official prayers to include both genders. Many predict that within a few years, even the sentence in the Creed (said during Mass) which so offends many women will be changed from "who for us men and for our salvation came down from heaven and became man" to "for us and our salvation came down from heaven and became truly human."

One might think that this progress would keep us women happy, at least for a few years, but that is not the case. As men often joke, now we uppity women are attempting to castrate God!

The Changing Genders of God

I am interviewing Jamie as her six-year-old son plays quietly beside us. She is telling me how she views God. "I don't mind using male pronouns for God," she explains. "But it bothers me to use 'man' and other male pronouns for 'us.'"

"I always see God as man, yet I know that God isn't a man," she continues. "God is whatever you think he or she is. What you call God is not going to change who God is. I would be uncomfortable if they started calling God 'she,' because that isn't how I see God, but I don't mind how anyone else sees God."

She is saying, "A lot of this is how we are brought up . . ." when a small male voice interrupts. "Mommy, I think God is a He." Her son's voice grows more emphatic, almost angry. "He is a HE!"

Although intellectually most of us do not have a problem agreeing that God is a spirit, neither male nor female, emotionally many people find this concept very difficult to internalize. I was surprised that almost every woman I talked to, regardless of her age, said she believed God was male when she was a child, whether that period of her life was only last year or 70 years ago. Using inclusive language for God is probably about where using inclusive language for humans was 20 or more years ago.

In actuality, the gender of God has not been all that relevant for many of us who grew up avoiding "God" (who we thought stern and judgmental) and praying instead to Jesus (as lover) and Mary (as mother).

"I view God as a man," Stacey tells me. "But I pray a lot more to Mary. I feel very close to her, because she is a female. Maybe she is the feminine side of God. And I have mentioned this to men, and they say they never even think of praying to Mary. 'Does that even count?' one asked me."

"We built May altars in grammar school," Catherine remembers. "I was doing feminist spirituality even back then. It took a long time to shift that idea of Mary. What has allowed me to understand the Blessed Mother as the goddess is having a different picture of pre-Christian and even post-Christian folk belief. Many of the holy days that the Church has are based on pagan seasonal rituals. I was really impressed when I realized that. I wondered why no one had ever told me before that Easter was a rite of spring. Getting this other picture of reality liberated me. Mary is not simply the mother of Jesus anymore. Unconsciously the Church hierarchy knew that the feminine had to be in it. And so Mary is that. But she is ranked as a 'lowly one,' not a goddess like Athena."

Unlike Stacey and Catherine, other women are having to make a conscious effort to expand their picture of God. However, once they succeed, they are finding the task spiritually and emotionally rewarding.

"I definitely feel God is more female than I did before," one woman, who admits she grew up in an extremely dysfunctional family, informs me. "I have such a yearning to be parented. I really want and need a mother figure to take care of me."

"I definitely have the need to stop thinking of God as only male," Terry, who also had a very abusive father, emphasizes. "I make a definite effort to use nonsexist terms when I pray out loud at Mass . . . not to say 'our father' but to say 'our parent.' It would be so easy to just stop saying it. After all, it says in the Bible, 'and God made them in his image, male and female.' Even in psychology they are talking about the male and female parts of the person."

"It would be nice to think of God as both father and mother," Jennifer sighs. "I got my image of God from my parents, and I relate better to my mother than I did to my father, and it would be easier for me if I had thought of God all along as both father and mother." She wishes that she had not been brought up to think of God as only male.

As the world gets smaller, and we have more contact with non-Christian beliefs from both Eastern countries and our own indigenous populations, many more images of God are becoming popular.

"My image of God is still in transition," offers Christi, who recently graduated from college. "It is sort of a spirit-orientated power source. I don't really have a picture in mind that means what God is."

"God is everything: mother, father, sister, brother," Linda explains. "I think a lot got lost in the translation from the original."

Although Jane K., now in her thirties, changed the language she used about God in college, she still "felt" God was male. Then, at one particularly rough time in her life, she had an experience while hiking in the mountains that she had never had before. "I felt that everything was falling around me, but the trees were still standing. And it was a real kind of Mother Earth experience. I found myself holding on to a tree, just bawling."

Since then, Jane's idea about God has changed drastically. "I don't have an image. It's universal, its creator, outdoor, trees, and nature."

Another woman, a "late bloomer" whose life as a teenager and young adult was extremely troubled and unconventional, related a similar experience that happened to her a decade later when she was struggling with the idea of coming back to the Church. "This enormous sense of love just poured in, and it was closer to me than my breath was. It was more real. It was personhood...and my clue, the secret message that made me know it was genuinely God, was that this person was genderless, because I had no way of thinking of that. It was not neutrality. I have no words to describe it. And I knew that forgiveness was not even an issue. That the love was so strong that it just swamps any distance between a person and God. It completely drowns it as if it were some small pebble at the bottom of the ocean. And that's when I knew that I had to get off the dime and figure out how to integrate this. Here I was in law school, and my right brain was doing jumping jacks!"

Listening to her talk, we can easily conclude that opening up our concept of God will ultimately be beneficial for all our spiritual lives.

"Our Father," the New Testament tells us, is the way Jesus taught us to pray, and no one is suggesting getting rid of this powerful and familiar way to talk to God. However, many women are experimenting with new and equally powerful ways to pray.

I first heard the following nonsexist adaptation of the "Our Father" about 10 years ago at a Golden Jubilee Mass for Sister Aileen Frances, CSJ, honoring her 50 years as a nun. She has since died. I do not know where she got this version; perhaps she wrote it herself. Regardless, I am sure she is pleased that we end our section on feminist spirituality with these words:

> Our Father, you are in heaven. Our Mother, you call us home. Our Brother, you are the first there. Our Sister, your kingdom come.
>
> Our Father, you are in my heart. Our Mother, I love your name. Our Brother, you love us so much. Our Sister, we do the same.
>
> Forgive us all the things we do, that break the chain of hands with you. Give us this day our daily bread and hold us close just like you said.
>
> Our Father, you are in heaven. Our Mother, you call us home. Our Brother, you are the first there. Our Sister, your kingdom come. Our Father, Our Brother, Our Sister, Our Mother, Our God. Amen.

NEW ROLES FOR WOMEN IN THE INSTITUTIONAL CHURCH

In this book we have given the reader a flavor of the feminist vision for the Catholic church, and predicted some of the changes that this vision is working to slowly bring about. The institutional Church itself has been working to include more women in both its rituals and its management as well. Anyone in contact with the Catholic church can easily see that much progress has been made to include women in many rituals as well as some of the lower echelons of Church management. Much remains to be done, however.

More Participation in the Liturgy

"When we were children," a woman tells me, "girls were told they could only go on the altar [past the Communion rails to the front of the church] the day they got married. It made me angry, because my little brother was an altar boy and he could go up there any day he served Mass." She obviously means during Mass or some other Church service, because women have been cleaning and preparing the altar since the Last Supper!

Another woman relates how, as a child, she learned all the Latin responses by heart and would get to Mass early each Lenten morning in the hopes that the altar boy wouldn't show up and the priest would let her say the responses to his Mass prayers. She had to kneel in the pew, of course, because girls weren't allowed up there with the priest.

"I can remember being told by a priest in the early 1960s that it was a mortal sin for a woman to be present in the sanctuary [altar area] of the Church during Mass," Ruth Wallace writes.[63]

Those of us who feel discriminated against because we aren't allowed to be ordained, or who angrily note the visible lack of women when three or four male priests huddle together on some special occasion to concelebrate a Mass, have either forgotten or are too young to remember how much worse things were 20 or 30 years ago. "Ex-Catholics" who have been out of the Church all these years are often shocked (many happily) when they happen to attend any Catholic service and see the number of women actively participating in each liturgy.

At the same time that Vatican II was telling the good sisters that they should become more involved in "the world," it was telling the laity that they should become more involved in the Church. Changes in liturgical practices led the way for this participation: Mass prayers switched from the Latin that few people understood to English or whatever the majority of the people in attendance preferred to speak. The altar was moved so that the priest could say Mass facing the people. Communion rails came down so there was no visual divider between the people and the altar. Occasionally, the altar was placed in the center of the Church so that the congregation could gather around the table. Laymen, followed shortly by laywomen, became lectors and read each of the changeable excerpts from the Bible during each Mass (except for the Gospel, which is still reserved for the priest). Soon both men and women were also being commissioned as Eucharistic ministers and were allowed to distribute the consecrated hosts (and sometimes wine) during Communion time, which by the mid-eighties were placed in each recipient's outstretched hand rather than on his or her tongue.

In many Churches these days, the entire congregation holds hands while they recite or sing the Lord's Prayer. A sign of peace was introduced after the "Our Father" (right before Communion time) and everyone present was urged to greet one another. Although many felt awkward at first, the sign of peace soon became a long and noisy exchange of handshakes, hugs, and even kisses which are greatly missed if for some reason it is skipped. In the 1990s, even those people who once objected to liturgical changes have, by and large, accepted them.

"I think that the participation at Mass is a lot better now then when we had the Latin Mass," Colleen remarks. "However, I was one of the first ones to scream about stopping the Latin Mass, but I've certainly changed my feelings about that."

"I saw the benefits of having English," Carol admits. "But I missed the Latin. Maybe on a spiritual level, the Latin was my way of praying in tongues. But fortunately, in my parish, the pastor was pretty careful about bringing in the changes slowly."

By now, many of the liturgical "experiments" of the 1960s and 1970s have become commonplace and there is a continued effort by many liturgists to reintroduce both symbols and procedures that take people back to the way things were probably done in the early Church. The core parts of the Mass (including the prayers, in whatever language) are the same in any Church throughout the world, but the music and the ambience depend almost entirely upon the talents and enthusiasm of the parish liturgy team, as well as the participants.

The same Church laws that prohibit women from being ordained also prohibit women from preaching and girls from being altar servers. But how these laws are enforced depends on the parish and, even more important, on how public the particular Mass will be.

Fifteen or so years ago, when my brother was ordained a Dominican, he asked his eighth-grade niece (my oldest daughter), who was also his god-child, to serve his first Mass. But instead of long black robes, he said he wanted her "to look pretty," and so he asked her to wear her new dress that she was also wearing to her eighth-grade graduation from a Catholic grammar school.

We approached our pastor and told him what was planned, and asked if she could "practice" at a few early morning weekday Masses (which had, at most, 15 or 20 people in attendance, almost all friends and neighbors) at our parish church, which was attached to her school. We didn't really think much about our request, until, to our surprise, our pastor told us no. Fortunately, before we had time to panic, we remembered that the Sunday Masses at the nearby Claretian seminary gladly welcomed visitors and let the children sit on the floor around the altar and take turns "helping" the priest say Mass. So we went there for a few Sundays and my daughter soon got all the practice she needed.

Fortunately, my brother's very crowded first Mass took place at a large, inner-city parish. He didn't ask permission, he just had her up there with him as his altar server. Since he had other women, including me, do the various readings, no one particularly noticed or cared that his altar boy was really an altar girl.

Even in the 1990s, I've never seen a girl altar server at our parish, but many parishes have them, despite rules to the contrary. Sheila tells me about her Church: "Lots of things are just evolving, like altar girls. Supposedly they're not allowed, but if our Church didn't have altar girls, there wouldn't be anyone up there."

As far as she knows, they just appeared without any big struggle or campaign to get them there. But for JoAnne, while studying law at Notre Dame, their presence was definitely a symbolic victory for feminism.

"I made the law school priest decide whether or not he was going to have female altar servers. The bishop had told him not to," she remembers, smiling. "But the priest knew it would cost him a lot if he said no, because I would be on his case forever. And after thinking about it for a while, he said yes. So I signed up to be the first female altar server. And a woman came up to me after that first Mass and said, 'I don't really know what is going on, but seeing you up there, I finally feel like I belong in the room.' On hearing this, the tears just came!" As she talks, JoAnne starts to tear up again.

In researching her book *Generous Lives*, Jane Redmont found that about half of the parishes that she visited have altar girls. She tells about one Midwestern parish where girls serve Mass every Sunday except those rare times that the bishop comes to visit.

"Preaching" is something very different, however. Although Ruth Wallace talks about women who are parish administrators giving sermons at a Mass, it is really less prevalent than having altar servers.

Sister Mary Margaret has been working together with a priest in a parish for the last five years, and she stresses the word *with*. "I won't work 'for' a priest anymore," she maintains. "I will work 'with' him or I won't work." But since they both like their bishop, who they claim is very liberal, they have decided that it is safer if they don't have her preach at Sunday Masses. "I do feel called to ordination," Mary Margaret confides, "but not in the clerical, power structure that exists."

There are many ways around the current rule against a layperson (even a man) actually giving the Sunday sermon at a Mass. All the priest has to do is say a sentence or two about the Gospel of the day and call his few words the homily, and then turn the microphone over to someone else who can talk about whatever he or she wants, as long as necessary. Or the priest can even leave his sermon out completely and go on with the Mass, and then have someone else "say a few words" after Communion time. If the event is a relatively private affair, no one even attempts to enforce who preaches.

My sister tells me that at large convent gatherings that have outsiders there, the presiding priest always gives the homily. But at events that are just for the sisters themselves, usually one of them does the preaching. I myself have "preached" at two Masses, once at my sister's 25th anniversary Mass for being a nun, and once (by proxy—I wrote the speech and had my sister deliver it) at the funeral of an aunt I had taken care of for many months before she died. I have been to countless other services where women preached, but they have always been "family affairs" and not a regular Sunday Mass open to the entire parish.

More Participation in Church Management and Service

According to a recent study, "About 20,000 lay people and religious are employed at least 20 hours a week as parish ministers in half the 19,000

Catholic parishes in the United States. This is in addition to those on the staffs of the parochial schools and those in support or maintenance positions. This number represents a dramatic change from a generation ago when there were few such parish ministers other than the organists or music directors or the parish visitors (catechists) in mission areas." [64]

Of these new ministers, 85% are women, and 60% are laypeople. More than half of them have a master's degree. Forty percent are involved in religious education, 27% are pastoral associates (the fastest-growing job description) who do many of the jobs that assistant priests used to do except say Mass or officiate at the other Sacraments. They perform a growing number of new social outreach jobs as well. Most of these women are married and white middle-class, or nuns, because they are often the only people who can afford to work for the $13,000 to $20,000 full-time yearly salary. [65]

However, these salaries I just quoted are substantially higher than those reported in another study, which claims that 92% of women in ministry are unpaid. Of those who do receive a salary, only 13% earn more than $10,000 a year, and 67% earn less than $5,000. [66]

Regardless of which study is more correct, there is no disputing the fact that no one works for the Church for the money. Often only suburban and middle-class parishes (or very large inner-city parishes) can afford to pay their lay ministers salaries.

Money is a very real problem for both sides of the equation, especially since other studies indicate that the average per family donation (in real dollars) is close to half of what it was 30 or so years ago. Furthermore, many parishes require their lay ministers to be "certified" by attending various classes and workshops in a certain field, another investment in both time and money.

I was waiting to interview the head of Hispanic ministries at a Catholic college when I overheard a prospective student discussing how she might come up with the tuition for a required course. Not only was she not getting paid for her many hours of parish work, her pastor was unable to reimburse her for any of the costs for her education. This angered and frustrated her, but she didn't seem to be considering giving up her ministry.

Financial necessities keep many interested women, particularly minority or single women, from answering a call to minister. The pastor of another woman I interviewed happened to mention to me that he was hoping she would agree to be the head of the Renew program that he wanted to start. "I know she has the time," he confided, "since she is unemployed."

I knew she would be thrilled at the opportunity, but suggested he find a way to pay her for some of the many hours this would entail since I knew her unemployment payments had run out. He looked surprised and reminded me of his very tight budget. When I told her about this conversation later, she thanked me profusely. "I would love that kind of a job, but I could never have brought money up to him," she remarked.

Another priest friend was complaining to me about the principal of his school. "But I have to take whoever the sisters send me," he sighed. He was shocked when I suggested that if he stopped expecting "slave labor" from the nuns and instead offered a fair salary to his school principal, regardless of her state in life, he, as employer, could then choose whomever he wanted to hire. However, such a pay increase for a nun would require going around the rules of his archdiocese, which arbitrarily (often in spite of input from women religious leaders) sets the stipends one may pay a religious employee.

Regardless of any talk about justice and fair wage practices, the truth is that many, many Catholic parishes throughout the country are in serious financial trouble, just as the entire Church is in trouble in many areas of the world, even the Vatican. Most people, particularly non-Catholics, don't believe this, and point to cathedrals and artwork, among other assets, which prove to them how rich the Church is.

In fact, the Church is "land poor" and many areas have an increasing problem in meeting day-to-day operating expenses, particularly since there are fewer nuns able or willing to work for the token amounts they once received. (My nun sister claims that she would not consider working for the institutional Church, and her order may soon not be able to afford to have too many of its members work for it either, considering how many retired sisters each working nun must now also support.)

As the need for social services, particularly in the inner cities, continues to accelerate, operating costs on every side skyrocket as well. Sister Ellen insists that despite the obvious need for more ministers in a Church where the clergy is aging and ill, declining in numbers, and generally considered overworked, the religious job market is really drying up.

"There are fewer openings each year from parishes and diocesan organizations," she explains. "The reasons cited are the economy, the need to trim the budget, and the high cost of salaries for religious. It is a fact that in our Midwestern state, nuns and ex-nuns are seeking a wage that is in parity with the laity . . . . But I wish to work with others in ministry, not for them. Collaboration in the work of building God's kingdom is a requirement for many of us today."[67]

It used to be that nuns were assigned to a job by their Superiors and were moved at will, often without any consultation. Salary was not an issue; it was considered part of their vow of poverty that it be minimal. But that was also when nuns had no other clothes except two habits to their name, and no one could tell if there was a run in a stocking. They relied on the laypeople for transportation. And there were many, many young hands, working many different jobs at once. But times have changed, and now there are cars, clothes, tuitions for advanced degrees, health care, and especially the many needs of the older nuns as each order becomes more top-heavy with retired sisters. All these are costly items that now become necessities if nuns are to continue their mandate to work and live among us in the modern world.

Suddenly their vow of poverty means learning how to economically care for each other while at the same time making preferential choices to help the poor. For the first time, an "unemployed nun" must often find her own job, not have one assigned to her, and feel the pressure of money and the lack of it. Today nuns, almost all of whom are middle-aged or older, are having to understand and worry about money, like other women have always had to do.

Parishes: The Center of Loyalty and Discontent

For most Catholic women who feel any connection at all to the Vatican, their loyalty is mainly symbolic. Often this can be said about their relationship to their diocese as well. Although many women insisted that one of the things they like best about being Catholic is the emotional and physical link their Church gives them to Christians throughout the entire world, in actuality, their local Church—their parish—is usually what they mean when they talk about "my Church." And for many, their like or dislike of their parish depends primarily on their like or dislike of its priests.

"In the nineties, I am once again very active in my Church," interior decorator Diane writes me. "I have found a pastor with whom I resonate and a way to bring my personal gifts to the church." When this priest left the parish, Diane was tempted to leave with him, but finally decided to first give the new pastor a chance.

Many priests themselves have as little to do with their chancery office as possible. And as the laity (who are hired by each pastor) take over parish jobs that priests and nuns used to do, there is even less need for priests to have much contact with the institutional Church downtown. Furthermore, women are not the only group of Catholics who are making up their own minds about Church teachings. Many priests are equally as doctrinally independent, which comes from dealing daily with hurting individuals, not with laws.

The result is, that while the Church of Rome may be being restructured from the top in a way that would appear geared toward erasing the spirit of Pope John XXIII and the teachings of Vatican II, the Church of the neighborhood is becoming more independent. "The Vatican and the bishops are leaving the Church," Father Harvey Eagan, a retired pastor, remarks with irony, confirming what many women have also told me.[68]

Most women who are employed by their parishes in these new jobs are proud of their new careers. Although one woman in particular, who had practically run her parish singlehandedly for many years, often "covering" for very inept and irresponsible priests, told me horror stories about parish work which finally caused her to look for another job, almost every other woman I talked to was extremely enthusiastic about her ministry. Dr. David DeLambo, whose dissertation was the study on new parish ministers for the National Pastoral Life Center, confirms my impressions. "We expected to find many more angry people, and to our surprise, and the surprise of groups I have lectured to about the study, our results show that over 90% of the lay ministers are satisfied in almost every category," he tells me. "Their satisfaction correlates highly with their spirituality. Many people get involved with these certification programs because they are interested in furthering their own spirituality. They are going to a professional program, but the professional program is geared towards their personal development."

By taking classes and then sharing what they have learned, not as guru but as participant, these women help form intentional faith communities for themselves and other interested parishioners. "I know my mother's participation began that way," David remarks. "When my father died, she was looking for a stronger support system, and she got involved in renewal in the parish, and that group became a community and they started doing things together, and started a social justice group."

However, only a few women parishioners that I interviewed who function primarily just as "women in the pew" were as enthusiastic about their parishes. Margaret is one, but then she is hardly an average woman in the pew because she is heavily involved in parish activities as a volunteer and her parish sounds like it is exceptional.

"We have a very active, spiritual program," she explains, "a parish council, all kinds of activities. We have people going into the seminary and the convent from here constantly, and those who don't make it come back and take up leadership roles in the parish. We have Anglo programs, Hispanic programs, prayer groups, youth groups. We feed the homeless. We are involved in ecumenical programs. We had 800 people at our organization fair last weekend."

Margaret claims that the success of her parish is due to the fact that they have three very holy priests. "They call us to holiness," she explains, "which is what their job description is."

They currently have 17 adults studying to become Catholics, and their CCD (the religious education program for public school children) has about 1,500 kids enrolled. Her own teenage son is a boarder in the diocesan junior seminary, which Margaret insists is for boys who are serious about their religion, not hermits, and, unlike years ago, encourages them to socialize with girls. Although Margaret works nights as a medical transcriber and has to sleep during the day, she is so enthusiastic about her parish that her evenings are reserved for Church groups.

Many other women, however, were so unhappy with their own local parishes that they have searched out a more compatible one. "Our parish is very orderly and quiet," relates Sharon, who also has had many run-ins with her pastor over the years. She prefers to go to Mass at a local monastery. "My healing [with the pastor] has been to consider that I go to my parish and see what I can give them, not what I get from them. But I have a need to have a little bit of warmth and joy and nurturing, so I go where I can get it."

But she also has good friends in the parish. "Priests come and go, but your neighborhood is going to stay the same, and that's your community," she explains. "And sometimes priests do change. I know a priest who was just impossible, and then he went on a Marriage Encounter Weekend as one of the presenters, and changed completely. He was at our church before we moved here, and he was one of the reasons we bought into this neighborhood. But then the pastor changed, and the new one was just like he had been before, so now some of us are saying, 'Maybe the charism of our parish is to convert the priest.'"

Cynthia used to be very active in her parish, but now she and her family go to Mass in a convent of social service nuns across town each weekend. "They have Mass in their living room, and we listen to real prayers of the faithful, from women who are working with real people. There are between 15 and 25 people there each Sunday, and it is very multiracial. The retired sisters live there and they like to have families come and join them. We are developing an intentional faith community, but I don't think that the sisters know that's what they are doing."

Although a priest comes from a nearby Church to say the Mass and preach the sermon, there is full participation from the rest of them as well. Cindy particularly likes her sons to see women being prayerful and spiritual. "I don't say anything, but I want them to experience that. I don't want them to think that men . . ." She stops and frowns. "How do you raise children in a church that hates women?"

Ann Z. and her husband are registered, paying members of the parish where they live, but they don't go to Mass there. "I don't care for the message in almost every sermon I have ever heard there," she explains. "The more I went, the less Christ-like I thought the priests and the community were."

She goes to Mass every Sunday and Holy Day of Obligation, and often even on weekdays, and daily rosary has always been a part of her life. Although she used to feel obligated to go to one parish and participate, she no longer does. "We go to different Churches each Sunday, depending on our other plans for the day. But our choices are definitely based on what the sermons are like, what the philosophy of the priests are, and what teachings they decide to emphasize. Before, I would not have understood anyone who was shopping around like this."

Several other women told me they had left their suburban parishes to join multicultural, inner-city churches. But for the most part, suburban parishioners and inner-city parishes have little, if any, contact with each other. Occasionally, two progressive parishes will link up with each other and exchange priests or their choirs for a Sunday. Or, at Christmas and Thanksgiving, a richer parish may send contributions of both food and money to their poorer neighbor. But for the most part, they are completely separate entities, which is a loss particularly for the suburbanites, who would find—if they ever ventured out of their upper-middle-class ghettos—that very often it is the inner-city parishes of the 1990s that have the most vitality.

Parish Councils

Although many women assume that a successful parish must have a good parish council, Margaret was the only woman I interviewed who was on one. To my knowledge, my own parish has not had one in any of the 28 years that we have been parishioners. We had a "pretend" one once, in the mid–1980s, as a result of an archdiocesan directive that told each parish to elect 10 representatives to an archdiocesan convocation.

Those of us elected concluded that this was the closest we would ever get to having a real parish council, and decided to act as if we were one. We really represented the huge spectrum of religious philosophies present in our small parish and immediately began to make enthusiastic plans and suggestions about new activities we were both willing and able to carry out.

However, our usually very tolerant pastor and not so tolerant deacon were very threatened by the group, and it soon became obvious that we were engaged in an exercise in futility. As soon as we discovered that "downtown" (who had set up the program) had no intention of actually letting the laypeople make any real decisions there either, we all slowly drifted back to our passive roles as "only people in the pew."

Our archdiocese does promulgate parish councils, however, and has a coordinator who puts on workshops for them. The paperwork they send me talks about the "1990s consensus building of a group of parishioners called together by a discernment process, who engage in overall planning for the parish that emphasizes spirituality." It claims that this is very different from the "majority vote" of "elected representatives" with "task-orientated" ideas of a few decades ago.

This distinction is really just academic when the pastor is unwilling to

give up any real control. Even our last pastor, who was theologically very liberal, refused to have one, despite how many times I brought it up to him. He
as well as many other priests, actually believe that parish councils just end up
causing a lot of problems.

Not only are most pastors afraid to give any real control to their parishioners, Bridget tells me that, according to Church law, parish councils can
only be advisory anyway. Cassandra had already given me the same information. Her pastor was not too happy with her, however, when she suggested
to the members of her parish council that they go into the rectory and look
in the book about Canon Law and find out that it really didn't matter a lot
about how they voted, because no one was planning to take their vote seriously anyway.

The result of these undemocratic processes is that many parishioners
refuse to spend hours in discussions about how to run a parish or a diocese
when they find out that no one plans to follow their recommendations anyway. And it is also very likely that this lack of democratic process also causes
the anger or, more likely, the indifference that is behind the falling weekly
cash flow ratios of many parishes. For it is only "when the parishioners get
involved in actually running the parish," Ruth Wallace found, "they become
part of the solution themselves, not only by their volunteer services, but also
by contributing more to the Sunday collection."[69]

Not everyone is that enthusiastic about democracy, however. Women for
Faith and the Family leader Sherry Tyree insists that the Protestant churches
in America are in decline precisely because of their democratic practices. It
obviously depends on each particular parish whether it is responsive to the
ideas of its parishioners, just as it depends on the "scientific" study that you
read whether the average Catholic really wants the Church to be more
democratic in its operations.

A June 1992 *Time/CNN* study claims that 83% of Catholic women are satisfied with the leadership of their parish priest, 80% are satisfied with the
leadership of their bishop, and 90% with the leadership of the Pope.[70] But
this survey talked to only 145 Catholic women, who obviously thought differently than most of the women I have interviewed. The women I have
talked to are more in accord with a Gallup poll conducted about the same
time. It claimed that 74% of people surveyed thought that elected parish
councils should decide parish policies, including the use of church funds;

68% agreed parishioners should choose their pastors; and 72% wanted bishops elected by priests and people—all practices in opposition to current Canon Law.[71] You can prove any point you want if you look around long enough for the "right" statistics.

The Feminization of the Catholic Church

Although many young men with priestly vocations are getting more conservative, many women in the Catholic church, especially those that now make up a large portion of the students who are studying theology and pastoral ministry in Catholic seminaries and universities, are getting more liberal. As these laywomen take over day-to-day local parish operations and programs out of necessity, they bring their feminine priorities and leadership styles with them. They look for spiritual and psychological support for themselves and the rest of the parishioners, and expect to operate through collaboration rather than authority. This often causes problems with the male cleric "old Church" pastor.

However, there are many liberal "new Church" (post–Vatican II) priests who are beginning to embrace feminine viewpoints and are suddenly finding themselves looking for emotional support and "connection" that go beyond a day on the golf course or a fishing trip to Mexico with fellow priests. Furthermore, "old Church" pastors frequently have become so burned out by the effort required to maintain their old practices in a changing world that they are happy to relinquish much of their work to the laity, if not any of their power. Priests also often find themselves in the untenable position of having unsupportive "bosses" downtown and in the Vatican who have outdated, even bad, management techniques and many of the people in the pew second-guessing their organizational pronouncements as well as their theological ones.

Priests are not the only group of males feeling the effects of the feminization of the Catholic church. Gone, or going, in many parishes are the men's clubs, the Holy Name societies, the sports teams for young men and their fathers, even the Knights of Columbus. The National Pastoral Life Center found that of all the possible contributions the new male and female ministers felt they were making, the ones that they felt least confident in providing were sensitivity to men's concerns and a way to involve men in the active life of the parish community. Parishes have yet to become adept at enabling parishioners who hold paid jobs to reflect on the linkages between their faith and work, or to find encouragement for creativity and integrity in their occupations.[72]

It is a vicious circle. With fewer males (as priests) to do the work, more women are doing it, which, in turn, often leads to less involvement by the men.

Women as Pastors

The new Code of Canon Law, published in 1983, made some provisions for the expansion of women's roles in the Church. While still excluding women from ordained ministry (as well as preaching or being altar girls), the new code opened the following positions to women on the diocesan level: diocesan chancellors, auditors, assessors, defenders of the marriage bond, promoters of justice, judges on diocesan courts, members of diocesan synods, and financial and pastoral councils. This also allowed women to become pastoral administrators in priestless parishes.[73]

By 1990 there were 210 parishes in the United States administered by someone other than a priest. Of these, 62% were headed by nuns, 22% were headed by deacons (men), 9% by laity, 6% by religious brothers, and 1% by a pastoral team. While worldwide, about 34% of parishes are without a priest, in the United States this number drops to around 10%, but the number is growing in both places.[74] And when there is no priest available to head a parish, more and more often the new "pastor" is a woman.

Ruth Wallace recently studied in depth 20 of these U.S. Catholic parishes administered by women. While she found that the majority of parishioners are very happy with their women "pastors," the ambiguity of the pastor role is a constant source of strain. Since these women cannot be members of the clergy (which includes deacons), they cannot legally give homilies (comment at Mass on the readings of the day), say Mass, baptize, or preside at marriages. Instead, each has to have a real priest come in on Sundays and for other sacramental occasions. The priest often tries to make it appear that the woman administrator has a larger spiritual role than she is actually allowed.

As one nun pastor explained, "This is the first time in any ministry I have been in where I have not had the credentials to do what I am asked to do.

Now we are asked, by the bishop, to be the spiritual leader of a parish and we can only do so much. We can't give absolution, even though we hear confessions all the time in the parlor. We can't anoint when we go to the hospital, even though we bless them."

Another nun pastor gave the analogy of trying to dig a hole without tools. "You need to dig this hole here, but I tie your hands, so do it," or "The tools are here, but you cannot touch them." She claims that she knows, deep down, that she is called to minister, and that is why she feels so bad that she has been given the job, but her hands are tied.[75]

Because a woman pastor has no aspirations to membership in the hierarchy of the Church, however, she can often stand up to a bishop better than a priest can because she feels she has less to lose. And the very fact that women are being assigned to these jobs and show strength in their positions is changing their image. "Even those parishioners who described themselves as traditional Catholics told me that they had changed their attitudes and actions regarding women in the church as a result of their experiences with their woman pastor," Ruth writes. "The overwhelming majority of the parishioners I interviewed no longer support patriarchy and gender discrimination, and they attributed their change of attitude to their women pastor.

"What is unique about woman pastors is the way they manage to transform constraints into opportunities in the daily enactment of their role," she continues. "Although many were resented when they first showed up, they viewed their problems as a challenge." Not being members of the clergy, they could identify with their parishioners better. Their leadership style, which incorporated their parishioners as peers, eventually led to a greater spirit of community in these parishes.[76]

Mary Leach, assistant to the chancellor at the University of Maryland, is in one such parish. She writes me: "I enjoy my parish, which is about as liberal as can be imagined and has no priest assigned. Its pastor is one of the most creative nuns it has been my privilege to know. She is heavily engaged in personal and parochial empowerment and meaningful social service activities."

Some parishioners feel only anger when the bishop sends them a woman instead of a priest. Their anger is probably less about the gender of their new pastor than it is about their feelings of rejection because their bishop doesn't think enough of their parish to send them a real priest. Many of these viewpoints appear to be changing, however.

"I think the nineties will see much more acceptance, not out of good will, but out of necessity, of lay women in ministry," Anne Brotherton concludes. "And that is going to raise even higher the issue of ordaining women, especially when women are the major churchgoers and the major church workers. Now they are going to be doing the kind of ministry that has been reserved only for priests and sometimes for religious women. So we are going to continually see the emergence of a new lay Church."

Slowly but surely, women are quietly working at integrating the chancery office (the business offices of the institutional Church) downtown as well. Some 30 or 40 dioceses throughout the country now have a commission on women, which is made up of women who study and offer guidance to the local hierarchy on women's issues. The number of dioceses with these commissions is growing so fast that the U.S. Bishops' Conference has put out a handbook to guide their development.

Women are now in charge of many kinds of institutional Church offices, everything from superintendent of schools to heads of charity and fundraising, and occasionally even the organizational head of the diocese. All report directly to a bishop, though. One fortunate change in Church policy is that 85% of the Vicars for Women Religious in the United States are now other women religious instead of male bishops, as they once were.

Sister Mary Glennon has been the Vicar of Women Religious in Los Angeles for several years and is the first woman in her diocese to have this job, which she took over from a bishop. She definitely believes her presence is making a difference. She reports directly to Cardinal Roger Mahony, whose office is only a flight of stairs away from hers. "Although both he and I prefer that I make an appointment to talk to him," she tells me, "I can go and knock on his door any time I need to." Her job description, as written in a pamphlet she hands me, is very diverse.

Despite her very busy schedule, she most graciously talked to me for close to two hours and was very frank and open. Although her greatest joy comes from her personal encounters with individual nuns who need her help, and she is very anxious to finish a degree in psychology so that she can better serve them, Mary also realizes that she is filling an important role as a "bridge" person in the institutional Church. Although she has more in common philosophically with the radical feminist nuns than they think, who may contend she "has sold out" by working so closely with the hierarchy, she also sees the necessity of having a woman like herself in the job.

"I know the men in the Church are changing," she tells me. "I go to the priests' council meetings every month. I have gone to the Archdiocesan Assembly of priests as well. We all know that we need each other. But it is women who have moved at a rapid pace. We have had to move fast. We have had to do our work. And unless we had to do it, we wouldn't have done it. The priests didn't have to. They saw us going off to all our meetings and they joked about it . . . . So it is only now that they are saying that the sisters are way ahead. The priests, and men in general, are seeing the light. Collaboration is certainly not just a woman's issue."

Laywomen are filling increasingly higher jobs in the chancery offices as well. Betty is a mother, wife, college philosophy professor, and nurse. Somehow she finds time to serve on her archdiocese Commission on Human Life. Although one of the male members of the group is internationally known and the leading theologian on this subject, Betty is the chairperson of the subcommittee on end-of-life issues. They began by studying the Vatican Encyclical on Euthanasia, and then looked at what various bishops all over the country have said, particularly about food and water withdrawal from a dying patient.

"Our work is to advise the archbishop about end-of-life issues as he informs his priests," Betty explains. "When he asks our opinion, I like to start my letters to him with: 'Thank you for asking.' I'm always amazed that, number one, I am allowed to be a chairperson of this subcommittee, and number two, someone would ask me for the response of the committee. In a male-dominated society like we have, I'm pleased to be asked my opinion. Things may be changing slowly, but at least they really are changing."

Each year, women are being asked to fill higher and higher levels of jobs in the U.S. Church, and if Milwaukee Archbishop Rembert Weakland (admittedly one of the most liberal bishops in the Church) has his way, women will be filling top Vatican jobs someday as well. In a December 6, 1992, op-ed piece in the *New York Times*, Weakland said that the top three positions in each of 21 Vatican offices (prefect, secretary, and undersecretary) are currently filled by cardinals, archbishops, and monsignors. "Women must be given places in these ranks," he wrote.[77]

Although no one is holding their breath until this happens, it is theoretically possible that it can, even if the ban on ordination is never lifted.

The Bishop's Pastoral on Women

When the U.S. bishops decided to tackle the subject of women in society and the Church in the early 1980s, I doubt they had any idea of how long it would take or the difficulties that would arise. As they have done when researching other issues, they decided to talk to experts on the subject, which in this case was women all around the country.

Innocently enough, they devised a process to ask Catholic women how they had been affirmed or oppressed by both society and the Church. What followed for many of the bishops was a conversion experience as they suddenly found out how far removed they were from the lives of the ordinary woman in the pew. For the first time in history, Catholic women not only had the opportunity but felt free to come forward and articulate their feelings to the whole Church without fear of discrimination or recrimination. The process was as exceptional and liberating for the women involved as it was for the bishops.

"We knew that we needed a process for the listening sessions," says Cindy, who was a leader of her diocese's committee, "and we knew that we needed rules for listening, because Catholics don't seem to have a good history about listening to anyone except authority. We wanted everyone to feel that they had their own authority by being created by God and living a life. So we set up the rules and the process, and we knew that the bishops were in big trouble. But they asked us to do it! And when we had the information all compiled and gave it back to the bishops, we knew that there was no way that they could handle what we told them!"

The first draft of the bishops' Pastoral on Women was a miracle. It was obvious that the bishops had actually been listening. Unfortunately, their hands were tied if they were to remain in good standing with the Vatican. While the bishops faithfully wrote down almost everything the women told them and even beat their breasts about the sin of sexism in the Church, they were unable to actually make or even promise to make any real changes.

What was written was a schizophrenic document full of many "yes, buts" that contradicted each other. If women had written it, we would have been ridiculed for our illogic. Instead, the bishops were censored by the Vatican for almost any attempt to offer solutions.

By November of 1992 the bishops' Pastoral on Women had been rewritten four times, each time getting more conservative but not conservative enough for some bishops and very traditionalist women. The radical feminists thought the pastoral should have been written about the sin of sexism in the Church and how to rectify it, which included allowing the ordination of women. The fundamentalists thought it should be about the sin of feminism.

"We have always said that the listening sessions were very positive," insists Maureen Fiedler of Catholics Speak Out. "The problem is that the bishops have since ceased listening to women and are listening to the Vatican. Each of the four drafts has become more and more Neanderthal. It has been an educational process for all the bishops, and the hearings were very beneficial in that they helped women to organize themselves in ways that they haven't done before. But now, it is not a pastoral on women's issues. It is a document on the Vatican's concerns. I think they ought to say that the process was good, but the product terrible, so scratch it."

Which is what they did. In November 1992 the U.S. bishops' Pastoral on Women became the first pastoral letter that came out of committee, was voted on by the bishops, and was then defeated. A core of progressive bishops persuaded prominent moderates that passage could do serious damage to Catholic women. Although 137 bishops voted for it and only 110 bishops voted against it, a two-thirds majority was needed to pass the measure. No one expects it to be voted on again.

How Women View the Hierarchy Itself

Very few women have personal relationships with bishops or cardinals, not even a clue about how these men spend their time, other than what they read in the newspaper. So it is as easy for many women to put down or make fun of the hierarchy, or even to discount their work entirely as it is for women to worship them in awe. "The hierarchy for me stops with Father Art," explains Jamie, a recent convert, talking about the associate pastor who baptized her.

"I love the Church I belong to," Ann Z. explains. "But it doesn't have very much to do with a bunch of bishops sitting around in conclaves talking."

But women who actually know these men up close and personal are much more charitable and positive than the average woman in the pew who has never met them. Dolores Leckey is a laywoman who works closely with many of the bishops at their U.S. headquarters in Washington, D.C. She has worked as the director of the Secretariat for Family, Laity, Women and Youth for 15 years, and she speaks highly of the many bishops she knows. She is particularly saddened when I relate to her that many of the women I am interviewing claim that the bishops and the rest of the hierarchy don't practice what the Gospel preaches.

"I have worked with these bishops," Dolores explains. "I can tell you of the struggles they go through. And I have met some of the holiest people I have ever known among the hierarchy . . . men who really will lay down their lives for anyone. And it is inspiring. The sadness is that some of them get caught in a kind of maintenance/administrative role, and people who are not close to them and do not work with them every day don't realize their inner struggles."

According to Dolores, the American bishops must do a balancing act in public, and they have to use the human tools at their disposal, which include the art of compromise. "They are trying to be true to several things: to their own inner selves, to the magisterium, to whatever is a workable solution to something, to their own conscience, and to the validity of the Bishop's Conference," she insists.

"They are balancing a lot of things. They are all trying to be men of integrity," Dolores continues. "And so they also know that there is a whole group of people who think that things are being lost. They want women to sit down and realize that. We all belong to the same Church. It is really not good for us to be judging the motives of other people. That is very dangerous and uncalled for. In most cases, on both sides of the spectrum, each side assumes that it has the whole truth. They are not dialoguing with each other, not trying to hear the other one, not trying to believe that this person or this group is really sincere. They are not willing to really look at each issue from the other side's angle."

Most of the women I talked to who actually knew a bishop personally shared Dolores Leckey's opinion. Patricia Miller was particularly vocal. "I am encouraged by the many, many bishops I have met personally who have a larger vision of the Church and who see the laity as part of that vision. And they see women as an important part of that vision. There are many courageous bishops who are speaking up for women, and for homosexuals, and for Native Americans, and for all of those people who can't speak for themselves. They are courageous men who are stepping forward, regardless of whether it hurts them politically in the Church. It makes me very proud to be a Catholic."

Patricia believes that the U.S. bishops reflect the total U.S. population, and if only 7% of American Catholics are conservatives (she prefers the word *traditionalists* because it is less political), then probably only 7% of the U.S. bishops share these views. She does not think that we are heading for a split between the U.S. Catholic church and the Vatican, because too many holy and talented bishops are working too hard to prevent such a thing from happening.

Papal Infallibility and Church Authority

Listening to the above makes me wonder if the only reason many of us Americans have such a bad opinion about the Vatican hierarchy is because we don't really know them. As much as she likes the U.S. bishops, it is the Roman Church—the Vatican—that frustrates Patricia Miller. "I feel they are out of touch with what's going on in the individual lives of many of the Church's members, and that their leadership is coming out of fear."

Many other women, those who are involved with official Church activities as well as average women in the pew, made identical comments. "The Pope, for many Catholic women, is a distant figure and not a subject of intense preoccupation," Jane Redmont found. "Several of the women I met expressed admiration for Pope John Paul II. More often women were highly critical or expressed a blend of criticism and admiration. John XXIII remained their favorite Pope."[78]

Few people know that it was not until 1870 that the constitution about the infallible teaching authority of the Pope was approved, or that 55 bishops who opposed this teaching left Rome the night before the vote so as not to embarrass the Pope or shame themselves by voting against the proclamation of this teaching.[79] Few people also realize how rarely the Pope speaks infallibly about a doctrine. It is a very specialized and rare process. Teachings like those against artificial contraception have never been declared as infallible.

Even though many American Catholics don't seem to take papal pronouncements all that seriously anyway, it is clear that Pope John Paul II does. In 1987 he declared that assent to the magisterium (the teaching authority of the Church) constitutes the basic attitude of the believer and is an act of the will as well as the mind, and that in the area of Church teaching, dissent is unacceptable. According to Father Michael Crosby, this means that instead of turning our minds and wills over to the power of God, the Pope wants us to turn them over to the magisterium.[80]

What *dissent* really means, however, is "public, publicized disagreement," which theologians are forbidden to do. They are free to believe—in private—whatever conclusions they come up with, and they may even confront the Pope and the magisterium, as long as this is all done very quietly. This is rather hard for a theologian, whose daily business is to lecture and write about his or her intellectual opinions and findings. It is not so difficult for most average women in the pews. As more and more American Catholic women become more educated, more accustomed to thinking for themselves, and more willing to assume the responsibility for making their own choices (which includes being willing to make their own mistakes), the infallibility of anyone has less and less relationship to their real lives.

"One of the things I find most offensive about the treatment of Curren and Hunthausen [a theologian and a bishop who were both censored by the Vatican during the 1980s] is the assertion by one of the archbishops involved that you can't tolerate what will confuse the simple faithful," Abigail McCarthy contends. "Well, there are no simple faithful anymore, due to television and the high level of education in the U.S."[81]

Archbishop Rembert Weakland agrees with her. In an address at the Catholic Press Association's 1992 annual meeting in Milwaukee, he asks:

> "Could I broach here a very delicate subject and one that no one writes about but that is very important? As I travel around the country, I find a growing disaffection from Rome . . . .
>
> It takes two forms. At times, it is rather just an expression of indifference to what Rome says. People just do not find that it matters much to them. I find this attitude very pronounced in the academic circles, but am always surprised to find it elsewhere as well at all cultural levels.
>
> In addition to this indifference, there is also a second group that shows much anger, and some degree of animosity toward Rome."

> The Protestant Reformation would never have been possible if there had not been a separation of affection from Rome on the part of clergy and laity long before the event that broke the ties.[82]

Archbishop Weakland obviously has his ear to the ground about what is going on in the American Catholic church these days. To give an opposing view, however, a few women I interviewed were enthusiastic about the Pope. Maria is one of them. "The Pope is our shepherd, and we are the sheep and we follow and we obey," she insists. "And it is wonderful having that submission to him. I am completely submissive, because I believe in everything he says. I think he is doing a wonderful job during a very difficult time. I am behind him 100%. I think he is a very spiritual man. He has tremendous insights. We only see one little portion, but he is seeing everything from a bird's-eye view, a worldview."

Needless to say, Maria does not represent many of the women I've talked to. The majority of them are like Carolyn, who respects the Pope for what he represents and considers herself a loyal Catholic, but would never dream of considering herself a sheep. For a while, Carolyn disagreed with the Pope on several different subjects, and she found herself feeling increasingly angry and alienated from the Church. Then one day, she realized that it was all her fault. "I stopped giving the institutional Church the power that I had given it before, but this was gradual. I had to realize that it was my own fault for having let this happen. It was not the institution that was imposing this on me; it was my own ego that was allowing the separation.

"I didn't feel the need for a ritual to get back into good standing," she admits, "but I felt that going to confession would be my admission to myself that I had allowed this barrier to be erected. And it was proof that I could accept some of the bad along with the good, because the good far outweighed the bad, and that I could accept that there has to be an institution for administrative purposes. Even though I may disagree with the institutionalization of some of these things, I can ignore all that. I must break through and not let that erect a barrier.

"Today I figure that the hierarchy are members of the Church the same as I am," Carolyn continues. "And we are all different. The Pope and the bishops are doing some things that I agree with, and some things that I don't, and I hope it all works out in the end. I'm not going to kiss their rings, but I'm also not going to let them keep me out of the Church!"

Christi, a recent college graduate, sums up what many women two and three times her age believe but have trouble explaining: "In grammar school and high school you were taught about the authority of the hierarchy, or the tradition of the hierarchy, as the guiding force, and how they set a pattern for your life. But in college, you begin to study the letters, the papers they wrote. You begin not to exactly criticize the teachings but to explore it all a little more critically. You stop just taking Church pronouncements word for word and instead try to first understand exactly what they are saying. Then you ask yourself, How does this apply to me personally? Is it something I can embrace? Or do I have to challenge it?"

In the 1990s most of the women who decide to challenge are doing so not out of anger but out of love. This reminds me of a time when things were difficult in my marriage, and I had gotten a single friend of mine to give me an extra key to her apartment, because I kept thinking that the only solution was for me to leave. Then, one summer afternoon when I was feeling particularly bad, I dove angrily into our swimming pool and began swimming laps furiously, crying, and all of a sudden it came over me: This is my house, my family, my life. And if anyone is leaving, it will not be me!

I was talking to a new friend—a highly visible woman in the Catholic church—during another interview, and she had almost the identical story. Comparing our experiences with our husbands to why we both stayed in the Catholic church, we suddenly laughed and agreed that the answer was obvious: We and many, many other women like us had finally decided to grow up at last!

CATHOLIC WOMEN AND SOCIAL JUSTICE

This book has discussed spiritual and moral issues that affect each woman as an individual, as a member of a particular family, and as a member of a specific group (the Roman Catholic church). But there is another relationship that many Catholic women consider equally, if not more, important to their personal salvation and spiritual life. That relationship is the connection of all people everywhere to one another simply because they are all children of God and members of the human race.

Most Catholic women take the commandment "To love your neighbor as yourself" very seriously, at least in principle. It is only when trying to apply these words to specific situations that it becomes obvious that this mandate may be not only the most difficult of God's laws to follow, but also the most controversial.

The catch-all term most often used today when talking about relationships among different people (particularly when the people involved are categorized by different ethnic, national, racial, or economic names) is *social justice*. However, the word "social justice" has come to mean far more than love of neighbor. Today this word implies that there are only a few people on the top, who are the "haves," and many people on the bottom, who are the "have nots." It denotes a worldview that the way to get into and stay in the top group is by systematically taking advantage of the people in the bottom group. It judges these systems—whether they be economic or political—as evil, or at least unfair. It attempts to change these systems by working with the poor in order to give them the needed tools and power to resist exploitation and thereby break the cycle of abuse.

As we have seen, one of the main reasons nuns left their cloistered convents in the 1960s was because Vatican II was telling them that their work was to be "in the world," not "shut off from the world" as many of them had thought previously. The change in everyday behavior that resulted from this new perception about their mission in life was particularly graphic. During World War II, many nuns were not even allowed to read about the war in the newspapers. By the time of the Vietnam War, their younger sisters (and some of these same, but now older, nuns) were actually among the protesters in the streets.

For many of these women religious, as well as for laywomen, Pope John XXIII's 1963 Encyclical *Peace on Earth*, and the Vatican II document *The Church in the Modern World*, were their personal call to active involvement in the struggle for social justice. Others credit well-publicized meetings of the Latin American bishops in Medellin, Colombia (1968), and in Puebla, Mexico (1979), for awakening them to the Catholic church's "preferential option for the poor."

"The message of Christianity has always been to love your neighbor," Pat Sears, who recently celebrated her Golden Jubilee as a nun, reminds me. "And we began to ask ourselves, 'How do you love?' And our reply was, 'You love by doing.' So we set up systems that would keep us informed about the issues of the day, and began to look for ways to influence the course of social justice so that we, and the world at large, could see that women religious were willing to work at making a real difference."

"Put your body where your mouth is" became the rallying call of many of these idealistic women. They began to lobby for government change and to set up information centers to awaken their own nuns to societal ills and proposed solutions, as well as to alert the public at large. Once informed, many began to dedicate themselves to the popular and not-so-popular causes of each decade. Nuns began to march, picket, boycott, fast, and campaign as well as teach, nurse, and pray. Martin Luther King, Jr., Cesar Chavez, John and Robert Kennedy, Daniel and Phillip Berrigan, Dorothy Day, Jane Fonda, and a host of other liberal leaders became their heroes.

Although for the most part they came from white, middle-class families, many of these sisters began to "romanticize" the disadvantaged. Even those who didn't could not dispute the fact that there was and is an ever-growing number of poor, both throughout the world and in the United States itself, in desperate need of help and inspiration.

"I picked a community to join that did not have any schools or hospitals," one woman, now an ex-nun, explains. "I did not want to belong to a community that had a vested interest in property and organizations or that would end up serving the upper classes.

"My commitment was with the poor in the missionary sense," she continues, repeating words I have heard from many other nuns. "It is difficult to understand Christian faith without connecting it to the social movements: human rights, protection of the undocumented, civil rights, health, and education. It is all connected together."

Each year, more and more of these dedicated and concerned women begged their communities to release them from their suburban teaching jobs so that they could move into the inner-city ghettoes to organize or just be present to the down and out.

As their social consciousness was raised, many began to feel guilty about the "opulent" lives they were living in the convent. I remember being invited in the late 1970s to meetings of the new social justice secretariat of my sister's community. Once there, I listened to women who were earning about $250 a month (almost all of which went to the convent to cover overhead) and who bought clothes at thrift shops and day-old bread at bakeries, beat their breasts because they thought they were too rich. Others, who were working overtime, often seven days a week, in urban ghettoes at new and exhausting jobs that were all understaffed and underfinanced, voiced similar fears that they were not doing enough.

And I, who had a stable upper-middle-class family of four children and a working husband yet often felt I was barely making it, could only listen to these women in complete disbelief.

Redefining Social Justice

This empathy with the poor and the marginalized soon led an especially enthusiastic, vocal, and educated group of Catholic women—a large portion of whom were nuns—to begin to define the term *social justice* as meaning much more than simple charity. To many of these women, social justice means advocating "structural change" of the white, male-dominated societal systems under which the Western world has operated for centuries, if not forever. Many took or are taking a second look at the government and what they consider to be the ruling class in the United States. Often labeling U.S. actions as imperialistic (particularly in Central America), they insist that U.S. support of the small, very powerful, and very rich upper class in many of these countries is keeping a large group of peasants (mostly indigenous) from any integration into the economic or political life of their country.

As early as the 1970s, long before it was politically correct to do so, these activist women began to talk about multinational corporations as being the real rulers of the world and to insist that many of the loans for development in Third World countries were saddling the people of these countries with such a continually compounding debt that they were becoming slaves of the World Bank.

Still calling for disarmament and peace in an increasingly violent world, these women activists have now taken up the cause of ecology. Most opposed the 1992 bombing of Iraq and today have serious doubts about the North American Free Trade Agreement (NAFTA) primarily because they fear it will throw peasants off their small farms and condemn them to a life of poverty-level wages in dark and dismal factories.

The average woman in the pew is both astonished and impressed at what these idealistic activist women have accomplished. While many laywomen like myself find pages of statistics about the difference between the "haves" and the "have nots" of the world so overwhelming that they feel paralyzed, others who read these same facts spring into action. Believing that nothing is impossible, they often do the impossible.

Twenty years ago, my sister Joanna did not know the meaning of the words *escrow* and *equity* and had never opened a bank account, written a check, or had a credit card. Now, the inner-city organization that she and Pat Sears started with an initial $500 donation from our parents has rehabilitated or built more than 75 housing units for the very poor in West Oakland, California; empowers tenants and their neighbors to take personal charge of their lives with a myriad of other services; and has an operating budget of more than half a million dollars per year, not counting what it spends on purchasing properties.

Scores of other nuns and activist laywomen have stories that are equally impressive.

Laywomen: Idealistic and Committed

By focusing on the awakening of American nuns to social justice, I don't want to denigrate the activism of Catholic laywomen. There are many, and three whom I interviewed particularly come to mind.

"When the *Catholic Worker Magazine* comes in the mail, I sit down and read it cover to cover, and stuff can be boiling over on the stove and I will let it boil until I finish it," Sheila confesses. She has taught English classes in Nicaragua four times over the past years and has recently opened an English as a second language school for immigrant women in her Northern California city.

Rose Marciano Lucey is another such activist. She and her husband were dedicated to working for structural change and world peace their entire married life, even while raising their large family. Now a widow in her mid-seventies, she has never watered down any of her convictions or activities.

"When the Gospel talks about feeding the hungry, it is not just about giving them food," she insists. "That's important, but you have to ask the deeper question: Why are people hungry? What did Jesus do? He tried to make a world where people are treated as human beings."

Her social justice ministries are too numerous to count, let alone mention.

Not a day goes by that Rose does not challenge those she meets or works with to examine their actions in the light of gospel values.

The younger generation of Catholic laywomen is not without their social justice idealists. Christi, a recent graduate from Santa Clara University, has joined the Jesuit Volunteer Corps (JVC). It is a one-year, renewable commitment to a simple lifestyle, social justice, spirituality, and community. As a JVC member, she is working with Catholic Community Services in Seattle, Washington, helping to organize a welfare rights coalition.

These three women have or have had husbands who are equally convinced about social justice issues and equally dedicated to solving social problems, or they are like Christi, single and childless. Although the average woman in the pew is also convinced about the necessity to love your neighbor, and sincerely wants to contribute to world peace and understanding, the scope of her idealism is far smaller, and she rarely is aware enough (or free enough) to blame the system.

Jane H., now in her mid-seventies, speaks for most of the women interviewed. "I was brought up that you should try to live a moral life, and do something for the world. It is important to leave the world in better condition than when you came into it and to consider other people. I am a great volunteer, and I believe in helping people, and I think that comes from my Catholic background."

Almost every woman I talked to told me about something that she personally was doing for someone in need. Jackie is a suburban mother of six adult children and has a growing number of grandchildren. She and her husband are often labeled as both ultrapolitical and religious conservatives, yet it would be impossible to count the number of times either one of them has reached out to help another parishioner or neighbor in need.

"My mother left me money when she died," Jackie mentions casually, "and I milled around and felt I had to give the money to someone. So when I saw a documentary on television about the Covenant House [a nationwide group working with homeless and exploited teenagers] I was very impressed and gave them what my mother left me."

Almost every other woman interviewed told of some personal charity or volunteer work, some as grandiose as leadership of well-known national and community organizations, others as simple but equally meaningful as shopping for a housebound neighbor.

Tension Among Catholic Women:
The Need for a Bridge Between Classes

However, many laywomen have ambivalent feelings when they hear social activists, even nuns, talk about radical social change. After all, many U.S. Catholic women today belong to the upper middle class and upper class privileged groups themselves and are among the very people that activist women are condemning for exploiting the poor. And all this action and absolute conviction about how to solve the problems caused by the uneven distribution of wealth and resources within the United States—never mind the entire world—makes the average woman in the pew feel not only guilty and uncomfortable (which is what the social justice activists want) but also "put down" because she can't (or doesn't want to) dedicate her own life and resources to all these causes. Furthermore, she is not completely convinced that her politically liberal sisters have perfected formulas that will really work to ensure that all people have a reasonably good quality of life. And, politically incorrect as it may sound, she may even suspect that some marginalized people, especially in the United States, may be in dire straits due at least partially to their own fault.

Jackie speaks for many of these women. "The social activist nuns have thrown all their eggs into one basket," Jackie complains sadly. "We need action that will bring different groups together, not widen the gap. This social justice business . . ." she shrugs and looks uncomfortable. "There is a need, I understand it. And I'd like to be part of it and help. But under the circumstances of people calling me names when I am trying to help . . ."

Jackie and her husband have managed to send six children to college but are far from rich. Their home, although on the beach, is small and old, purchased years ago, and was remodeled often (the garage is now a bedroom) to fit their growing family. She shakes her head, sighs, and continues.

"There has to be a better way. I was very poor as a child, but I never knew I was poor because everyone else was just the same as I was. But today there is a fostering of people begrudging what other people have. And I hate it. It has taken away our charity and our desire to help. Because we consider that everyone has their hand out.

"And it is very distressing," Jackie continues. "The minute something goes wrong, they call us names. They call us racists, etc. We always come across as these rich, fat cats. No one sees how we are struggling to raise our families, too. All this activism certainly doesn't seem to be helping people to love one another."

Even some of the older nuns in religious communities, who are dreaming of a peaceful retirement, feel threatened by their activist sisters when they talk about turning convents into shelters for the homeless, or make other equally creative, and equally idealistic, suggestions.

Fortunately, most activists in the convent these days are trying very hard to be sensitive about the needs of their older nuns. They are becoming far more tolerant of any unraised consciousness and different opinions, whether about social justice, women's issues, or the internal workings of the institutional Church. And, in fact, many older nuns also can be found among the politically radical.

And it is easy to see why so many women religious are attracted to the promises of enlightened socialism. Nuns (and order priests and brothers) belong to the only organizations in the world that are, in the 1990s, happily and successfully living a communistic lifestyle. So it is difficult, if not impossible, for them to understand, let alone relate to, the problems of middle- and upper-class women whose lives and fortunes are determined by the strengths and weaknesses of capitalism.

Unfortunately, the more involved activist women become with the very poor and marginalized, the less they are able to fathom the very real problems of the middle class. Not only do they lack any comprehension of the economic realities encountered by those who own small businesses or are self-employed (particularly when a recession hits hard and long), they find it hard to imagine the difficulty, if not the impossibility, of one member of a family proposing drastic lifestyle changes for its other members. And despite how it sometimes may seem, there is more to life than money, or the lack of it. The average woman in the pew, regardless of her class, believes that everyone has similar moral decisions to make each day which appear to have little, if anything, to do with personal or worldwide economics.

Although activist nuns—and other formerly middle-class women who are dedicated to social justice causes—should be able to serve as bridges and translate the realities of the lives of the different classes to one another, they often don't. Many of them are ashamed of their middle-class roots and even more ashamed of their middle- and upper-middle-class relatives. Or at least they sometimes act that way. So they have less and less contact with the very group that must be converted to social justice causes and ways of thinking and acting if any progress is going to be made in solving the problems created by poverty.

I don't mean to imply that Catholic nuns should give up their preferential option for the poor, or desert the inner cities. There is only so much each person can do, even overprogrammed and workaholic nuns, and I respect their decision to devote their lives to the poor, whom they see as needing them the most.

However, they should be aware of how much their absence is being felt by the middle class. One of the reasons why there are so few young women are entering the convent these days is because upper and middle-class high school and college women have little if any contact with these idealistic role models.

It is not only adolescents who are missing them. Upper and middle-class adults are equally in need of inspiration and example. And what all of us, regardless of our class, probably need the most is education about and contact with other people whose culture and/or circumstances are different from ours.

"My husband and I tried to interest our suburban parish about Nicaragua and other social justice issues," Sheila tells me, "but not many seemed to care."

"The last time I was at Mass at my parents' parish, the priest was preaching against building barns to store your wealth," Christi relates. "He was telling people that they should be giving 10% of their wealth to help the poor. And he was making many people in the Church uncomfortable. And my impression was that, when the pastor finds out what he said, the priest won't last. But the message the priest was giving was the message I got every day at my Catholic college."

Despite the rhetoric of many activists, all those who make up the middle and upper classes are not "bad" or "selfish" people. In fact, many are both generous and concerned. But they lack opportunity and know-how, as well as motivation, to bridge the gaps between neighborhoods. Anything that activist Catholic women can do to introduce the more privileged to the economic and social realities of the disadvantaged will be an important service, not only to the poor but also to those better off. Yet to be effective, "bridge people" need to remember to look at all people with at least close to the same amount of charity and understanding, even tolerance, that they show to the poor and the marginalized.

Keeping an Open Mind

It is hard to know if disasters, human tragedies, and crimes that occur each day in our world are really getting worse and more numerous, or if television just makes it seem that way. One hundred years ago, people only experienced and knew about what happened within a few miles of their homes. Now, a terrorist attack, famine, or a war continents away feels like it is happening right next door. Just as soon as we start to make up our minds about who's at fault, or what an obvious solution must be, another TV or newspaper report gives us another, and opposing, view.

So some women, even a few of those who consider themselves liberal activists, are coming to the conclusion that as nice as it would be to have another "list" of "correct" responses for every situation (like we once had about moral issues), there are no longer any easy or automatic answers for the increasingly complex political and economic problems of modern life either. Nor can any of us—whether we be conservative or liberal or some blend of both—afford to consider that our version of reality and our proposed solution to a problem is the only one that will work. Although few will deny that what the world needs is a quick and massive increase of the "We are all in this together" philosophy of life, no one suggests that such a radical idea is going to be easy to promote, much less accomplish.

MULTICULTURALISM: THE CHALLENGE OF THE COMING CENTURY

However, many Catholics believe that their Church really does have the ingredients to become a successful model of how to combine many different people, from many different cultures, backgrounds, and economic classes, into an organization that both celebrates diversity and encourages spiritual unity. Although no one thinks that this is or will be an easy task, several women gave me examples of how diverse groups within their Church are already beginning to learn from one another.

"One of the most amazing sessions of the Listening Process that we did for the U.S. bishops in the mid-eighties was in East Los Angeles," Cynthia recalls. "Once again, my life was changed by what I learned there. The missionary sister running the session took our process that was middle class and turned it into a happening for women who were poor, who didn't speak English, and who were new arrivals to the United States. They showed us how to get these women to open up, and the women really got into it. And they not only said the same things that women all over our diocese said, they taught us many things as well."

Sofia is a pastoral assistant in a parish that is also predominantly Spanish speaking. "We are working hard at establishing *communidades de base*, which are like renew groups," she tells me. "And these are very life giving. Many of our parishioners were in similar groups in their Latin American villages. Their faith is a big part of their lives, not just an hour on Sunday. Even the poorest of the poor were used to helping each other in their country of origin. That is exactly what is beginning to happen here. It is circular, not top-down. They are bringing a lot of positive energy to the Church here in the United States."

The values of solidarity, community, and deep spirituality which these immigrants are bringing to the grassroots are what theologians like Mexico-born Maria Pilar Aquino, who specializes in liberation theology, are bringing to our universities and scholarly religious publications. "I am convinced of the transformative capacity of Christianity," Pilar explains. "Christianity is re-encountering its own identity in Latin America. The rebirth of Christianity is now happening in the poor and the oppressed. I find no other explanation than that we are discovering that Christianity is a liberative source, that it can dialogue with our ancient cultures. And if it is open to them, it can survive.

"And more and more I am explaining myself within the worldview of our native cultures," she continues, "and the mixture of European and Indian cultures that we have become. In the very Roman Catholic church, I have found I can believe in the new earth, the new creation, through the promises of the Gospel, the promises of Christianity, as well as the teachings of our native religions.

"I believe what the poor believe, what the oppressed believe, and what all the people who want solidarity believe," Pilar explains. "We share the vision of what the Church and the world can be. It is this utopian vision which is pushing us, updating our movements every day. And we can experience all of this within the Roman Catholic church."

It is not only Latin Americans who are making multiculturalism both the challenge and the opportunity of the coming new century. In large archdioceses like Los Angeles, Mass is currently being said in as many as 130 different languages, and even small dioceses are becoming increasingly diverse.

"We only have 16 different ethnic groups here in Oakland, but they each want their own Mass in their own language," Rose Marciano Lucey relates. "And I see that as the much bigger struggle that is before us: How are we going to make all of these groups part of the total Church?"

In response to her own question, Rose is helping her diocese plan a joint celebration for all its ethnic groups. "Each community is going to make a model of the houses that they used to live in, and share their culture with one another. And that is the revolution that is going on in this country. People haven't woken up to it yet, but a new world is happening . . . . It's the First World and the Second World and the Third World, all together in a new combination that is the New World.

"And all of these groups have both rich and poor in them," Rose explains. "There is only one world, and there is only one gospel, and we kid ourselves into thinking that we are separate. And that's what scripture is all about."

Despite the upbeat words of Cynthia, Sofia, Pilar, and Rose, understanding and appreciation of both the differences and similarities between distinct groups of people do not come easily. As the number of ethnic groups continues to multiply in the United States (even within the Catholic church) each year, this new multiculturalism becomes more challenging, even to liberal feminist activists. Events at the Women-Church Conference in Albuquerque in April of 1993 show us some of the difficulties that must be faced.

To the casual observer, as well as to many of the volunteers who had worked diligently to put on the event, the conference appeared to be bending over backward to be inclusive. For months, the organizers of the weekend had insisted that recognizing multiculturalism be one of the paramount goals of the gathering. They had given more than 500 scholarships to women who had requested them. Women representing many different ethnic groups were invited to speak at the workshops and plenary sessions. At the closing event, different women were scheduled to sum up their experiences at the conference and to offer ideas for Women-Church's continuing agenda. Instead, only women from minority groups came forward, each claiming that much of her own personal experience at the conference had been one of discrimination, even racism, not good will or unity.

These protests had a snowballing effect, and it soon became apparent that if you were from a nonwhite group and didn't come forward to say you had been slighted, you would feel that you were betraying your ethnic group. One of the primary objections made was that although the organizers and speakers presented a picture of what appeared to be a rainbow of ethnic groups and races, the majority of the women in attendance were white and middle class.

The minority women were both articulate and passionate. As they spoke, a nervous hush fell over the assembled audience.

And I think I speak for most of the white women in attendance when I say that my first reaction was of hurt, confusion, and disbelief. I had no idea what, if any, specific instances of discrimination they were referring to, and I particularly felt sorry for the organizers of the event, who appeared to have worked overtime to be respectful of differences and to be inclusive.

After the event, my sister and I sought out several of the minority women and asked them to explain what they had been talking about. Their responses were particularly enlightening and caused me to change my mind about what the emotional session had really meant. In the end I concluded that the conflict was the most significant, as well as the most positive, event of the entire weekend: The minority women had felt secure enough—"in" enough—to risk letting other women see, experience, and understand their truth, even when they knew their words would sound harsh.

"We're tired of having to come and 'perform' for liberal white groups, so that you will feel good about how liberal and inclusive you are," was one of their messages. "We have lots to teach you. But if you want to learn, dare to come among us and sit quietly in the corner as the student, not as our saviors."

As I reflected on their words, they suddenly began to make more sense, and it occurred to me that they were once again proving the truth of one of the main themes of this book: the need to listen to and work with one another.

Growing Up At Last

And so, as the countdown to the 21st century begins, Catholic women everywhere are not only coming to a better understanding about their own inner truths, but following the examples of one another and daring to speak this truth out loud to each other, to men, and even to the institutional Church itself.

What they are learning is this: There are no simple or even obvious answers to the world's large and seemingly overwhelming problems, or even their own small but equally difficult ones. There are only individual efforts, which, as they are joined together one by one, gain momentum and strength. There is as much a need for tolerance—on all sides—of mistakes and weaknesses as there is for the courage to make hard choices, personal adjustments, and even structural changes.

For a time, many of us, even nuns, have been so busy "saving the world" that we have had little time left for prayer and meditation. However, a growing number of Catholic women, including the social activists, are beginning to realize they need a strong inner sense of truth and balance, of centered spirituality, within themselves if they are going to be strong enough to survive, let alone make a real difference.

Some of us are finding this strength in traditional ways when we meet with Christ and our neighbors around the altar at daily or weekly Mass. Some are finding it in other Eucharistic moments at support groups with other women and when joining hands in solidarity with those in need. Most Catholic women are looking for and finding spirituality and growth in all of these places, and other sources of inspiration and peace as well.

Within the multicultural and very diverse organization that is the Catholic church—which we believe is formed by and through the Holy Spirit which lives in all of us—we should be able to find hundreds of opportunities for human solidarity and spiritual growth. And, as grownups, we must first blame ourselves if we don't.

CHAPTER FOUR

The Good News
and Bad News About
the Catholic Church

One of the main questions that many people, particularly those who are not practicing Catholics themselves, ask about women and the Catholic church is, "Why do modern, liberated, and educated women of the 1990s stay in, let alone convert to, a church that is so blatantly patriarchal and which often appears to be anti-woman?" This is a good question, one that many committed Catholic women ask themselves at least occasionally.

Sofia is a perfect example of the kind of woman that many would never believe could stay a Catholic. Married for the second time and now a young grandmother, she calls herself a radical feminist and insists that there are many areas of Church policy she cannot support. "I can truthfully say that every day I quit the Church maybe once or twice," she says, grinning, her smile contagious. "But I'm still here. I wouldn't have it otherwise."

Not only is Sofia still a Catholic, she left the Church as a teenager and returned about 10 years ago when she was in her late thirties. Furthermore, she is often a daily communicant and is employed by the Church full-time as an assistant pastor.

"But I sometimes find it necessary to scream from the inside," she confesses. "And if they don't like it, they can tell me, and then I can decide if I will continue a Catholic or not. But I have never had a problem being a feminist. I am careful about what I say to whom. I don't want people to be uncomfortable, that is just common courtesy. I don't like running around riling people up....I don't believe that is my function in life at all. I just want to be the most useful that I can be in my own life."

All of the women interviewed for this book also strongly identify with their Catholic religion and enthusiastically endorse what they consider are its basic teachings. Yet, as we have seen, many disagree with certain interpretations of the institutional Church about how its teachings are to be lived in the world today. But usually their quarrel is with upper Church management or a particular priest, not with Christ, God, the Holy Spirit, or even with most of the Church's members or many of its teachings. Only a few of the women quoted in this book are like Catherine, who reports that she has actually left the Church.

"I left when I began to understand that my good work was benefiting the institutional Church, that they were looking good, because I, as a nun, was doing certain things," Catherine, an award-winning photographer and filmmaker, explains. "And I didn't want to support the way the Church is managed. There is not the kind of collaboration that I am willing to work with. Since it is not there, I won't participate in it.

"I spent years trying to raise consciousness about this, thinking that once they understood . . . . Like if a doctor tells someone they have a heart condition and can't smoke anymore, you would assume that person would stop smoking. So I thought the men in the Church would change once they understood. I thought all I had to say to them was, 'Hey, guys, you are excluding me,' and they'd say, 'Oh, I didn't realize that. I'm sorry, let's fix it.' But that wasn't the case."

The conflict between her needs and expectations and her reality was too great for Catherine to resolve, and she no longer calls herself a practicing Catholic, but agrees she probably would check "Catholic" on a hospital admission form. However, many other women told me ways in which they simply and quietly work around problem areas in their particular parish or job situation. Others insisted that they were not that unhappy with the status quo. But even women like Catherine, who have "left" the Church, still believe in and try to practice the core truths of Christianity. As often as not, it is their very dedication to these basic truths that caused them to leave the Church in the first place, because they came to believe that the Catholic church as an institution often does not practice what it is preaching. Their leaving proves their support of the principles of Catholicism, rather than the opposite.

Jane Redmont agrees with me, "If the remarkably diverse group I interviewed (in *Generous Lives*) is any reflection of the roughly 30 million people it represents," she contends, "there is little crisis of unbelief among American Catholic women. The message of the Gospel, the person of Jesus, the power of the Holy Spirit, the presence of God in the world: These are rarely factors in disaffection from the Catholic church. For many, it is the contradiction between the message of Jesus and the lived experience of the institutional Church that it has become too much to bear."[1]

Andrew Greeley puts these ideas even more concretely. "To understand contemporary American Catholicism, one needs to think of religion as imaginative and indeed poetic behavior . . . that confers identity. In such a situation it is utterly rational to continue to be Catholic no matter what the damn fools who are your leaders might do."[2]

WHY PEOPLE COME, WHY PEOPLE STAY

Those who stay are staying not out of fear or even guilt, but out of strong emotional and intellectual attachment to the truth as taught by Jesus, and a deep love for a tradition that has proven it is able to span all ages and all cultures.

Those of us who went to Catholic schools used to spend hours in apologetics class where we argued about and tried to prove all sorts of things about God and our Church. Yet today our faith is rarely based on any of these intellectual arguments.

Whether there really is a God, or whether Christ was (is) God, and a myriad of other long and involved theological questions have little relevance to our daily lives. But what is relevant is the messages that Christ brings to us, and the connection to one another and to the spiritual that we feel when we try to live up to Christ's teachings. And most of us suspect that even if the philosophies of God's love for us, the value of life, the worth of each human person, and the ethics and moral viewpoints that we, as Christians, believe in were proven to have been fabricated by some giant Big Brother to keep us all in line (an opiate of the people, like atheists and communists supposedly insist), it would not matter. They are simply the way that most of us who call ourselves Catholic think we should all live our lives and, much more important, the way we WANT to live our lives.

Even though we know we often fall short of these ideals, we never doubt that these principles are of ultimate importance to all people everywhere. While we Catholic women realize that others—be they Jewish, Muslims, Buddhists, Hindus, Native Americans—may be called to connect with God and the rest of humanity through other histories and rites, we find our connection through rituals, like the sacrament of the Eucharist, which have spoken to us personally all of our lives. These practices and beliefs link us in a special way to the many generations that have come before us and will come after us. They also connect us to other members of our Church who live in every corner of the earth.

What Is Best About Being Catholic?

The two main things that the women I have interviewed find appealing and essential about the Catholic church are its liturgy (the rituals of Catholicism) and its message of love of God and neighbor. Their comments were both numerous and inspiring.

Maria experienced that love in a particularly potent way when her young daughter lay dying of cancer in their home many years ago. "We were all kneeling beside her, saying the rosary, sending her off," she explains softly, her eyes beginning to moisten. "And my parish priests were there with us. That is why my Church is so important to me. They were always here."

Women talked about many different personal spiritual experiences. "I pray at the extremes of feeling," Carolyn remarks. "Either very happy or very sad." Carolyn goes to daily Mass, which she says helps her have the strength she needs to live out her Christian values each day.

"I find the Gospels to be absolutely contemporary. It is amazing how relevant they are. If I miss going to Mass, it throws me off-kilter," she insists. "It gives me a specific period during the day when I can get away from the telephone or whatever I am doing and concentrate on the spiritual. It is like people who run every morning. Most of the time it gives me a little calm, and reminds me what is important."

Mass also plays a very important part in Diane's life. She particularly likes "seeing God alive in people at Mass and in the greater world around me. There is a profound sense of hopefulness in the Catholic church," Diane explains, "because we are all seen as God's daughters and sons. We all have value. We are all sacred."

Diane is now studying creation spirituality and finds that it has deepened her sense of the sacred to include all life on the planet, and has helped her bring together within herself the values of the Church, the peace movement, and her childhood in Nebraska.

Diane loves the sense of soul that she has gotten from being Catholic. "It is a sense of a deeper dimension within myself which I can feel growing. The Church helps me to learn to love, to grow in the spiritual gifts: honesty, goodness, reconciliation, and kindness. I respect the Church for standing up for the sacredness of life—all human life—even though I disagree with it on birth control and to some degree abortion. I love the sense of God in the community which is so much a part of the new Church . . . the sense of oneness with my friends."

Jane H.'s experiences are different from Diane's. She admits that she doesn't always get much spiritual help at Mass. "But once in a while I do get inspired and I live for those moments," she insists. "And I would go to Mass if there weren't any sermons at all. I get my spiritually out of the liturgy of the Mass and the basic philosophy that I must follow."

Convert Sara is particularly enthusiastic. "I am so grateful of the people who have come through my life," she insists, "because I am a changed person. I am so happy that I am a Christian, that I am Catholic, and that it has introduced me to the priests and the wonderful people. I feel different and totally blessed."

Sherry is equally eloquent about her feelings. "The prayers, the Mass, the rituals, the stations of the cross, they all represent a place in my life where I really feel I am talking to a creator and He or She actually hears me. I don't see it as all symbolism. I really feel I am with God and talking to God in Mass."

Women from every spectrum of the rainbow of political religious beliefs like being a Catholic for much the same reasons. Marian K. probably considers herself a radical feminist, but she is also an Irish Catholic, which is an even a stronger source of her identification. "The Eucharist and what it means to me still keep me at a particular church I can live with. I need to gather with others who believe in Jesus to share the bread and wine which are also signs of community. I could wish for a smaller community of women, to share our lives but I don't have such a Eucharistic community." So, like many women, she does the best with the church she has at hand.

Many Catholic women bring fond memories from their childhood to the altar with them each time they go to Mass. "As a child, I loved the traditions, genuflection, incense, the Latin. It was so organized, and my family was the opposite of that, and so it attracted me. I also felt that I belonged, because my family had been Catholic, and that was what I was supposed to be," many different women told me in many different words.

This connection with God, this sense of family tradition, is what Betty particularly seeks for her children. "I want my children to have some kind of religious experience like I had," she explains. "Children today, as we do, need something to fall back on."

Betty and her family live in an area of Southern California which is often subject to intense and rapidly moving brush fires. "I remember during our last terrible fire," she continues. "I drove out with my kids down a road, and there was fire coming on both sides and over us. The girls were shrieking with fear, so I told them to pray. They began to yell the Hail Mary. And that was what got us through. It gave us energy and power to go through the fire, even though we should not have been able to get through there. Intellectually, it had nothing to do with it perhaps, but it was something they could do to help us get the car through. And that's what we want: something that will help us through the hard times. You need some kind of structure."

As a nurse, Betty is convinced, from experience, that those who believe in God have a much nicer exit from this world than those who, not believing, fight and struggle horribly against death.

Bridget is becoming a nun for the spiritual help and inspiration she has found in her new community. "I want to live and work with a group who wants to make it work, that believes in extending the Kingdom, in making it real. And that's the only place I feel like I will be able to get the kind of support I need to do it. I can't do it by myself."

Jane B. also has felt her faith deepen and grow because of other Catholic women that she has met. "They convert me by their example," she explains. "They don't even have to open their mouths." She goes on to mention by name women in her parish whose faith and dedication have inspired her to get more involved in parish work, daily Mass, and other forms of spirituality.

For Cassandra, it is the social justice messages of Christ that call her most compellingly. "I have responded to the Gospel, to Jesus and the values that Jesus holds before us. And I see a man sent from God—God incarnate—who goes counter-culture. Jesus says, 'I didn't come to follow the law, I came to break the law. And if you follow me, you will find yourself turned upside down.' In the Gospel, Jesus includes women in ministry. He affirms the efforts of the women, and he goes against the culture in a way that got him into trouble, that got him killed.

"That's the Gospel that I follow," Cassandra explains. "Not the system that I find oppressive . . . a system in which half the population is not recognized as mature, in which women are dismissed or lumped together with children, animals, and property, under a patriarchy."

Pilar, now a doctor of theology, was once a nun. But even before that, she was a teenage girl in Mexico. Number two in a poor family of eight children, the Catholic church and its teachings about social justice gave her both identity and direction. "I always felt moved to compassion by the very poor families who lived in San Luis Sonora, Mexico, where I grew up. The Catholic church played a very important role in my life there. At age 12, I started to be a catechist. It put me in an environment so that I could do something for others. It was the one space where I felt completely accepted."

More than a few women are "hooked" on being Catholic out of a profound respect for its potential. And they believe that the Catholic church is far larger than its hierarchy, far stronger and more spiritually potent than even the sum of all its parts.

"We have to claim our roots, in Jesus' story," Theresa explains. "And that is why people can stay, because we have hopes about what can be . . . because we can look to the past and see what has been."

"I would be uncomfortable without the framework of the Catholic church . . . the basic teachings that have been a part of my life as a Roman Catholic," Sister Mary Luke Tobin says. "I think that Roman Catholics comprise such a large part of the world's population that we as Catholics can do a lot of good, and I don't see any advantage of jumping out of that into some other denomination. People in those other denominations are looking to us Catholics for guidance, for spirituality, for prayer.

"The fullness, to me, seems to be within this magnificent tradition," she explains. "And I will say that every once in a while it has to have some correctives. I don't think that God is standing there saying that everything the Catholic church does or teaches is right. I'm not saying that at all. I am saying that I am grateful for the tradition itself, because there are great things in it. I have all the great mystics and saints that I can consult. And I am not consulting them for their morality, but for their insights, to lead me into the ways of God, which is what religion should be about."

As we talk, we discuss the fact that no matter how hard some men in the Church may be trying to reign people back into "old church ways" after Vatican II, they can't ruin a good thing! Pilar has told me that many of the Latina women whom she works with feel sorry for the hierarchy, pity for the priests and bishops who are unable to accept the gift of women's insights. Mary Luke thinks that many of these men are actually operating out of fear. "And I sympathize with them to a degree. They have to find a way so that it doesn't look like they are giving up and saying that there are no moral rules. That is the trouble with moral rules. People think you are giving them up, and that there are none, that everything goes. And that's not what's happening at all."

In her work at the Thomas Merton Center in Colorado, Sister Mary Luke Tobin sees a growing thirst for good spiritual information and material. "I get a lot more calls to assist spiritual direction these days, and a lot more calls from people who are writing books and articles and asking questions." She believes that more and more people are realizing that they ultimately must make their own decisions, but at the same time they are asking for guidelines, for inspiration, along the way.

WHAT TO DO ABOUT CHURCH LAWS: A DIFFERENCE OF OPINION

Women particularly seem able and willing to hold two opposite opinions on a subject at the same time. They can praise the stability brought about by Church traditions, and insist on the truthfulness and importance of the moral vision that their Church gives them, and at the very same time insist on recognizing the knowledge that comes to them out of their own lived experiences as equally valid. They love the Church for always being there through every age, and at the very same time they can demand that it also be flexible. While they acknowledge that these two views held together may cause a lot of tension, they do not believe that they are contradictory.

All Catholic women look to their Church for inspiration. Some, however, only want it to "cheerlead" them into heaven with broad and vibrant brushstrokes about morality. Other, more traditional women, happily accept specific instructions and advice.

"The Catholic church is my way of getting to heaven," Jackie insists. "If there is a heaven, the guidelines of this religion will get me there. The Church has made a difference in how I live my life." She considers that the Church, which has been in the morality business for some 2,000 years, knows much more about morality than she, and she is grateful that its teachings are very specific.

Jennifer is younger than most of Jackie's children, but she also is looking to the Church for direction in her life. She claims all Church laws are ideals that no one, not even the Church, believes you can follow all the time, but that help keep an individual's—and the world's—moral standards high.

But several years ago, away from family and friends, when she first started graduate school, Jennifer did not have the support system for her religion that she had taken for granted at home. So when she began to seriously date a nonpracticing Jewish man, she resented the emotional problems and confusion that they had, which she blamed on her religion, and she stopped going to Church.

She soon discovered changes taking place in her that she did not like. Without her knowing it, going to Mass each Sunday had given her the nourishment she needed to be the kind of person she wants to be. Hungry, she returned, anxious to come to a mature understanding and appreciation of her Catholic faith. "Right now the teaching part of it is more important to me than the Eucharist," Jennifer explains. "But what is most important to me is my attitude toward other people."

Martha, a psychologist and teacher as well as a wife and a mother, also looks to the Church for guidance in many areas. "As we get older, we fine-tune how to make moral decisions. But I think that the Catholic church has the most mature, and best thought-through moral judgments of any religion. The issues are clear and they make sense . . . except maybe concerning sexual issues, and they are improving enormously on that, at least on what priests will advise you."

Martha insists that, for her, religion is no longer about "sin" but about "growing." "I do think that the Church provides wonderful ways for me to grow," she explains. "First of all, many parishes are giving information, lectures, and classes that help you with your family . . . ideas that are appropriate and consistent with modern psychology. There are not very many hell and brimstone, guilt-producing sermons anymore. Priests are much better trained in modern-day psychology. The Church gives all sorts of people ways to help them grow in their ability to reach out to others. Social justice issues . . . the Church is pretty much the leader in that field. Even the conservative bishops are into social justice. It is well organized and there is a lot of it."

Martha considers the conservatisms of the Vatican to be necessary. "It grounds us. We don't want to become nothing. We do want consistency. The Vatican provides leadership and hopefully allows some struggle . . . kind of like parents of adolescents. It keeps us from becoming independent too fast. We may be adults, but we are a lot of people, with different ideas, and we need someone to keep the boundaries. And the fact is that no one forces you to be Catholic. The Catholic church *is* about something definite. If I don't want that, I can leave it. Start my own church if I want to. But that doesn't mean that I think that everything that the Pope says is necessarily correct."

But for Martha, as for many women, "what holds it all together is the liturgy. I just love the Mass. It has all the artistic and sense-filled mystery. It also hooks back to previous times and connects you to God, both in general and in the past, and all around the world at the same time."

Highly educated Catholic women seem to be as enthusiastic as "average" Catholic women are. Psychiatrist Nancy tells me that although Freudian psychology tries to integrate God out of your life and claim that belief in God is an indication that you have dependent needs that are unmet, she personally believes just the opposite.

"There is only so far you can get by integrating God out. You cannot put together a complete picture of the human psyche without putting God in. I am a fairly well-adjusted person because I have gone through all this time integrating God *in*, and I feel rich!"

Patricia Miller finds exciting the debates and discussions that new ways of thinking about morality provoke. "The Catholic church is an intelligent, solid-based church when it is at its best," she explains, "Even though some would say that we aren't allowed to discuss and debate, we are doing it, and it is our faith which has empowered us to do this." What she particularly likes about being a Catholic is the universality of the Church. "I am at home in a Vietnamese community in California as I am in a European-based community in Boston!"

TURNING TO JESUS IN TIMES OF PERSONAL CRISIS

Many women relate that, to their surprise, in times of crisis, they immediately found themselves in a Catholic church, kneeling before Jesus in the Blessed Sacrament, regardless of how many years they had been away or even how angry they had been when they left.

"I was gone from the Church for 25 long years," Sofia relates, "because of some serious spiritual questions I had about how we were living as a Church. I underwent a really traumatic, personal agony, a darkness, by being away. I refused to have anything to do with the Church. And then something happened that made me realize how very, very alone I was, and I was called—that's the only way I can say it—to run to the nearest Catholic church I could find, because I almost committed suicide."

Fortunately, once there, Sofia was welcomed by a wonderful priest. "He was the most relaxed person I had ever met, with a good sense of humor," she recalls. "He encouraged me to go to Mass. And then I realized how much our Church had changed."

When Maria left the Church, she angrily took her four young children and her husband with her and found a new way of relating to life through a New Age 1970s group called The Foundation of Human Understanding. She found the values that it taught uplifting and very useful, the people friendly, supportive, and compassionate. She never thought she would return to the Catholic church. "I felt I was growing spiritually. I didn't miss the Church at all," she says.

However, one afternoon, on the highway near their home, she and her husband passed a car that had obviously been in a serious accident, because it was completely totaled. They recognized the car as belonging to their oldest daughter. In complete panic they raced home and happily found their daughter had escaped from the accident unhurt and was safe.

The next thing Maria knew, she was kneeling in her old Catholic church before the Blessed Sacrament in tearful prayer, giving thanks and promising that the whole family would return. "When I came back I found that I had changed," she tells me. "When I left, I had been judging everyone. I was completely unloving. But when I returned, my anger had all been washed away."

She found she could accept people as they were—even priests she had disagreed with before—and instead of being upset because they and the Church were not meeting her needs, she realized it was up to her to give something to the Church instead. "My new attitude was because I had grown up," she explains.

Cynthia left during the 1960s. "I feel like I was away because I was not allowed to practice my Catholicism when I was a Catholic," she explains, "because my Catholicism was not fitting into the parishes that were all around me. In Arizona, we experienced a drunk priest. Then when we tried to go back to Mass another time, there were all these Knights of Columbus with their swords, and it was during the Vietnam War, and it didn't make sense. I felt that there was no place in the Church for me."

But 13 or so years later, now with two young sons, Cindy came back. "My sons are what made me come back," she recalls. "And I remember telling the priest in confession that I had come back because I had forgiven the Church for its sins. It was face-to-face, and the priest looked at me and smiled. And I said, 'I know I sound uppity here, but that is what I had to do to come back to the Church, I had to forgive it . . . and now I am asking you to forgive me.'"

Although many women told me they have come back to the Church and started practicing again without first going to confession, Cynthia needed a ceremony, a ritual, to mark that she was returning—"that, like it or not, I'm back," she says, grinning.

Although baptized as a child, JoAnne had lived an actively dysfunctional life while a teenager and in her early twenties. "I thought I was going to hell in a handbasket, no matter what I did," she explains. She was also actively anti-Catholic much of this time. Even so, the only law school she applied to 10 years later was Notre Dame. "I chose it because it was Catholic, but I couldn't admit that, even to myself."

Once there, she found herself drawn to the Mass that was celebrated in the law school lounge each Sunday evening. "The priest also taught me torts," she remembers. "He was Irish and gorgeous, and I fell in love with him as a priest, watching him celebrate Mass. I didn't go to the Eucharist or anything like that, but I would watch him from a dark corner. And after about three months of this, I finally realized I wasn't in love with him, but I was in love with whatever changed him from a law school teacher to what he became when he celebrated Mass. My mind was blown. This guy, who was basically your male chauvinistic pig asshole, would turn into . . . his face changed, and he gave great homilies. Every single one of them rang in my ears. After a while I noticed that he was directing some of his stuff at me, sitting in the audience. He also said Friday Masses at noon. And I told him that I wanted to come, but not under any false pretenses . . . that I didn't know what I was doing there."

When JoAnne discovered that there was some power at work turning him into the very strong, prophetic teacher he became during Mass, she started thinking seriously about the Catholic church for the first time in her life. "I went and talked to another priest, who was a wonderful guy, and the first thing he said was, 'I really admire your courage in seeking God in an institution that will not welcome you because you are a woman.'"

JoAnne admits she went through a major struggle in order to get to a point where she was able to let go and believe. "I started going to different Eucharists, and reading like mad, and seeking spiritual direction. I was convinced that I was losing my mind, because I didn't know what was going on. I had never heard the word *conversion*. To me that was what happened to St. Paul when he got knocked off his horse, and it hadn't happened since."

JoAnne claims she often felt embarrassed about suddenly becoming religious, especially since she had major problems with the patriarchal Church and had been an atheist. "I didn't even have a language to use about what was going on with me. So I did something that I had never done: I went into the Sacred Heart Chapel, and there were tourists in there. It is not much of a place to pray, but I did, and I knelt down and I let the tears come, and I couldn't really pray with anything verbal in my head, because I couldn't really commit to the notion that God was real. I was really jumping off a cliff. And so I just said, 'If you are there, help me!' And I got bowled over by God's response."

JoAnne began to go to the library to find out what strange, psychological disorder she had. "That's when I discovered all this stuff about conversion, and I said, 'Yes, that's how I feel! That's exactly what's going on.' I read everything they had and got more and more involved, and finally, the Sunday after Thanksgiving, I just decided to go to Communion."

Most of the women I talked to who are recent converts don't have stories quite as dramatic as JoAnne's, but they all turned to Catholicism at a certain crisis point in their lives, and all were met immediately by the welcoming and nonjudgmental arms of their parish priest.

Lauren was in the middle of a difficult divorce from her abusive husband. So she turned to the Catholic church, which had always attracted her, and found the priest there full of empathy.

"I spent a lot of time with him," she relates. "I was going through a custody suit while I was learning to be a Catholic in RCIA, and everyone was very supportive." Lauren claims she looked into many other religions also, and that if you compare religions the way she has, you will find that all religions have certain issues that are difficult to accept, or that you don't agree with, but "You don't throw out the whole lunch because you don't like the peas! The fact that there are a few issues I can't agree with doesn't mean that I can't be Catholic."

When Jamie was in the hospital having her baby, she put down "Catholic" on the hospital form because even though she was not baptized and not really brought up a Catholic, her parents had been Catholic before she was born.

One day, when her son was about two, some Legion of Mary members knocked on her door and asked her if she was Catholic, and she said yes. They invited her to Mass at the nearby Church and put her into contact with a neighbor who was going there also.

"As soon as I walked in, I knew this was for me. I was hooked!" she explains. "I said I want to be a part of this more than anything, and I want my son to be a Catholic, too. I had gone to other churches, searching, and many of them were upset because I had a small kid. One even made me leave because he was crying. But at this church, kids were crying and were still welcome, and I said, 'This is like a family, this is wonderful.'

"I started going every Sunday and I had my son baptized," Jamie continues. "I didn't even know you could be baptized if you were an adult, and go to Communion, or be confirmed. I didn't know that there was anything like RCIA, or that I could become a real part of the Church, until I read a notice in the Church bulletin one Sunday," she relates. "Then I found out that I could become an actual member of the body of the Church—forever—like I could have as a child. I got very excited and thought, *Wow! now I can really become a part of the Church.*"

Jamie got to know the priest very well and felt very accepted by him. "I would cry on his shoulder about my past sinful life," she remembers, "how horrible I was, and he would say very calmly, 'Why? You wouldn't have an abortion when everyone was telling you to do so. And you love that child more than life itself. Why would you feel bad about yourself?'"

Jamie feels that she is lucky to be a Catholic in the 1990s. "I can come fresh to the Church, with no preconceived ideas about what it teaches. Today is the Church that I love . . . . This is the Church that I want to raise my child in."

DESPITE LOVE, THERE STILL IS ANGER

Even as women are telling me wonderful things about the Catholic church, they are also explaining their frustrations with different aspects of the Church that they admit they love. However, few women suggest that these complaints mean that they should stop being Catholic.

As we have seen, extremists on both ends of the spectrum come in for the most criticism and stir up the most anger, particularly any person who insists on putting down another's personal views, whatever they may be.

Sherry Tyree hates the word *dialogue,* which she insists many liberals really use in order to manipulate a situation. "Not only has it become trite as a word, but it is now used as a weapon," she remarks. "I call it 'Let's dialogue and then do it my way.' I have had this happen to me, where I am talked to death by someone who has no intention of seeing my point of view."

I didn't ask her if, in the same conversation, she was open to seeing the other side's point of view as well. For despite what Sherry says, most of us believe that the word *dialogue* should be used only by people who recognize that there really may be two sides to an argument . . . that both sides may contain at least some partial truth. But that is a thought which is always easier for the 80% of us who are in the middle to entertain than for the 10% on each of the far ends to profess.

Almost every woman interviewed had at least one personal gripe about the Church. I don't consider this bad news, but good news, because the very fact that women care enough to feel frustrated and angry proves how important the Catholic church and the teachings of Jesus have become to their lives.

Many women mentioned, and probably rightly so, that many priests no longer seem enthusiastic about their jobs. "The first priest that I ever got to know as a real person—enthusiastic but fallible—was our last pastor," Jane B. tells me. "And he was forced to leave our parish. It is a crime that they are not using his talents. The biggest problem in the Church today is in the hierarchy and in the administration. My advice to the priests and the hierarchy is that they should act the same way toward us as we are to act to one another. I see a tremendous lack of caring and making people feel valued."

"I think maybe 90 families have left our parish Church in the last eight years since we've had this pastor," Sharon tells me. "The interdenominational faith group near us is now 40% ex-Catholic, because people are looking for a community for their families and not finding it. None of my children goes to church anymore, and I think maybe it is because they can't find what I found in the Church in St. Louis, where we used to live. We made a real effort to get the kids involved, and invited the priest to our house, and lots of other things, but he made no effort to personally welcome them. Our kids wouldn't give him a second chance. I've given him lots of chances."

Laurie, in her late twenties, and her husband live in California half a continent away from Sharon but find their parish much the same. "We have been going to the same Church for four years and have never really gotten to know anyone, even though we have been trying hard to seek people out," she explains.

"My parish provides almost nothing," Toni remarks, "unless you have a child in the school. I am a lector at Mass on Sundays, I get involved, and I still don't have a community."

As we talk, and I share almost the exact same feelings about my parish, we both confess to one another that, of course, we should not be complaining but instead should be doing something about this lack ourselves. When nothing is happening in a parish, it is always easier to blame the problem on the priests than on yourself.

But Cassandra is a master catechist of her diocese and has been very active in several different parishes, and she knows many more priests than most of us do, and much more intimately, and her words are harsher than many of us would ever even think. "There are a handful of priests that I respect and admire, because they work hard, and they take their commitment to their vows and to the people seriously. It is wonderful to see them working. But the greater majority do as little as they can get away with. They do minimum ministry with maximum perks. It is not the gospel. It is more getting away with everything they can, and maybe no one will notice. It is very discouraging," Cassandra insists.

She tells a long and sad story about a friend of hers, who, with her husband, was very active in their parish. She was dying from cancer. One morning, when it became obvious that she would not last out the day, her husband called the rectory in search of a priest to come to their home. But it was a weekday morning, and not one of the three in residence could be found.

So Cassandra went and held the dying woman's hand and blessed her as she died. "Two hours later the pastor shows up, explaining that he didn't know it was so serious or he would have come earlier. And I'm not talking about even the average woman in the pew . . . or someone who just pops in on Easter and Christmas. This was a woman who worked for the Church every day. Her husband was president of the Parish Council," she fumes. "Some priests seem to believe in ministry only at the convenience of the minister. And I have a problem with that."

Some women who have explored other denominations bring back ideas about improvements that they think the Catholic church should make. Stacey wants desperately to remain a Catholic, but she has been going with a new boyfriend to a very famous Protestant church and tells me all about it excitedly.

"I tell my mom that I always leave this Protestant service so psyched up," she relates. "And my mom says, 'Well, that's not the job of the Catholic church . . . and I find myself thinking, *Why isn't it?* I've always been told if you don't get anything out of the Church, it is your fault, but if they had someone who was enthusiastic . . . . I just don't get the feeling that many priests are enthusiastic anymore."

Stacey had gone to a series of lectures at her Catholic parish, which she had really looked forward to. "The priest just listed all these virtues. I felt like I was in a catechism class. We never sat down and said, 'Let's discuss how we apply that in our real life.' We also had a speaker come to our young adult group on medicine and ethics. And I thought that would be great. But they ended up getting a priest who got up there and said, 'This is what the Catholic church teaches,' and that was the end of any discussion."

Stacey claims that although she has gone to Mass on Sunday all her life, she can barely remember the sermon or the readings afterward. Yet she finds herself thinking about what she heard in her new Protestant church all week long. "When I left last week," she admits, "I left with little notes written down, and I was so charged up, with things to do personally, that were relevant to my real life. This is the first time I have ever been involved with another religion."

So far Stacey has resisted the temptation to leave the Catholic church officially, but another lifelong Catholic, more than twice Stacey's age, confesses she has started attending a very liberal Episcopalian church near her home, although she still writes down "Catholic" when she is asked to name her religion on a hospital form.

"I was in a parish where nothing was happening, as far as I could see, except what the laypeople were doing by themselves," Rose Catherine relates. "And many of the priests seemed threatened. They seemed to want to go back to the old ways.

"I was in Church one morning," she recalls, "and the priest preached a sermon right out of the turn of the century, on hell, fire, and damnation, and completely ignored all the young children in the Church. And in the middle, I, a relatively mild-mannered person, got up and walked out, something I didn't think I would ever do."

She went down the street to the Episcopal church and found the music good, their Eucharist beautiful. "I found they had a vision that included everyone—baptized, unbaptized, sexual orientation, whatever. And then I saw a woman priest was saying Mass and there were also women acolytes. I've never thought of myself as a feminist, but it really made a difference. And this church is known all over the city for its social outreach program to help the poor and those on the margin of society. And I met women in their eighties and nineties who had a thought in their head. They were involved, sometimes more radically than the middle-aged were. And when they told me that I could join their parish without giving up what I was, I did. So now I am a Catholic who happens to be going to an Episcopalian church."

Some women are upset about specific organizational or ceremonial changes in the Church today. Colleen particularly complains that kids must wait until their midteens to be confirmed, that it no longer happens during grade school anymore. "It takes two years of classes, in your parish, outside of school," she remarks. "So no wonder we are losing a lot of kids. If you are 16 and a junior in high school, and have a job, a car, are dating, with all kinds of school activities, you don't have time to go to confirmation class."

Other people like the changes and are upset because they think they have not been fully implemented. "What frustrates me is the reluctance to accept the changes of Vatican II," Sara maintains. "Liturgically, people fight it, priests and nuns fight it. I don't understand what they are so afraid of. If they could just get past the fear of thinking that they are doing something wrong, it could be so wonderful."

Like Sara, Margaret is also a very faithful volunteer at her parish each week. It is not the priests but other women who irk her. "What makes me the angriest is the patronizing attitude of the nuns, because we are just laywomen, or of the female professional staff, who look on us as just workers . . . . The prejudice, the patronizing, and I am feeling this from women more than men," she maintains. "It may be because I am dealing with more professional religious women than men, or that they feel more threatened by laywomen. I don't know."

Although definitely a most committed and enthusiastic Catholic, Margaret claims that what she dislikes most about the Church is that a little bunch of people think they have the truth and are hoarding it to themselves and refuse to let the laypeople in on the good news of what the Church is all about. "One of my biggest gripes is the patronizing that is being done by Church leadership, treating us like we don't have enough brains to make our own decisions, and telling us what God wills for us," she complains.

Terry, now grown up, is far less angry at the Church today than she was as a child. "My father was a lector and very involved with the Church," she recalls painfully. "And here he was the pillar of the Church on the outside, and at home he was beating us all up . . . especially me, who stood up to him, but he even hit my mother once when she was pregnant. And then I'd go to church and see him standing at the altar doing all the readings, when women still weren't allowed to do that, and he was considered so holy, and was even made a Grand Knight . . . and it used to make me livid, that these men would dress up like that and I imagined them all going home and beating up their families, like my Dad did."

As a grownup, Terry has resolved this conflict by giving up her family (whom she hasn't seen in many years) and getting closer to and more forgiving of her Church. Singlehandedly, with little official Church support, she started a Newman Club for the Catholic students at the university where she taught until recently.

As a teenager, Terry was angry because she felt the Church was denying her own intelligent appraisal of her family situation. As a psychologist, Toni sees many women from families like Terry's. She wishes that the Church would be more honest in letting people know that one's own conscience plays a large part in making moral decisions.

"I think the Church encourages a cloak of silence," she maintains. "And by not allowing the truth to be said and by not explaining that perhaps there isn't always only one right solution to a problem, or by refusing to admit that even the hierarchy themselves are not 100% certain about an issue, this cloak of silence paralyzes people with guilt and anger."

Toni claims that while she uses other techniques, her model of doing therapy is to help people develop their ability to hold more than one idea at a time about a situation, even if it feels contradictory. She wishes that there would be official Church acknowledgment that confusion does exist and that sometimes decisions are not all black or white. "Then when I am working with a person around a problem area that has to do with her spirituality or her understanding about the Church's teachings, it would be easier to help her if I could show her how the Church itself is trying to come up with answers."

COPING WITH FRUSTRATION AND NURTURING OUR SPIRITUAL LIVES

Just as Catholic women are coming to the conclusion that they are ultimately responsible for deciding the morality of each of their individual actions, they are also realizing that they must be equally responsible for the growth of their own spirituality. Gone forever are the days when "Father said" or "Sister said," or even "the Pope said" are acceptable answers. Furthermore, women are beginning to understand that they can no longer blame only the priests in their parish if they themselves feel spiritually hungry.

"Before I was just not that involved," Anne D. explains. "I did things that I had to do, and there was a whole lot I did not know. But I have learned that people need to get involved. Things are not going to happen unless you make them happen. You can't rely on the priests to make it happen. They need help, they need guidance, they need friendship."

Anne maintains that the laity, especially women, have great power and don't even know it. "If we can befriend a priest and have some knowledge about a subject matter, it can have great impact. Each of us has gifts, and we must use and honor them," she insists, adding, "You really have to work the system. Inside is more important than outside. And you might be able to make change . . . . There is always hope of change."

Many women, even intense feminist women, are beginning to recognize that they must take some "quiet time" for themselves at least occasionally in order to hear God's voice within. With a lot of help from therapy and friends, Barbara Tandy claims she is finally realizing that she is a human "being," not a human "doing."[3] Margaret is striving very hard to do the same. She was, and probably still is, a workaholic volunteer, both for her family and for her Church.

"The leaders that I ran into in the Church were very heavy on 'This is God's will for you, Jesus will be disappointed in you if you don't do this or that.' And I think for many years that was the whole thrust of my spirituality, getting out there in the trenches and doing as much I could until I dropped from exhaustion," Margaret explains.

But about 12 years ago, Margaret woke up. "I realized that the only thing that matters is how close I am to Jesus on the last day of my life and whether he will recognize me as his friend or not. Since then, I have turned my life entirely around. I went through two years where I did nothing except read scripture or pray. And now I am at a place where I have a good balance. I still tend to go overboard in action, because that's where my roots are. I get out and start working and working and working, and then I have to say, 'Wait a minute, where is Jesus in all of this?' Then I have to backtrack.

"But I am doing better at being a more balanced person," Margaret concludes. "I don't buy into other people's guilt trips anymore. If they tell me this is what I ought to do, I say, 'Fine, that's your opinion, but this is what I *know* I have to do.'"

Even social justice activists are finding they need to find a way to develop a centered, personal prayer life. "You couple the old convent ethic of work, work, work, with the American ethic of achieve, achieve, achieve," Bridget explains. "No wonder people burn out." She refuses to do that anymore, although it worries her what the other women in the convent that she has just joined will say. She wants to work only four days a week and is afraid that may not go over very well with some parts of her new community, because she doesn't plan to do something "socially useful" on the days she is not working.

"One of the reasons I want to join the convent is for contemplative, spiritual support," she insists. "And it is impossible to be contemplative, spiritual, and always working."

Most women are both standing up for themselves and at the same time refusing to be angry anymore. "The big problem with anger and rage," psychiatrist Nancy explains, "is that it is energy that is directed in a noncreative way. Anger is useful to a certain point, and beyond that it tends to be destructive, and there is a necessity to understand yourself, and contain it, and to harness it, so you can use it for a creative purpose."

Many women whom I have talked to agree with me that they have less anger these days and much more inner direction. For many, their anger came from intense feelings of hopelessness and frustration. Now, instead of beating their heads against a wall, they believe that change is happening, not by continual confrontation, but by slowly chipping away at outdated structures and beliefs. As one nun explains, "What the women religious of North America are saying is, 'Keep voices down and discussions open. Let's talk things out with patience and resolve.'"[4]

Not only are women religious (nuns) sticking together more than ever before and presenting a united front to the hierarchy, they are also learning how to be diplomatic without giving in. Whenever they have to meet with Vatican or other Church officials, they role-play first, remembering to avoid words that they should not use because they evoke such hostility, words like *team, empowerment,* and *dialogue.*[5] Once women internalize the idea about their own responsibility, it is much easier to ignore other people who treat them as if they aren't able to think or act for themselves.

"I try very hard not to get angry anymore," Rose Marciano Lucey explains, "because I realize that we are all fallible, and if I get angry at the Church, I have to be angry at myself, and I am trying not to be angry at myself, because I am totally responsible for myself and my beliefs and how I accept the Gospel and my Church."

"What do I do about my anger?" Sofia restates my question before she replies. "I believe that I am a prayerful person. I try to bring peace to others. And if I am to be in a really centered place, I have learned I need to make room in my daily life for prayer and meditation. I used to go to daily Eucharist, but I can't do that right now." So she does other things, like read and talk to people. She thinks it is very important that she stays inside the Church.

One of the ways Sofia has found to nourish her own spiritual life and convictions is by becoming a "nonvowed" lay member of an order of nuns. Most likely the wave of the future for many religious congregations, the order that

Sofia has joined also accepts men, and Sofia's husband is studying so that he can make that commitment soon as well. This is an increasingly available and popular way for women and men to find a small faith community for themselves. The order that Sofia has joined now has more than a hundred associates, mostly women.

Many women also pointed out that each of us is responsible to search out situations that we find nourishing. For some it is a support group, one made up just of women, or one that includes men as well. For others it is taking classes. Many mentioned the encouragement and growth they have gotten by reading books about spirituality. Others go to retreats on a regular basis, have found themselves a personal spiritual director, or buy or borrow audiotapes on spiritual subjects which they play while driving to and from work.

"How do I cope?" Sister Hortense asks. "The more frustrated I get with the 'highly,' the more I try to get in touch with the 'lowly.' That is why I was so happy to be able to take my sabbatical in Africa last year, and see how little they care about the hierarchy. In many instances they are first-generation Christians, and they care more about Jesus."

Each year Sheila and her husband go to a retreat with the Franciscan Father Richard Rohr in New Mexico. "Wild horses couldn't keep me away from that," she tells me enthusiastically. "I meet all these people who are really wonderful and who really do create faith. So that's what keeps me in the Church, and I can't let all these little, nitpicking stuff bother me. I just look at the larger picture."

"The bottom line is being responsible for yourself and not letting yourself become a victim," Sharon insists. This means refusing to let people who claim they "have the only truth" try to railroad you into some behavior that, in your heart, you know is wrong for you, regardless of whether the person trying to direct you is from the far left or the far right.

Feminist theologian Rosemary Radford Ruether has some specific ideas on how to cope with membership in an institution that sometimes is not run as well or as inclusively as we would like. She suggests we look around to find a local Church that is doing a fairly good job of being sensitive to justice and love and join it. Or, gather a few friends and create a community for prayer and discussion. Or, come up with some combination of these two ideas. But most important, Rosemary believes we need to avoid places, people, or activities that make us angry, hurt, frustrated, or bitter.[6]

The Good News and Bad News about the Catholic Church

Artist Rosemary Luckett copes by no longer volunteering at her local Church. "I feel like the Church will have to reach a crisis point before the people wake up and make the Church what they need it to be and what Jesus would like it to be," she writes me. "So I've stopped trying to 'save' it in its present form. I have stopped making deals with the male celibate clergy and stopped giving money. Instead, I do volunteer work for the Women's Ordination Conference; I give money to the poor and other organizations; and I read what seems right to read instead of what I 'should' read so that I can do my volunteer church work better. In addition to plunging wholeheartedly into my artwork, a friend and I started a women's discussion group that meets biweekly and is open to women of all faiths. Soon I may investigate a couple of independent (underground and home-based) churches in northern Virginia, although there are enough people like myself to start one here for ourselves if we had the energy to do it."

Rosemary insists she will keep looking for her own faith community until she finds one in which women share "their gifts on an equal footing with men from leading the assembly to washing the dishes to making decisions."

Jo'Ann De Quattro suggests that people who are unhappy about a certain pastor or parish should stop putting money into the collection each Sunday and instead write a note about why they aren't contributing and drop that in instead.

"I know a church where the pastor would not work with the people," her friend and fellow worker, France, volunteers, "and so the parish council got together and established an escrow account. Then they sent a letter to the archbishop saying that until there was a change, there would not be any money. And it worked . . . within a year they had a new pastor!"

Cassandra says she still feels anger, but she is coping by refusing to put herself in Church situations that are dangerous to her mental health. However, by standing up for herself, she finds she is no longer welcome at her parish. So although her husband still is a Eucharistic minister at Masses there, Cassandra no longer attends. Instead, they have gathered a dozen or more other Catholics together and have Mass each week at a different person's home. They found a priest, who is no longer able to practice in a public church because he is married, to help lead this intentional small faith community they have begun.

Barbara and her friends had a similar idea almost a decade earlier, only they did not look for a male priest, nor did they label their service Eucharist. "It was never our intent to create an alternate Mass," she explains. "We deliberately chose Friday night because we didn't want to get into competing. And what we said was that we wanted people to be nourished by ritual. And we were aware that we spent a lot of our lives going to meetings about things that we believed in, but we wanted to do something that was personally nourishing to us. We also agreed that everyone would chip in a few dollars and we would send out for dinner, so that no one had to cook."

This group still exists today, and it still meets on Friday nights as a women's support group. "We had a round coffee table," Barbara, who no longer lives in the Southwestern city where the group takes place, remembers, "which became the most sacred space I know. We would start with the ritual, and then share afterward. And we never called it Mass, although at various times people might say, 'This is really Eucharist.' But we didn't want to label or define it. The group was about half nuns and half laywomen. We had a woman in her seventies, and a few in their early twenties. We were very selective. It was by invitation only. And we didn't talk about issues—we did that lots of other places, but not here. This was only for our own spiritual nourishment."

There are almost as many ways of taking responsibility for one's spiritual growth as there are women in the Church. The important thing is not *how* they are doing it, but that they *are* doing it. Sister Theresa Kane, president of the Leadership Conference of Women Religious in the 1970s, was the first person to publicly tell Pope John Paul II about the pain that many Catholic women feel because their Church excludes them from full membership. Ten years later, in a speech only to women, she challenged them as she had once quietly and respectfully challenged the Pope.

"We need to grow inwardly and outwardly," Theresa Kane declared. "We need to cry out with courage and with rage whenever we experience any aspect of our lives, be it in society or in Church, that does not create or nurture such equality, or that in any way suppresses, denies, or trivializes such equality. As women, we need to continue our deepest desires, to be creators, to be initiators, to be assertive, to be adventuresome, to be bold, pioneering spirits, in the same spirit as our foremothers and foresisters. We accord by our very nature to be authors of our own destiny."[7]

WHY WOMEN STAY

By now it should be obvious that many Catholic women have declared their ownership of at least half of the Roman Catholic church. Only a few of the women I have talked to really have left the Catholic church. By far the greater majority insist on staying, but many on their own terms. Their words are thought-provoking and inspiring.

"It is a rich tradition and I do believe if we can get to the point where we are really following what the Church stands for, there is an awful lot to offer," Agnes Anne Schum remarks. "I believe that if there is to be change, I have to do it from where I am. Sometimes it is out of stubbornness, and other times it is just wanting to hang on to my heritage."

"I am a Catholic from the beginning. It is who I am," insists France. "I cannot stop being a member of my own family. And in the same way, I can't stop being a member of the Catholic church."

"I don't just walk out of the Church and forget it. I am baptized, and I have a right to be here," explains Cassandra. "It is where I have been called to interface with God. And that's how it is. They may not like me, or my style. But that is their problem. I'm not always wild about their style."

Marian K. still dreams that by staying, she might "help make one small, not giant, step forward for humankind."

"There are lots of things that bother me, but I don't know that leaving it is any less hypocritical than staying with it," Ann Z. has decided, "or believing that there is a foundation in Christ and that I don't have to leave this Church just because some of its male leadership is misguided."

"There is something about the Catholic church that draws me to it," Sheila explains. "It stands for social justice, and charity, and the corporal works of mercy, and solidarity. The Catholic church I see myself belong to is not the little narrow hierarchy that says you can do this and you can't do that. I see it in a larger sense.

"I was talking to a man in the airport when I was leaving Nicaragua," she recalls, "and he was saying he was an atheist. I told him I was a Catholic, and he said, 'You know, I've been thinking since I've been down here, the people that I have met with true faith in this world are all Catholics, so there must be something to it. And if I were to ever join a religion, I'd be a Catholic.'"

"Being a Catholic has nothing to do with the men who are running the Church," Cynthia insists. "It has to do with Jesus. The men are trying to make it revolve around them, but they can't. I used to have automatic respect for the authority of the Church. Now, I feel sorry for them, for the men, that they are not moving on. But I can't wait for them anymore, and I am sorry about that. But the urging in my soul is such that I cannot stay where they want me to stay, especially when God is telling me to go somewhere else. It's not that I am doing this out of a whim. It has taken me a lot of years."

Betty probably sums up what many, many women told me: "If you don't like the way an organization is run, you don't quit it, you fight to make it better."

It is amazing that in a world that appears to be drowning in violence, materialism, and despair, so many, many women care so much about their faith and are working so hard to make God's promises come alive for everyone. Their commitment comes not out of habit, nor fear, nor guilt, but only out of enthusiasm for the vision of Christ and his followers for the last 2,000 years.

Perhaps some who read this book will consider that many of the women I have interviewed are "Pollyannas" and overly optimistic, or at the very least are "whistling in the dark."

However, most of the women who are enthusiastic about the Catholic church admit that their vision is of a utopia that, intellectually, they realize may never be achieved, certainly not within their lifetime. Nevertheless, it is a vision that excites and compels them to try, once again, to share what they believe and love.

Donna Mahoney explains it beautifully: "We are alive in the most exciting times for women in the Church," she says, smiling, her eyes sparkling with enthusiasm. "Every day brings new possibilities, new promises. We are living in a time of transition with one foot in the old and one foot in the new. It will be our challenge to take our Church and society into the next generation, into the next decade, into the next millennium, holding hands with other women and men committed to the gospel values of peace, justice, equality, and love."

Few Catholic women of the 1990s, now grown up at last, would not want to be a part of this new vision.

EPILOGUE

When I started working on this book, I was an interested Catholic but not a particularly spiritual or inspired one. When I would meet someone who was gung ho about her personal religious life, particularly if she frequently went to daily Mass and other nonmandated public prayer groups or hung around her parish church, I tended to write her off as sticky sweet and overly pious. Although I was too polite and sophisticated to call her a nerd, even quietly to myself, in truth that was where I relegated most people, even nuns, who openly claimed to frequently being in touch with the Holy Spirit. Even the occasional meaningful religious experiences of my own were not something I wanted to admit to anyone else, much less talk about.

Although probably no one would have called me an average woman in the pew, it was primarily my close relatives in religious life that set me apart, rather than any particular belief, experience, or commitment of my own. Partially because of the familiarity I had with a side of the Catholic church that few laypeople get to see, and more because I am naturally nosy, I had spent a long time "studying" the Catholic church, or at least clipping out articles and collecting books on the subject. I was fascinated by the changes in the Church over the last 40 years, and in particular with how women were evolving. But my interest was primarily sociological and academic, and I did not feel like I had much, if any, part to play in these changes other than that of observer.

I was particularly interested in contrasting my life as a wife and mother with my twin sister's life as a nun. As a "closet" feminist who was not particularly liberated in real life, I got a vicarious thrill out of reading about the actions of courageous, committed, and assertive women and wishing that it would not cost me too much to be one. Having missed the sixties completely, I had a nagging desire to find a cause to fight for, but not enough nerve to actually do so. Another obstacle preventing me from becoming an activist was my annoying habit of seeing both sides of almost every issue. And although many friends would probably consider me outspoken, the truth was that I often was only outspoken about an aspect of a particular belief that I thought the listener would agree with.

Still there was no way that I had any doubts about the sinfulness of the Catholic church's official teachings prohibiting artificial birth control for married women and ordination for any woman. Here were two causes even a fence sitter like myself could adopt, but I seemed to have neither the courage nor the drive to do so. And although I occasionally complained that I did not belong to a small faith community, I was not spending much energy looking for one.

But all that was before I began this project. Researching and writing *The Catholic Woman* has changed me significantly. This book was begun, at least partially, as an angry feminist exposé. Somewhere along the way it turned into an upbeat cheer. It was the women I talked to who made this difference, and I thank them.

They have given me a community of women all across the country, those I interviewed as well as the many thousands of women just like them that I now know they represent. Even if I never talk to many of these women again, I will always be grateful that they are out there. I hope you, the reader, will feel like part of this community as well.

Despite the fact that many disagree about different "Catholic" issues, almost all of the women interviewed have deep and meaningful spiritual lives which they respect and enjoy and are not embarrassed or afraid to talk about. They have often inspired me by both their words and deeds, and I hope they have inspired you as well.

Writing this book has been a multifaceted learning experience. It has taught me not to arbitrarily jump to conclusions about what some woman may think about a subject, but instead to ask her first to tell me what she believes. It has helped me focus my thoughts and forced me to come to personal conclusions and to publicly admit them. No longer can I pretend that I am not a feminist, at least a moderate one.

Most important, writing this book has deeply affected my personal spiritual life. I find I am going to Mass much more often than before, and that I feel "hungry" if I don't manage to attend at least a few mornings during each week. Rather than give into the anger that I used to feel at some of the pronouncements of the Catholic hierarchy, I find myself instead marveling at the resilience of women to stay in a group that often speaks, as well as acts, as though it does not want us. I find myself applauding our ability and our tenacity to sift through illogical rubbish, not to prove a point but to keep coming up with the many spiritual treasures that are buried there.

Epilogue

Since writing this book was in addition to rather than instead of my normal work routine, it should have made me feel even more fragmented than usual. Instead, I found myself becoming more focused, more centered, more balanced and more spiritually grounded than at any time I can remember.

Again partially because of women I interviewed, I have begun to make an emotional commitment to an inner-city group of Catholics (mostly women) who meet every morning for Mass in a small chapel of a home that was once their parish convent. This Church is very convenient, only a block or two from my office, and although I, white and upper middle class and probably by far the most theologically liberal, am definitely the "minority" member of this group, I can feel it becoming my faith community. Until recently primarily African-American, this parish is now close to 50% Hispanic.

For quite some time I have been feeling a need to do something concrete to signify that I wanted to be considered a member of this faith community. Now the perfect opportunity appears to be presenting itself. I have been asked to help organize a parish "bilingual" language class where the African Americans will study Spanish and their Hispanic neighbors English. Although I have taught both these subjects before in more formal academic settings, putting these two parish groups together will be an exciting experiment that we will all be improvising together. Learning two languages is obviously not our primary goal!

Perhaps this class will turn out to be so much fun and so successful that we'll end up inviting suburbanites to stay in town after work and join us. But because of what I have learned while writing this book, I am not planning to get caught up in directing this group, but only to remain open to how and if it will evolve.

A final word to you, dear reader. I hope this book has begun to help you recognize and appreciate the wide rainbow of views held by Catholic women who consider themselves practicing and loyal members of their Church. I hope when someone asks you, "How can educated, modern Catholic women participate in such a patriarchal institution as the Catholic church?" you will have some answers at your fingertips. Even more important, I hope that reading this book will give you the courage and the energy to both name and honor your own spiritual visions and realities, while at the same time respecting the truths of others, even if and when they may differ from your own.

APPENDIX A:

Biographies of the Women Interviewed

Although conversations with many other Catholic women have contributed to the facts and insights presented in this book, the following is a brief résumé of each of the women I have actually quoted. Each woman was given the opportunity to decide how she wished to be identified. Often, in the text itself, only first names are used, for brevity's sake, and so this list is in alphabetical order by first name. Last names are included in the text for women who are nationally well known, who specifically requested that their entire name be used, or who are quoted that way in the book from which I got their quote. In the text, *Sister* is only used about 25% of the time in front of a name of a nun. Letters after a name mean that the woman belongs to that particular Community of Religious Women. The best way to find out more about a woman who is quoted is to look for her name in the list below. Women whose quotes are taken from another book are not on this list.

Agnes Ann Schum: A Sister of Loretto and a certified enneagram teacher, a member of the Women's Ordination Conference, Ann is interested in transforming the Catholic church into an institution that is truly Catholic.

Ann Z.: A lifelong member of the Catholic church, Ann is a college graduate who has been a wife and mother for 24 years and a teacher in public education for 14 years.

Anne Brotherton, SFCC: An associate professor of sociology and ministry at the Jesuit School of Theology at Berkeley, and a member of Sisters for Christian Community, Anne is the author of *The Voice of the Turtledove: New Catholic Women in Europe*, which was published in 1992 by Paulist Press.

Anne D.: A wife, mother, and religious educator, Anne serves as the director of the CCD (Confraternity of Christian Doctrine) in her parish.

Barbara: A leader in developing workshops and retreats on women's spirituality and ritual since the early 1970s, Barbara has served for the past several years in a top national leadership position in her congregation of sisters.

Betty: Once a nun, now a wife and mother as well as a nurse and college professor, Betty is chairperson of the End of Life Committee of her archdiocese.

Bridget: She recently joined the convent, has a master's degree in theology and has worked in various capacities in public and Catholic schools.

Carol: Mother of 11 children, active in the United Way, Operation Rescue, and Community Interdenominational Bible Study, Carol plays the organ, organizes her parish's quarterly rummage sales, and is involved in a myriad of evangelization activities.

Carolyn: A lawyer with her own private practice, Carolyn spends much of her free time in parish work, where she particularly enjoys writing the petitions (Prayers of the Faithful) that are read from the pulpit at each Sunday Mass.

Cassandra: A dynamic Christian woman of integrity and vision, Cassandra is struggling to help her Church live up to its potential in the 21st century.

Catherine: A nun for 25 years and now married, Catherine is a talented photographer and film director and has recently produced and directed a video series on older women.

Christi: A recent college graduate, Christi has joined the JVC (Jesuit Volunteer Corps) and has recently been accepted to law school. She plans to work eventually in some aspect of public service law.

Cynthia Yoshitomi: Married with two teenage sons, Cynthia is a human relations consultant for the National Conference of Christians and Jews as well as for the Green Circle Program, which fosters understanding between different groups within society.

Colleen: Mother of a large Catholic family, Colleen calls herself a conservative Catholic and dedicates many hours each week to her parish and other charitable causes.

Diane Hewitt: An enthusiastic Catholic, divorced mother of three adult children, and a commercial interior designer who specializes in church environments, Diane has recently been chosen to prepare her diocese's cathedral for its yearly ordination ceremony.

Dolores Leckey: A nationally known writer and lecturer, Dolores has been the director of the U.S. Bishops Secretariat for Family, Laity, Women and Youth for many years.

Donna Tiernan Mahoney: Author, speaker, and doctoral candidate, Donna is the second vice president and women's concerns chairperson of the National Council of Catholic Women.

France White, SCHJ: A staff member of the Peace and Justice Center of Southern California, France is an accomplished artist whose art reflects her social justice values.

Hortense: A nun for over 30 years, Sister Hortense is a catechist, longtime Catholic elementary and secondary school teacher and administrator, past employee of a diocesan office, and former member of endless Church-related task forces and committees.

Jackie: A committed Catholic who has been very active in her parish, Jackie is a staff member of the Department of Education and Academic Affairs of a major national art museum.

Jamie: A recent convert, young wife, and mother (recently of twin daughters), Jamie hopes to be a doctor one day.

Jane B.: Referring to herself as "a perpetual pilgrim," Jane is a wife, mother and grandmother and has been active in her parish for more than 30 years.

Jane H.: Now a retired public high school principal, Jane has been active in her local parish for many years.

Jane Kirchner: A graduate of St. Thomas University in pastoral ministry, Jane completed her master's degree in international peace studies at Notre Dame and has recently become the Catholic campus minister at the University of LaVerne in California.

Jennifer: A young Catholic scientist, Jennifer is trying to find a spiritual balance between the strictly traditional morals and values of the Catholic church and the modern, secular, individualistic goals of the world in general.

Jo'Ann De Quattro, SNJM: A cultural Catholic feminist who struggles for human liberation as a staff member of the Peace and Justice Center of Southern California, Jo'Ann has been active in many social justice and feminist causes.

JoAnne: A lawyer who has been a prosecutor in the district attorney's office in a small town, JoAnne is trying to decide if she should enter the convent and calls herself "an incipient radical feminist."

Kathy: A wife and mother of five young children, she is self-employed as a lecturer on parenting and other family and spiritual issues.

Laura Grimes: Married and in her late twenties, Laura is a Ph.D. candidate in systematic theology at the University of Notre Dame.

Lauren: A recent convert, Lauren is a mother and a licensed speech-language pathologist.

Laurie: A product of Catholic school education, including a Catholic college, Laurie is currently taking time off from her job as a public school teacher in order to stay home with her young daughter.

Linda: Unemployed after years as a manager of a large insurance office, Linda has always been single and draws religious comfort from her Pentecostal roots and her Catholic daily Mass.

Liz: Involved in parish activities as diverse as finance and the OCIA (Order of Christian Initiation) program, Liz describes herself as a Catholic woman who continues to question, to hope, to celebrate, and to grow.

Margaret: Married and the mother of three teenagers, Margaret has been active in parish ministry for more than 26 years and is currently director of OCIA and chair of her Parish Pastoral Council.

Maria: Once a timid wife and mother, now a radical activist, Maria combines counseling for life outside an abortion clinic with helping to feed the homeless and is the organizer of a prayer group in her parish that particularly asks for healing from the Blessed Mother.

Maria Pilar Aquino: Author of numerous articles about Latin American women, Pilar is an assistant professor of theological and religious studies at the University of San Diego, president of the Academy of Catholic Hispanic Theologians, and a member of the Ecumenical Association of Third World Theologians.

Marian Bramble: Mother of both a priest and a nun, Marian is also a grandmother and great-grandmother who has been a faithful Catholic all her life and has been particularly involved in helping to improve race relations in her neighborhood.

Marian K.: An 80-year-old, single, retired professional Catholic woman, Marian is a national consultant to the Women's Ordination Conference and continues to work for the elimination of the evil of patriarchy as the way to bring justice to women in the Church.

Martha: Married with two adult children, she is an intern in the field of marriage, family, and child therapy.

Sister Mary J. Glennon, CHF: A nun for more than 40 years, she currently serves as chair of the Western Region of Vicars for Religious, represents the western United States on the National Executive Committee of Vicars for Religious, and has been the Vicar for Religious in the Archdiocese of Los Angeles for more than six years. Recently, Mary was elected Assistant to the Director General in her own community, the Sisters of the Holy Faith, an international community based in Dublin, Ireland. She assumes her new position in January, 1994.

Mary Leach: A lay Catholic, feminist, and founding board member of the Women's Ordination Conference, Mary works in administration at the University of Maryland.

Mary Anne Vincent, CSJP: A talented writer and staff member of the Peace and Justice Center of Southern California, Mary Ann is also a genealogist who has traced her family back to the 16th century.

Mary Margaret: A woman religious, Mary Margaret has chosen to minister in parishes as her way of furthering the role of women in the Church by personal example.

Sister Mary Luke Tobin, SL: A Sister of Loretto in her mid-eighties who works at the Thomas Merton Center for Creative Exchange in Denver, Colorado, Sister Mary Luke Tobin explains that participating officially as an "auditor" at Vatican II and sharing the spiritual insights of Thomas Merton opened her eyes to making free and authentically autonomous decisions.

Sister Maureen Fiedler, SL: Codirector of Quixote Center, Maureen is a justice-seeking feminist attempting to call all who claim a Roman Catholic tradition to embrace Jesus' teaching of gender equality and to apply teachings on justice to the internal life of the Church itself.

Nancy: An adult and child psychiatrist with her own private practice, Nancy has an appointment to the clinical faculty of the USC School of Medicine in the departments of Psychiatry and Family Medicine.

Patricia Miller: A Catholic educator, Patricia is the creator and author of a video and print series on sexuality, and is also a sexuality consultant to lay and church groups, including the U.S. bishops.

Pat Sears, CSJ: Cofounder and longtime codirector of an inner-city low-income housing and self-help group, Pat maintains that education has always been the focus of her life, both in the classroom as a teacher and in society at large through her many social-action activities.

Rebecca: A young, committed Catholic, Rebecca is a second-year student at a Catholic university.

Rose Catherine: Once a nun and a teacher for more than 20 years and now a member of the laity, Rose Catherine has recently retired from her job as a writer/producer of religious and other value-oriented educational material for both children and adults.

Rose Marciano Lucey: Now in her seventies, this mother of nine and grandmother of many is a founding member of the U.S. Christian Family Movement and the National Peace Academy. She has been a lay representative of the Catholic church throughout the world (including Russia), a founder of the Hope Group for Women's Rights, a member of Questers (Catholic Women for Constructive Change), a board member of Jubilee West (an inner-city self-help housing group), and a volunteer at the Center for AIDS.

Rosemary Luckett: Artist, pioneer, and prophet, Rosemary gives simple and elegant voice through her work to the experience of women who struggle to assume their birthright in the Catholic church.

Sara: A convert who is very active in school and parish work, Sara teaches aerobics and is taking a diocesan course on liturgy in order to help the changes of Vatican II be fully implemented.

Sister Sean Patrice, CSJ: Sean Patrice has spent 30 years educating Catholic grammar-school children and encouraging them to be passionately involved in making life better for people in accordance with their Catholic beliefs.

Sharon Nelsen: A devoted Catholic, artist, and poet, this creative mother of five recently began work on a master's of theology at a midwestern Catholic university.

Sheila: A convert who has been very influenced by the social teachings of Dorothy Day, Sheila retired early so she could work with the Catholic Worker Movement and begin a language school for poor Hispanic women.

Sherry Tyree: One of the founders of Women for Faith and the Family, a national Catholic women's organization started in St. Louis, Missouri, in 1984.

Silvia Cancio: Although once active in her parish, Silvia has since become very disillusioned with the male power structure in the Catholic church and now teaches women's studies at the University of Cincinnati and is active in "Women-Church."

Sofia: A pastoral assistant in an inner-city parish as well as a wife, mother, foster mother, and grandmother, Sofia has an intense commitment to social justice and describes herself as being "in the process of becoming."

Stacey: A newly divorced yet still devout Catholic in her early thirties, Stacey has an M.B.A. and works in finance.

Terry: She is currently working on her dissertation about the spirituality of 19th-century American women writers but still misses her former volunteer work as Catholic campus minister at a major Protestant university.

Theresa: A Benedictan nun, she is a Eucharistic minister and an administrator of a Catholic feminist organization.

Toni: A psychotherapist for a Catholic Family Counseling Agency as well as in her own private practice, she has worked with more than a hundred Catholic women and many of their family members to help them resolve spiritual and emotional conflicts.

Vivian: A member of the Immaculate Heart Community (an ecumenical group of women and men who attempt to live the gospel of nonviolence in today's world), Vivian teaches in an inner-city alternative school, is a leader in creation spirituality and Pax Christi groups, and is an officer in the Interfaith Council for the United Nations.

APPENDIX B:

A Feminist Liturgy

This feminist liturgy—and many other similar and equally creative feminist liturgies—can be found in a collection of such celebrations entitled *Liberating Liturgies*, compiled and published by the Women's Ordination Conference, P.O. Box 2693, Fairfax, VA 22031; 703-352-1006. The following liturgy, created by Mary Ann McGivern, is reprinted here with permission from the Women's Ordination Conference.

CELEBRATION OF BEING IN THE MIDDLE OF THINGS

INTRODUCTION: This is a celebration of being in the middle of things: a 25th Anniversary. Twenty-five years doesn't seem very long at all. It is a point, though, of reflection. We eat and drink and sing and dance and be merry, not because we're finished or even in a particularly good place, but because sometimes it is good just to stop and say "This is where we are" and to rejoice together over our very existence.

SONG: "How Can I Keep From Singing," a Shaker Hymn (or another song of your choice)

REFLECTION: By Celebrants or Celebrants and participants

SONG: "Bread and Roses" (or another song of your choice)

PETITIONS: Individual prayers of petition may be offered here. The response is "We cry out to the living God, come live among us."

OFFERING OF RICE CAKES, WONDER BREAD, TORTILLAS, FRESH BAKED BREAD, SWEET BREAD AND WINE (other items of significance to the group may also be included here)

RESPONSE: We offer bread and wine to God and to each other. We offer ourselves to God by giving ourselves to one another. May this offering of our lives be accepted by God. Let us each, in union with God and with one another, accept our gift in God's name and offer in God the gift of peace.

EXCHANGE OF PEACE: (When this time of sharing is complete, all gather in a circle)

SONG: "Old Devil Time" by Pete Seeger (or another song of your choice)

RESPONSE OF THE COMMUNITY: We thank you God for your gifts. We know who you are by these gifts: wheat and grapes and trees and bricks for houses and our friends who give us strength.

We remember the women and men who have lived and died in you: Jesus who was born in a stable and died on the cross; Gandhi who clung with his whole being to the knowledge that killing was wrong; Dorothy Day who knew it would be foolish to live anything less than what she believed. (Others, famous and unknown, may be mentioned here who have gone on before us in the way of truth and love.)

CELEBRANTS: The bread and wine are holy because we have blessed them with our lives. So let us break bread together and drink wine in memory of all those who live and die in God. (Instrumental music is played as the bread and wine are shared.)

FINAL BLESSING

CLOSING SONG AND DANCE.

APPENDIX C:

An Experience in Awareness

WOMAN: WHICH INCLUDES MAN OF COURSE

There is much concern today about the future of man, which means, of course, both men and women—generic "Man." For a woman to take exception to this use of the term "man" is often seen as defensive hair-splitting by an "emotional female."

The following experience is an invitation to awareness in which you are asked to feel into, and stay with, your feelings through each step, letting them absorb you. *If you start intellectualizing, go back to the step where you can again sense your feelings. Then proceed. Keep count of how many times you need to go back.

1. Consider reversing the generic term MAN. Think of the future of WOMAN, which, of course, includes both women and men. Feel into that, sense its meaning to you: as a woman. As a man.

2. Think of it always being that way, every day of your life. Feel the ever-presence of woman and feel the non-presence of man. Absorb what it tells you about the importance and value of being woman. Of being man.

3. Recall that everything you have ever read all your life uses only female pronouns—"she," "her"—meaning both girls and boys, both women and men. Recall that most of the voices on radio and most of the faces on TV are women's when important events are covered on commercials and on late talk shows. Recall that you have only two or three male senators representing you in Washington.

4. Feel into the fact that women are the leaders, the power centers, the prime movers. Man, whose natural role is husband and father, fulfills himself through nurturing children and making the home a refuge for woman. This is

only natural to balance the biological role of woman who devotes her entire body to the race during pregnancy: pregnancy, the most revered power known to Woman (and man).

5. Remember that the body of woman is the ideal: especially her genital construction. By design, female genitals are compact and internal, protected by her body. Male genitals are so exposed that he must be protected from outside attack to assure the perpetuation of the race. His vulnerability obviously requires sheltering.

6. Thus, by nature, males are more passive than females, and have a desire in sexual relations to be symbolically engulfed by the protective body of the woman. Males psychologically yearn for this protection, fully realizing their masculinity at this time, and feeling exposed and vulnerable at other times. A man experiences himself as a "whole man" when thus engulfed.

7. If the male denies these feelings, he is unconsciously rejecting his masculinity. Therapy is thus indicated to help him adjust to his own nature. Of course, therapy is administered by a woman, who has the education and wisdom to facilitate openness, leading to the male's growth and self-actualization.

8. To help him feel into his defensive emotionality, he is invited to get in touch with the "child" in him. He remembers his sister's jeering at his primitive genitals that "flop around foolishly." She can run, climb and ride horseback unencumbered. Obviously, since she is free to move, she is encouraged to develop her body and mind in preparation for her active responsibilities of adult womanhood. The male vulnerability needs female protection, so he is taught the less active, caring, virtues of homemaking.

9. Because of his vagina-envy, he learns to bind his genitals, and learns to feel ashamed and unclean because of his nocturnal emissions. Instead, he is encouraged to dream of getting married, waiting for the time of his fulfillment, when "his woman" gives him a girl child to care for. He knows that if it is a boy child, he has failed somehow, but they can try again.

10. In getting to the "child" in him, the early experiences are reawakened. He is in an encounter group entitled "On Being a Man" which is led by a woman. In a circle of 19 men and 4 women, he begins to work through some of his deep feelings.

What feelings do YOU feel he will express?

*How many times did you have to go back?

NOTES

Chapter One:

1. p. 480, *Whatever Happened to the Good Sisters?: A Collection of Real Life Stories,* 1992, ed. Kathleen Fitzgerald and Claire Breault, Whale's Tale Press, 160 Wildwood, Lake Forest, IL 60045.

2. p. 227, Ibid.

3. p. 309, Ibid.

4. p. 228, Ibid.

5. p. 211, Ibid.

6. p. 2, Ruth Wallace, *They Call Her Pastor,* 1992, State University of New York Press, New York.

7. pp. 145, 146, Lora Ann Quinonez and Mary Daniel Turner, SN de N, *Transformation of American Catholic Sisters,* 1992, Temple University Press, Philadelphia.

8. *Liturgy* technically means any official, public church ritual, but it is most often used as a synonym for Mass. In the 1990s, however, it has come to mean any public spiritual ritual, even those prayerfully created and performed by women.

9. p. 87, Doris Althoff Kozlowski, in *Whatever Happened to the Good Sisters?*

10. pp. 14, 61, Rose Marciano Lucey, *Roots and Wings: Dreamers and Doers of the Christian Family Movement,* 1987, Resource Publications, San Jose, CA.

11. p. 47, Ibid.

12. p. 201, Andrew Greeley, *The Catholic Myth,* 1990, Macmillan Publishing Company, New York.

13. pp. 272, 273, Rita Bresnahan, in *Whatever Happened to the Good Sisters?*

14. p. 217, Barbara Ferraro and Patricia Hussey with Jane O'Reilly, *No Turning Back,* 1990, Poseidon Press, New York.

15. p. 266, Ibid.

16. p. 156, Margaret Murphy, *How Catholic Women Have Changed,* 1987, Sheed and Ward, Kansas City, MO.

Chapter Two:

1. p. 96, Sandra Schneiders, IHM, *Beyond Patching*, 1990, Paulist Press, Mahwah, NJ.

2. p. 19, "U.S. Catholic," April 1985, quoted in *How Catholic Women Have Changed*, p. 12.

3. p. 135, Michael Crosby, *The Dysfunctional Church: Addiction and Codependency in the Family of Catholicism*, 1991, Ave Maria Press, Notre Dame, IN.

4. p. 50, Ibid.

5. p. 109, *Beyond Patching*.

6. p. B5, *Los Angeles Times*, April 24, 1993, reported by Religious News Service.

7. p. 110, *Beyond Patching*.

Chapter Three:

1. Donna Tiernan Mahoney, keynote address, Insights Into Women's Issues Conference presented by the Committee on Women's Concerns, Diocesan Council of Catholic Women, September 12, 1992, Lake Worth, FL.

2. p. 13, Sidney Callahan, "Conscience needs community," *Church*, Fall 1992, National Pastoral Life Center, New York.

3. p. 134, Jane Redmont, *Generous Lives: American Catholic Women Today*, 1992, William Morrow and Company, New York.

4. pp. 135, 211, Ibid.

5. p. 9, quoted in *Voice of the South West*, November 1992, Gallop, NM.

6. p.15, quoted in "Rome's birth control conceptions flunk real world test," Father Joseph Gallagher, *National Catholic Reporter (NCR)*, September 4, 1992.

7. p. 24, Gerry Dunphy, letter to the editor, *NCR*, December 4, 1992.

8. Quoted in "Pope reaffirms tough birth control stance," *NCR*, November 15, 1988.

9. p. 5, Gallagher, *NCR*, September 4, 1992.

10. p. 94, *The Catholic Myth*.

11. p. 94, Ibid.

12. p. 70, *Roots and Wings*.

13. p. 96, 23, *The Catholic Myth*.

14. p. 91, Ibid.

15. p. 49, 50, *Human Sexuality*, U.S. Catholic Conference, Washington, DC, 1991.

16. p. 6, Dawn Gibeau, "Families testify about prolonging life, death," *NCR*, December 18, 1992.

17. p. B3, *Los Angeles Times*, January 2, 1993.

18. p. 97, *The Catholic Myth*.

19. pp. 97, 98, 104, Ibid.

20. p. 196, *Generous Lives*.

21. p. 23, Ibid.

22. p. 117, *The Catholic Myth*.

23. p. 23, 24, *Generous Lives*.

24. p. 117, *The Catholic Myth*.

25. pp. 13, 14, Greeley, *NCR*, November 10, 1989.

26. p. 22, *Time Magazine*, December 14, 1992.

27. pp. 17, 18, Tom Fox, *NCR*, November 13, 1992.

28. Ibid.

29. p. E1, *Los Angeles Times*, January 6, 1993.

30. To learn more about her views, see Patricia Miller (in Bibliography).

31. p. 248, *Generous Lives*.

32. p. 1, Russell Chandler, "Striving to serve God and family," *Los Angeles Times*, September 19, 1990.

33. pp. 250, 277, 287, *The Catholic Myth*.

34. *NCR*, March 22, 1991.

35. p. 151, Ruth Wallace, *They Call Her Pastor: A New Role for Catholic Women*, 1992, State University of New York Press.

36. p. 156, Donna Tiernan Mahoney, *Touching the Face of God: Intimacy and Celibacy in Priestly Life*, 1991, Jeremiah Press, Boca Raton, FL.

37. pp. 119, 120, Uta Ranke-Heinemann, *Eunuchs for the Kingdom of Heaven*, translated by Peter Heinegg, Doubleday, New York, 1990.

38. p. 1, Carolyn Moynihan Bradt, "Evidence exists: Women were priests and bishops in the first five centuries of the Church," *New Women, New Church*, Vol. 13, No. 2–5, May-October 1990.

39. p. 6, Arthur Jones, "Gallup poll results unlikely to please Vatican," *NCR*, July 3, 1992.

40. p. 6, Richard A. McCormick, SJ, "Changing my mind about the changeable Church," *Churchwatch*, Call To Action Quarterly Progress Report, October-November 1990 (originally published in *The Christian Century*, August 8–15, 1990).

41. pp. 524-527, "Women in the Ministerial Priesthood," *Origins* 6:33, February 3, 1977, as quoted by Rosemary Chinnici on p. 7, in *Can Women Reimage the Church?* 1992, Paulist Press, New York.

42. p. 44, *Can Women Reimage the Church?*

43. p. 247, Catherine Mowry LaCugna, "Catholic women as ministers and theologians," *America*, Vol. 167:10, October 10, 1992.

44. p. 3, Dorothy Vidulich, "Women's pastoral buried after 10 years," *NCR*, December 4, 1992.

45. p. 17, Father Ron Luka, "Is 'Do this in memory of me' mere rhetoric?," *NCR*, November 25, 1988.

46. p. 3, Pat Windsor, "Poll: Most Catholics confused about the Eucharist," *NCR*, March 20, 1992.

47. p. 1, Bernard J. Cooke, "The Eucharist, a threatened species," *NCR*, May 11, 1990.

48. p. 14, Bernard J. Cooke, "Entire faith community performs Eucharist," *NCR*, May 18, 1990.

49. p. 17, Ruth McDonough Fitzpatrick, "A discipleship of equals," *Creation*, September/October 1990.

50. p. 236, *The Dysfunctional Church*.

51. p. 12, Bernard J. Lee and Michael A. Cowan, *Dangerous Memories: House Churches and Our American Story*, 1986, Sheed and Ward, as quoted by Ruth McDonough Fitzpatrick, *Creation*, p. 17, September/October 1990.

52. p. 283, *Generous Lives.*

53. p. 351, *Whatever Happened to the Good Sisters?*

54. p. 3, Joan Turner Beifuss, "Feminist theolgians organize, make gains", *NCR*, April 13, 1984.

55. pp. 56, 57, *Can Women Reimage the Church?*

56. p. 244, Catherine Mowry LaCugna, *America*, Vol. 167, No. 10, October 10,1992.

57. pp. 12-14, *Beyond Patching.*

58. p. 36, Ibid.

59. p. 91, Ibid.

60. p. 105, *How Catholic Women Have Changed.*

61. p. 51. "The war Against feminism," *Time Magazine*, March 9, 1992.

62. p. 3, Phyliss Willerscheidt, "What is inclusive language?," *Catholic Women*, May/June 1992.

63. p. 324, *Generous Lives.*

64. p. v, Philip J. Murnion, *New Parish Ministers*, 1992, by National Pastoral Life Center.

65. p. vi, Ibid.

66. p. 240, Catherine Mowry Lacugna, "Catholic Women as Ministers and Theologians," *America*, October 10, 1992.

67. p. 580, *Whatever Happened to the Good Sisters?*

68. p. 1, Tim Unsworth, *NCR*, October 19, 1992.

69. p. 178, *They Call Her Pastor.*

70. p. 65, Richard Ostling, "Cut from the wrong cloth," *Time*, June 1992.

71. p. 6, Arthur Jones, "Gallup poll results unlikely to please Vatican," *NCR*, July 3, 1992.

72. p. 12, *New Parish Ministers.*

73. *p. 6*, They Call Her Pastor.

74. p. 13, Ibid.

75. p. 143, Ibid.

76. pp. 165–168, Ibid.

77. p. 7, *NCR*, December 19, 1992.

78. p. 245, *Generous Lives*.

79. p. 77, *The Dysfunctional Church*.

80. p. 77, Ibid.

81. p. 250, *Generous Lives*.

82. p. 20, Archbishop Weakland, quoted in *NCR*, May 29, 1992.

Chapter Four:

1. p. 272, *Generous Lives*.

2. p. 7, *The Catholic Myth*.

3. p. 126, *Whatever Happened to the Good Sisters?*

4. p. 161, *How Catholic Women Have Changed*.

5. p. 111, *Transformation of American Sisters*.

6. p. 22, Rosemary Radford Ruether, *NCR*, July 17, 1992.

7. 1989 speech by Sister Theresa Kane to the Leadership Conference of Religious Women.

BIBLIOGRAPHY

Abbott, Walter M. (Ed.). *The Documents of Vatican II*. New York: The American Press, 1966.

Aburdene, Patricia, and John Naisbitt. *Megatrends for Women*. New York: Random House, 1992.

Armstrong, April Oursler. *What's Happening to the Catholic Church?* New York: Doubleday, 1966.

Bolen, Jean Shinoda. *Goddesses in Everywoman: A New Psychology of Woman*. San Francisco: Harper & Row, 1984.

Brotherton, Anne (Ed.). *The Voice of the Turtledove: New Catholic Women in Europe*. New York: Paulist Press, 1992.

Chinnici, Rosemary. *Can Women Reimage the Church?* New York: Paulist Press, 1992.

Clark, Linda, Marian Ronana, and Eleanor Walker. *Image Breaking/Image Building: A Handbook for Creative Worship with Women of Christian Tradition*. New York: The Pilgrim Press, 1981.

Crosby, Michael H. *The Dysfunctional Church: Addiction and Codependency in the Family of Catholicism*. Notre Dame, IN: Ave Maria Press, 1991.

Daly, Mary. *Beyond God the Father: Toward a Philosophy of Women's Liberation*. Boston: Beacon Press, 1973.

Daly, Mary. *The Church and the Second Sex*. San Francisco: Harper & Row, 1968.

Dwyer, Maureen (Ed.). *New Woman, New Church, New Priestly Ministry*. Proceedings of the Second Conference on the Ordination of Roman Catholic Women, November 10–12, 1978, Baltimore, MD.

Faludi, Susan. *Backlash: The Undeclared War Against American Women*. New York: Crown, 1991.

Ferder, Fran. *Called to Break Bread? A Psychological Investigation of 100 Women Who Feel Called to Priesthood in the Catholic Church*, Quixote Center, Mt. Rainier, MD, 1978.

Ferraro, Barbara, and Patricia Hussey with Jane O'Reilly. *No Turning Back.* New York: Poseidon Press, 1990.

Fink, Peter E. (Ed.). *The New Dictionary of Sacramental Worship.* Collegeville, MN: The Liturgical Press, 1990.

Fiorenza, Elizabeth Schussler. *Discipleship of Equals.* New York: Crossroad, 1993.

Fitzgerald, Kathleen, and Claire Breault (Eds.). *Whatever Happened to the Good Sisters? A Collection of Real Life Stories.* Whales Tale Press, 160 Wildwood, Lake Forest, IL, 60045, 1992.

Gallagher, Chuck. *The Marriage Encounter.* New York: Doubleday, 1975.

Gilligan, Carol. *In a Different Voice: Psychological Theory and Women's Development.* Cambridge: Harvard University Press, 1982.

Greeley, Andrew. *The Catholic Myth: The Behavior and Beliefs of American Catholics.* New York: Macmillan, 1990.

Hunt, Michael J. *College Catholics, A New Counter Culture.* New Jersey: Paulist Press, 1993.

Kennedy, Eugene. *Tomorrow's Catholics, Yesterday's Church,* San Francisco: Harper & Row, 1988.

Larsen, Earnie, and Janee Pagnegg. *Recovering Catholics: What to Do When Religion Comes Between You and God.* San Francisco: Harper & Row, 1992.

Lieblich, Julia. *Sisters: Lives of Devotion and Defiance.* New York: Ballantine Books, 1992.

Lucey, Rose Marciano. *Roots and Wings: Dreamers and Doers of the Christian Family Movement.* San Jose, CA: Resource Publications, 1987.

Mahoney, Donna Tiernan. *Touching the Face of God: Intimacy and Celibacy in Priestly Life.* Boca Raton, FL, Jeremiah Press, 1991.

Miller, Patricia. *In God's Image: Male and Female,* and *Parent to Parent,* video and print series, may be ordered from Franciscan Communications, 1229 S. Santee St., Los Angeles, CA 90015; 1-800-984-3600.

Muggeridge, Anne Roche. *The Desolate City: Revolution in the Catholic Church.* San Francisco: Harper & Row, 1986.

Bibliography

Murnion, Philip J. *New Parish Ministers: Laity and Religious on Parish Staffs.* National Pastoral Life Center, 299 Elizabeth St., New York, NY 10012-2806, 1992.

Murphy, Margaret. *How Catholic Women Have Changed.* Kansas City, MO: Sheed and Ward, 1987.

Ohanneson, Joan. *Woman: Survivor in the Church.* Minneapolis: Winston Press, 1980.

Quinonez, Lora Ann, and Mary Daniel Turner. *The Transformation of American Catholic Sisters.* Philadelphia: Temple University Press, 1992.

Ranke-Heinemann, Uta. *Eunuchs for the Kingdom of Heaven.* Translated by Peter Heinegg. New York: Doubleday, 1990.

Redmont, Jane. *Generous Lives: American Catholic Women Today.* New York: William Morrow, 1992.

Reese, Thomas J. *Archbishop: Inside the Power Structure of the American Catholic Church.* San Francisco: Harper & Row, 1989.

Schaef, Anne Wilson. *Women's Reality: An Emerging Female System in a White Male Society.* San Francisco: Harper & Row, 1981.

Schneiders, Sandra M. *Beyond Patching.* Mahwah, NJ: Paulist Press, 1990.

Steinem, Gloria. *Revolution from Within.* Boston: Little, Brown, 1992.

Tannen, Deborah. *You Just Don't Understand: Women and Men in Conversation.* New York: William Morrow, 1990.

U.S. Catholic Conference. *Human Sexuality: A Catholic Perspective for Education and Lifelong Learning,* Publication #405-8, Washington, D.C., 1991.

U.S. Catholic Conference. *Lineamenta: Vocation and Mission of the Laity in the Church and in the World Twenty Years after the Second Vatican Council,* Publication #959, Washington, D.C., 1985.

U.S. Catholic Conference. *The Many Faces of AIDS,* Publication #195-4, Washington, D.C., 1987.

Upton, Elizabeth. *Secrets of a Nun: My Own Story.* New York: William Morrow, 1985.

Wallace, Ruth. *They Call Her Pastor: A New Role for Catholic Women.* State University of New York Press, 1992.

Weaver, Mary Jo. *New Catholic Women: A Contemporary Challenge to Traditional Religious Authority.* San Francisco: Harper & Row, 1985.

Weaver, Mary Jo. *Springs of Water in a Dry Land: Spiritual Survival for Catholic Women Today.* Boston: Beacon Press, 1993.

Winter, Michael M. *Whatever Happened to Vatican II?* London: Sheed and Ward, 1985.

Women's Ordination Conference. *Liberating Liturgies,* 1989; WOC, P.O. Box 2693, Ste. 11, Fairfax Circle Center, 9653 Lee Highway, Fairfax, VA 22031; 703-352-1006.

INDEX

Ratzinger, Cardinal Joseph, 44
RCIA, 64, 208–209
Reconciliation, 115, 133, 143, 171
Redmont, Jane, 67, 95, 100, 108,
    137, 159, 177, 197
Riots, L.A. 1992, 134
Rohr, Richard, 218
Ruether, Rosemary Radford, 39,
    52, 218

S

Sacraments, 114–115, 117,
    122–123, 134, 161, 170
Schneiders, Sandra, 38, 51–52, 148
Sensus fidelium, 63, 66,
Sex education, 104–106
Silvestro, Marsie, 36
Sipe, Richard, 103
Sisters Formation Movement, 11
Social justice, 180–189, 201, 204,
    216, 221
Sterilization, 81–82
Surrogate motherhood, 82

T

Tarsicius, Saint, 132
Teenage pregnancy, 104
Tuite, Marge, 30
Turner, Mary Daniel, 14

V

Vatican II, 15–19, 32–33, 54, 58,
    61, 63, 76, 95, 120, 157, 164,
    202, 213

W

Wallace, Ruth, 157, 160, 168,
    170–171
Weakland, Archbishop Rembert,
    173, 178
West, Rebecca, 151
Willerscheidt, Phyllis, 152
Women Church, 52, 130, 142,
    144–145, 191–192
Women for Faith and the Family,
    22–23, 28–29, 48–50, 66, 69,
    116, 130, 168
Women priests, 114–129, 160,
    173, 213
Womens Ordination Conference,
    25, 36, 52, 119, 120–131, 128,
    219
World Bank, 183